UNITED NATIONS CONFERENCE ON TRADE AND DEVELOPMENT

TRADE AND DEVELOPMENT REPORT

2023

Growth, Debt and Climate:
Realigning the Global
Financial Architecture

United Nations

Geneva, 2024

United Nations publication issued by the
United Nations Conference on Trade and Development

UNCTAD/TDR/2023

ISBN: 978-92-1-002908-7

eISBN: 978-92-1-358486-6

ISSN: 0255-4607

eISSN: 2225-3262

Sales No. E.23.II.D.24

Policy priorities

The *Trade and Development Report 2023: Growth, Debt and Climate – Realigning the Global Financial Architecture* identifies five core policy priorities:

- Reducing inequality.

- Balancing the priorities of monetary stability with long-term financial sustainability.

- Regulating commodity trading generally, and food trading in particular.

- Addressing the crushing burden of debt servicing and the threat of spreading debt crises.

- Providing reliable access to finance and technology transfer to enable the energy transition.

Specific policy recommendations for a development-centred global debt architecture

1. Increase concessional finance through capitalization of multilateral and regional banks, and issuance of special drawing rights.

2. Enhance transparency in financing terms and conditions, using the digitalization of loan contracts to improve accuracy.

3. Revise the UNCTAD Principles for Responsible Sovereign Lending and Borrowing to motivate and underpin the importance of guiding principles throughout the stages of sovereign debt acquisition.

4. Improve debt sustainability analysis and tracking to reflect the achievement of the Sustainable Development Goals and empower country negotiators with improved data on their potential for growth and fiscal consolidation.

5. Enable countries to utilize innovative financial instruments such as sustainable development bonds and resilience bonds. Develop rules for automatic restructurings and guarantees.

6. Enhance resilience during external crises, for example by implementing standstill rules on debtors' obligations in crises, and create a space to enable the avoidance of debt distress.

7. Encourage borrowers to share information and experiences, drawing inspiration from private creditor coordination.

8. Initiate work on a more robust debt workout mechanism and a global debt authority.

Contents

Foreword xi

Abbreviations xii

Explanatory notes xv

Overview xvii

Chapter I

Current Trends and Challenges in the Global Economy 1

   A. Introduction 3

   B. Global growth landscape: divergence under the clouds of uncertainty 5

   C. Leading economies in an interdependent world 9

   D. Corporate capture and the demise of fiscal policy 12

   E. Credit, investment and the role of monetary policy 15

   F. Inflation and distribution 19

   G. Labour costs and inequality 23

   H. Conclusion 25

   References 30

Chapter II

International Markets: Trade, Capital Flows, Commodities 33

   A. Introduction 35

   B. Trade 35

     1. Review of recent cyclical developments in international trade 37

     2. A new paradigm of international trade? 40

     3. Revisiting the distributional impacts of trade 44

     4. Conclusion 49

   C. Commodity Markets 51

     1. Oil and natural gas 52

     2. Minerals and metals 52

     3. Food 53

   D. Global financial conditions and developing country vulnerabilities 54

     1. Capital flows to developing countries: Recent developments 54

     2. Debt and development distress in developing countries: Insights from the frontier market economies 57

   References 68

Chapter III

Food Commodities, Corporate Profiteering and Crises: Revisiting the International Regulatory Agenda...71

A. Introduction..73

B. Food as an asset: hedging, speculation and profiting from crises....................................76

C. Of loopholes and loopholing 84

    1. Dodd-Frank: an opportunity missed..85

    2. Global food traders: Commercial hedgers or financial institutions? 88

    3. How to differentiate between financial and commercial companies, using the "asset dominance" ratio 90

D. Regulatory Lessons 92

References 97

Chapter IV

Reforming the International Financial Architecture: The View from UNCTAD 101

A. Introduction..102

B. Towards a development-conscious international financial architecture.................................103

C. How to deliver development finance? Historical approaches and contemporary trends..................109

D. Solvency, sovereign debt relief and restructuring: Evolving challenges and ongoing advocacy 110

E. Conclusion 113

References 114

Chapter V

Realigning the Global Debt Architecture to Work for Developing Countries...............................117

A. Introduction..119

B. Regulating debt to address key system failures?...121

C. Life stages of sovereign debt 124

D. Transformational proposals 126

    1. Strengthening transparency across the sovereign debt cycle..126

    2. Debt management and debt sustainability analyses and tracking 131

    3. Debt workout and the global debt authority 133

E. Resilience in the debt life cycle 138

    1. Buffers to support resilience...138

    2. Anything but debt?..139

    3. Measures that create respite 140

F. Recommendations for transforming sovereign debt and a way forward...................................140

References 141

Chapter VI

The Need for Financial Reform for Climate-Aligned Development 145

  A. Introduction 147

  B. The underlying causes of financing gaps in a climate-aligned development agenda 147

     1. Private finance and the "missing trillions" 147

     2. The forward march of fossil fuel finance continues 148

     3. The role of public banks and funds in financing the shift to climate-aligned development 151

  C. Steps forward 154

     1. Scaling up additional public finance 155

     2. New and evolving market-related instruments 160

     3. Divestment and redirection of existing funds 163

  D. Changing the record: Building a consistent financial ecosystem that aligns climate
      and development finance 167

  E. Conclusion 169

  References 170

List of figures

I.1	Private investment is slowing down sharply again	5
I.2	Real GDP levels recovering separately	8
I.3	Rushed withdrawal of fiscal support: Post-2008 and post-2020	13
I.4	Globally: Rising profit share, shrinking fiscal space	15
I.5	Central banks have only partly retrenched from the pandemic expansion	16
I.6	Though real rates have rebounded they remain low in some developed countries... but credit conditions are considerably less favourable in developing countries	16
I.7	Investment and credit remain decoupled	18
I.8	Inflation rates have remained in line with historical standards in most developing countries	19
I.9	Inflation rates are down in developed countries and some prices are falling	20
I.10	Profit shares have increased above their long-term rising trends	22
I.11	Wages have not kept up with inflation	23
I.12	Post-pandemic, real compensation in the United States still has to recover	24
II.1	The sharp swing of supply chain pressures after their COVID-19 highs	37
II.2	Maritime freight rates have returned close to their 2010s average	38
II.3	International air passengers flying high: But Asia still not at cruising altitude	39
II.4	Global trade: Merchandise is declining while services appear more resilient	39
II.5	The paradox of United States-China trade decoupling	41
II.6	During the pandemic, export concentration strengthened further in more than half of surveyed developing countries	46
II.7	Increasing asymmetries of trade benefits: After the COVID-19 shock, profits of top 2,000 multinational enterprises further increased while the global labour income share continued to shrink	48
II.8	Commodity prices have moderated since 2022, but many products remain at historical levels	51
II.9	Capital flows to developing countries have been very volatile in recent years, with portfolio investments turning highly negative in late-2021 and early-2022	55
II.10	Equity fund flows to emerging market economies rebounded in early 2023	56
II.11	Significant appreciations of several emerging market currencies in the first half of 2023	56
II.12	Frontier markets contribute less than 10 per cent of developing countries' total output but carry 20 per cent of the external public debt	59
II.13	In the years after the global financial crisis, returns of non-investment grade bonds usually outstripped those of investment-grade bonds	59
II.14	Frontiers filling the vacuum in the non-investment grade segment	60
II.15	Frontiers' bond issuance was on the rise during the last decade until the COVID-19 shock	60
II.16	The reliance on private creditors for external financing of frontier market economies has strengthened	61
II.17	External public debt of frontier markets has grown faster post-financial crisis	61
II.18	Frontier markets' public finances are under heavy pressure after a decade of debt accumulation	62
II.19	Frontier markets' external debt service drains export revenues	62
II.20	Frontier markets are at the forefront of compounding crises	63
II.21	Growing number of frontier markets moving into debt distress	64
II.22	COVID-19 and other financial shocks increased debt vulnerability of frontier markets	64
II.23	Emerging and frontier markets face a wall of debt repayments from 2024 onwards	65
III.1	Profits of main energy and food traders increased dramatically in 2021–2022	73
III.2	Food as an asset: Price and volatility high again	76
III.3	Most exchange-traded agriculture derivatives are traded in Asia and North America	78

III.4   Profits of the "ABCD" food companies surge during periods of price volatility..............................79
III.5   Food price volatility increases during crises 80
III.6   Financial operations drive profit growth in the food trading sector..81
III.7   Hedging and speculation in OTC commodity markets..83
III.8   Large food traders become unregulated financial institutions 92
V.1   An evolving debtscape: Growing reliance on private credit 120
V.2   Unpacking the sovereign debt black box 125
V.3   Pitfalls along the path: The phases and failures of sovereign debt 126
V.4   Transformational goals along the sovereign debt life cycle 127
VI.1   Fossil fuel finance unabated even after the Paris Agreement 150
VI.2   Mature financial centres most involved in keeping fossil fuel finance alive and kicking 151
VI.3   The catalytic role of public banks and funds to finance the transition to green projects 152
VI.4   The downward slide in global development finance...155
VI.5   Despite years of multilateral pledges, fossil fuel subsidies fly high 163

List of boxes

I.1   Is a just transition possible in a low growth environment?..26
I.2   Inflation targeting: the history of the 2-per cent target 28
II.1   South–South trade cooperation: recent developments around the BRICS and the Global System of Trade
       Preferences initiative 50
II.2   Recent trends in official development assistance 58
III.1 It's all in the footnote: Dodd-Frank and financial regulatory arbitrage 86
IV.1   The Horowitz Proposal for a multilateral interest equalization fund: Fit for the green transition? 106
IV.2   UNCTAD and the Paris Club: 40 years of cooperation..111
V.1   Digitalizing loan transactions through an International Loans Repository 129
V.2   UNCTAD and the evolution of a global debt authority as an institutional mechanism 134
V.3   Private creditor coordination – lessons for borrowers?..136
VI.1   Targeting climate and fossil fuel finance inequalities..156
VI.2   Learnings from South Africa and the Just Energy Transition Partnership.....................................161
VI.3   The case of Indonesia: Financing reform of the palm oil and fossil fuel sectors............................166

List of figures in boxes

I.B1.1 Energy efficiency has increased since 1980 in most economies..26
I.B2.1 Inflation targeting is complicated by the difficulty of making correct projections............................29
VI.B1.1 Developed country banks originate the bulk of credit support to fossil fuel companies, except in China.........157

List of tables in boxes

I.B1.1 Spending on energy is a small fraction of total spending in most countries 27

List of tables

I.1	World output growth, 1991–2024	6
I.2	Developing countries have been generating critical global demand	8
I.3	Inflation eases at different rates across countries, due to their economic structures	21
II.A.1	List of frontier market economies	67
III.1	Global food trading companies: Number of subsidiaries	89
IV.1	The UNCTAD vision for reforming the international financial architecture	105
VI.1	Even a small reduction in subsidies would help, as producer subsidies total $51 billion	164

Foreword

Today, we see setbacks in indicators on poverty, hunger and gender equality, to mention just a few. The financing gap for the Sustainable Development Goals in the global South – which totalled $2.5 trillion in 2015 – now amounts to $4 trillion. Nearly half of all humanity, or 3.3 billion people, lives in countries that spend more resources on debt servicing than on funding health or education. At this pace, only 15 per cent of the Sustainable Development Goals will be achieved by 2030.

The *Trade and Development Report 2023: Growth, Debt and Climate – Realigning the Global Financial Architecture* identifies three specific global challenges that have crystalised during the year 2023. Weak global growth, divergence between major economies and between developing countries, as well as the increased role of geopolitical factors, indicate that we are witnessing a change in the nature of global interdependence, or a transition from the period of hyperglobalization to one of polyglobalization.

In its current phase, globalization is more decentralized, moving from a system dominated by a few global powers to a network of regional poles, big continental economies in the South and the rise of various plurinational forums. Competitive multilateralism appears to be replacing a universal one. This new phase of globalization is marked by inequality within and between countries, premature deindustrialization (with stagnation in employment) and a lack of resilience in the international system, with trade and investment lagging behind.

Between 1990 and 2010, at the peak of hyperglobalization, foreign direct investment expanded sevenfold and international trade, fourfold, while access to the Internet reached 30 per cent of the world population. In 2023, the growth of global trade remained below historical levels, with trade in intangible assets and services outpacing trade in manufactured goods, which has been hovering in negative territory. Asymmetries in the gains from international trade and related problems of market concentration have played a role in exacerbating the decline in the global labour income share. Foreign direct investment has stagnated since the 2008 crisis in the vast majority of developing countries.

These are dangerous trends. The Sustainable Development Goals are much more than a set of targets – they make up our latest shared agenda in a world that is more polarized than ever, a world that desperately needs solidarity, cooperation and multilateralism. The global economy does not have a trade structure adapted to a context in which all the poles are making industrial policy.

This can be a risk in the long term, especially for small countries that depend on multilaterally agreed rules-based international trade. In the context of polyglobalization, the countries that have been marginalized historically in global decision-making should be given a voice. The UNCTAD flagship *Trade and Development Report* has been presenting ideas and solutions to empower this voice and close the developmental gap. As the challenges analysed in the *Trade and Development Report 2023* show, our greatest task has scarcely begun.

Rebeca Grynspan
Secretary-General of UNCTAD

Abbreviations

ADR	asset-dominance ratio
AfCFTA	African Continental Free Trade Area
AMIS	Agricultural Market Information System
ASCM	Agreement on Subsidies and Countervailing Measures
BEPS	base erosion and profit shifting
BOGA	Beyond Oil and Gas Alliance
CAC	collective action clause
CBAM	carbon border adjustment mechanism
CBDR	common but differentiated responsibilities
CERES	Coalition for Environmentally Responsible Economies
CFTC	United States Commodities Futures Trading Commission
CHIPS	Creating Helpful Incentives to Produce Semiconductors
CIF	cost, insurance and freight
CIFT	Committee on Invisibles and Financing related to Trade
CRA	credit rating agency
DAC	Development Assistance Committee
DMFAS	Debt Management and Financial Analysis System
DSA	debt sustainability analysis
DSSI	Debt Service Suspension Initiative
EBITDA	earnings before interest, taxes, depreciation and amortization
ECB	European Central Bank
EMBI	Emerging Market Bond Index
EME	emerging market economy
ESG	environmental, social and governance
EUDR	Deforestation Regulation of the European Union
FDI	foreign direct investment
FME	frontier market economy
FOB	freight on board
FSB	Financial Stability Board
G20	Group of 20
G77	Group of 77
G90	Group of 90
GATT	General Agreement on Tariffs and Trade
GCEL	Global Coal Exit List
GDIP	Green Deal Industrial Plan

GDP	gross domestic product
GFANZ	Global Financial Alliance for Net Zero
GFC	global financial crisis
GFSN	global financial safety net
GNI	gross national income
GSCPI	global supply chain pressure index
GSP	General and Special Principles
GSTP	Global System of Trade Preferences
GUO	global ultimate owner
GVC	global value chain
HIPC	heavily indebted poor countries
IAEA	International Atomic Energy Agency
ICMA	International Capital Markets Association
IDA	International Development Association
IEA	International Energy Agency
IEJ	Institute of Economic Justice
IFA	international financial architecture
IFF	illicit financial flow
IFRS	international financing reporting standards
IIF	Institute of International Finance
IIJA	Infrastructure Investment and Jobs Act
ILR	international loans repository
IMF	International Monetary Fund
IPCC	International Panel on Climate Change
IRA	Inflation Reduction Act
ISDA	International Swaps and Derivatives Association
JET IP	Just Energy Transition Investment Plan
LDC	least developed country
LNG	liquefied natural gas
MDB	multilateral development banks
MDRI	Multilateral Debt Relief Initiative
MFN	most favoured nation
MiFID	European Union Markets in Financial Instruments Directive
MNE	multinational enterprise
NBFI	non-bank financial institutions

NDC	nationally determined contribution
NGEU	Next Generation E[uropean] U[nion]
NGFS	Network for Greening the Financial System
NZIA	Net-Zero Industry Act
ODA	official development assistance
OECD	Organisation for Economic Co-operation and Development
OPEC	Organization of the Petroleum Exporting Countries
OTC	over the counter
PNG	private non-guaranteed
PPG	public and publicly guaranteed
PRGT	Poverty Reduction and Growth Trust
RPK	revenue-passenger kilometre
RTA	regional trade agreement
SDGs	Sustainable Development Goals
SDR	special drawing right
SEC	United States Securities and Exchange Commission
SDFA	Sustainable Development Finance Assessment
SDT	special and differential treatment provisions
SIDS	small island developing State
SNAP	Supplemental Nutrition Assistance Program
TDR	Trade and Development Report
TRIMS	Agreement on Trade-Related Investment Measures
TRIPS	Trade-Related Aspects of Intellectual Property Rights
VAT	value-added tax
WTO	World Trade Organization

Explanatory notes

Classification by country

The classification of countries in this Report has been adopted solely for the purposes of statistical or analytical convenience and does not necessarily imply any judgement concerning the stage of development of a particular country or area.

There is no established convention for the designation of "developing" and "developed" countries or areas in the United Nations system. This Report follows the classification as defined in the UNCTAD Handbook of Statistics 2023 for these two major country groupings (see https://hbs.unctad.org/classifications/, accessed on 20 December 2023), which is based on the classification applied in the "Standard Country or Area Codes for Statistical Use", known as "M49", maintained by the United Nations Statistics Division (see https://unstats.un.org/unsd/methodology/m49/, accessed on 20 December 2023).

For statistical purposes, regional groupings used in this Report follow generally those employed in the *UNCTAD Handbook of Statistics 2023* unless otherwise stated. The data for China do not include those for Hong Kong Special Administrative Region (Hong Kong SAR), Macao Special Administrative Region (Macao SAR) and Taiwan Province of China.

References to "sub-Saharan Africa" in the text or tables include South Africa unless otherwise indicated.

Other notes

References in the text to *TDR* are to the *Trade and Development Report* (of a particular year). For example, *TDR 2020* refers to *Trade and Development Report 2020* (United Nations publication, Sales No. E.20.II.D.30).

The term "dollar" ($) refers to United States dollars, unless otherwise stated.

The term "billion" signifies 1,000 million.

The term "trillion" signifies 1,000,000 million.

The term "tons" refers to metric tons.

Annual rates of growth and change refer to compound rates.

Exports are expressed at freight on board (FOB) prices while and imports are reported at cost, insurance and freight (CIF) value, unless otherwise specified.

Use of a dash (–) between dates representing years, e.g. 2019–2021, signifies the full period involved, including the initial and final years.

An oblique stroke (/) between two years, e.g. 2019/20, signifies a fiscal or crop year. A dot (.) in a table indicates that the item is not applicable.

Two dots (..) in a table indicate that the data are not available or are not separately reported.

A dash (–) or a zero (0) in a table indicates that the amount is nil or negligible.

Decimals and percentages do not necessarily add up to totals because of rounding.

OVERVIEW

Global economy: Stalling into 2024

The year 2023 is likely to be seen as an inflection point in a fragile and uneven global recovery, post-pandemic. The entire world economy, except for North Africa and Central and East Asia, has slowed since 2022. With projected growth in 2023 of 2.4 per cent, the world enters 2024 at "stall speed", matching the definition of a global recession. Divergence of low growth trends between key regions, as well as within the BRICS countries (Brazil, the Russian Federation, India, China and South Africa) and the Group of Seven indicates that there is no clear driving force to propel the world economy onto a robust recovery track. Without adequate coordinated policy responses or mechanisms, today's diverse and compounding shocks risk being transformed into tomorrow's systemic crises. In the face of new challenges to the international political economy, this scenario is a threat to the multilateral system and to global economic stability. Policymakers need to engage on multiple fronts to chart a stronger, more resilient trajectory for the future.

The year also saw a mix of economic outcomes. On the one hand, inflation, while still above pre-pandemic levels, is coming under control in many parts of the world. The banking crises of the second quarter of 2023 did not lead to financial contagion and commodity prices are down from their 2022 peaks. A small improvement in global growth is expected in 2024, but it is contingent on recovery in the euro area and on other leading economies avoiding adverse shocks. On the other hand, three sets of structural problems threaten global long-term stability and economic resilience:

(a) Diverging recovery paths in the context of slower growth across major regions;

(b) Deepening asymmetries in income and wealth;

(c) Growing pressures of indebtedness and thinning policy autonomy in developing economies.

These three factors add to an increasingly complex interplay between economic, climate and geopolitical risks. Against this background, prospects for developing countries are especially concerning. Development requires a favourable external environment based on robust global demand, stable exchange rates and affordable financing. The ability of developing countries to accelerate growth, strengthen productive capacities, decarbonize and meet their financial obligations is fundamentally dependent on steady, strong global demand. Today, however, international policy coordination is driven by central banks that focus primarily on short-term monetary stability over long-term financial sustainability. This trend, together with inadequate regulation in commodity markets and continuous neglect for rising inequality, is fracturing the world economy and splintering off developing countries, undermining their ability to thrive.

"A strategy of sustainable and balanced growth becomes less feasible if high levels of debt and inadequate financial regulation threaten financial stability and food security, while, in parallel, income is increasingly retained by global corporations rather than workers."

Against this background, 2024 is unlikely to show substantial improvement. A strategy of sustainable and balanced growth becomes less feasible if high levels of debt and inadequate financial regulation threaten financial stability and food security, while, in parallel, income is increasingly retained by global corporations rather than workers. In the face of a crisis, previous coordination efforts have tended to ignore sectors or countries that are not considered systemically relevant, thus compounding the very crisis they sought to resolve. This mistake should be avoided at all costs.

The *Trade and Development Report 2023* presents an alternative response. It outlines an approach based on balancing the pace of disinflation and the impact of high real interest rates not only against inflation indicators, but also in relation to economic activity, employment, income inequality and fiscal stability. Yet in the current framework of international financial architecture, policy space is easily curtailed by movements in the asset markets. This has heavy impacts on social policies, investment and employment generation. In an interconnected world in which developing countries are potential engines of economic growth, policymakers in advanced economies should consider the damage that high interest rates can cause to long-term investment, both in terms of structural change and climate adaptation as well as debt sustainability.

To address these problems, this Report identifies five core policy priorities:

1. **Reducing inequality.** This should be made a policy priority in developed and developing countries. This requires concerted increases of real wages and concrete commitments towards comprehensive social protection. Monetary policy is not to be used as the sole tool to alleviate inflationary pressures. With supply-side problems still unaddressed, a policy mix is needed to attain financial sustainability, help lower inequalities and deliver inclusive growth.

2. **Balancing the priorities of monetary stability with long-term financial sustainability.** In light of growing interdependencies in the global economy, central banks should assume a wider stabilizing function within this landscape.

3. **Regulating commodity trading generally, and food trading in particular.** This needs to be done internationally, using a systemic approach developed within the framework of the global financial architecture.

4. **Addressing the crushing burden of debt servicing and the threat of spreading debt crises.** To do this, the rules and practices of the global financial architecture need to be reformed. The mechanisms, principles and institutions of global finance should ensure reliable access to international liquidity and a stable financial environment that promotes investment-led growth. Given the failures of the current architecture to enable the resilience and recovery of developing countries from debt stress, it is crucial to establish a mechanism to resolve sovereign debt workouts. This should be based on the participation of all developing countries and include agreed procedures, incentives and deterrents.

5. **Providing reliable access to finance and technology transfer to enable the energy transition.** This would require not only fiscal and monetary agreements among the Group of 20, but also agreements within the World Trade Organization (WTO) to implement technology transfer, and within the International Monetary Fund (IMF) and World Bank to ensure dependable financing. Without eliminating the incentives and regulatory conduits that make cross-border speculative investment so profitable, private capital is unlikely to be channelled to measures to help adapt to climate change.

Global growth landscape: Divergence under clouds of uncertainty

In 2023, the global outlook was shaped by four main factors. First, international prices of oil, gas and food returned to late 2021 levels, eliminating a powerful driver of inflation. However, retail prices in many countries remained higher than pre-pandemic averages, putting pressure on household budgets. With supply-side drivers of inflation largely addressed, Governments should in principle be able to tackle profiteering more effectively. Yet, the policy actions currently observed mostly involve central banks continuing to signal the likelihood of high interest rates.

Second, the United States of America, accounting for a quarter of the world economy, displayed resilience during two years of rising consumer price inflation (April 2020–June 2022). This was despite a year and a half of blanket disinflation policies (11 interest rate hikes in 18 months) and sporadic financial market disruptions. Key parts of the economy, buoyed by employment and nominal wage growth, have sustained consumption and spending. At the same time, although unemployment reached historic lows, the employment rate remains at recession levels, standing at 58 per cent of the population, and for many, wages remain very low.

Third, in China, lifting of the remaining COVID-19-related restrictions helped sustain the recovery that began in 2022 and which revamped industrial production. The country's economic growth relies less on exports than in the past and the Government continues to enjoy considerable fiscal space. However, persistent weaknesses in the real estate sector pose challenges, including potential financial stress, reduced job creation, constrained consumer spending and delayed investments. Escalating geopolitical tensions are disrupting the dominant position of China in key global value chains, clouding prospects in some of its frontier technology sectors, at least in the short-term. Authorities have responded to slower than expected growth with a mix of monetary expansion, supply-side incentives and regulatory tightening. The overall impact of the chosen policy responses and their spillover effects, particularly on neighbouring economies, remains uncertain.

Fourth, concerns over growth prospects in China should not divert attention away from the deteriorating economic health of the European economy. With a share of the global economy similar to that of China (approximately 18 per cent in purchasing power parity, higher at current exchange rates), the global consequences of the slowdown in Europe are at least twice as weighty as those of the slowdown in China.

"With a share of the global economy similar to that of China, the consequences of the slowdown in Europe are at least twice as weighty as those of the slowdown in China."

At the current juncture, larger emerging economies are unlikely to provide a robust offset to slower growth in advanced economies. With tighter monetary policy, low investment and limited government spending, the world economy is experiencing a lacklustre recovery reminiscent of the aftermath of the 2007–2009 financial crisis. Of particular concern, given the ambitious development and climate targets set by the international community with a 2030 delivery date, growth in almost all regions in 2023 and 2024 is also set to fall below the average for the five-year period before the pandemic. Latin America stands out as an exceptional example of the trend, facing an even more challenging situation due to its particularly weak growth prior to the pandemic.

Trends in international markets

During 2023, developments in the international trade and finance system were influenced by uncertainties. These include a tighter monetary stance by central banks in advanced countries, a more geostrategic policy approach to international economic relations, the growing influence of industrial policy on trade strategies of major economies together with multiple geoeconomic risks. In addition, several structural weaknesses that pre-date the COVID-19 shock have become particularly significant for developing countries. These relate to the growing concentration of export markets and related asymmetry of income distribution, a slowdown in investment and an unsustainable burden of debt, the widening technological divide and the mounting costs of the climate crisis and related challenges around the energy transition.

The intertwining of immediate and long-term concerns poses significant governance challenges for today's interdependent global economy. Increasingly, the principles of the rules-based multilateral trading system are being contested. This trend is unlikely to fade, given the diminishing prospects of achieving the kind of harmonious and stable order required to meet the goals of the 2030 Agenda for Sustainable Development and the targets of the Paris Agreement. Whether, and how, policymakers will meet these governance challenges over the coming months will determine whether the world avoids recession in 2024. Resolving these governance issues also depends on developing countries sidestepping a "lost decade" and the multilateral system avoiding further fracture and ending the current decade in more robust health.

Reshaping global trade

After a rollercoaster ride in 2020–2022, global trade in goods and services points to a subdued expansion of 1 per cent in 2023, significantly below world economic output growth. This is also lower than the average growth registered during the last decade, itself the slowest average growth period for global trade since 1945. In the medium-term, trade is heading back to its subdued pre-crisis trend; in the near-term, despite the resilience of global trade in services, it will remain sluggish, as the growth of merchandise trade hovered in negative territory throughout 2023.

The asymmetry of gains from the international trading system, apparent in both advanced and developing countries, has been building into a backlash against the rules of global governance and, increasingly, the very idea of free trade. This backlash is prompting policymakers to reassess their strategic prioritization of the role of trade. A new trade lexicography reflects these shifts, with terms such as "fragmentation", "deglobalization", "slowbalization", "reshoring", "nearshoring", "friendshoring", "de-risking", "decoupling", "open strategic autonomy" and "new industrial policy" peppering current discussions around trade policy.

"The asymmetry of gains from the international trading system, apparent in both advanced and developing countries, has been building into a backlash against the rules of global governance and the very idea of free trade."

New export controls have also reflected the shifting sentiment around trade policy across the globe. These have covered three types of non-mutually exclusive objectives: (a) securing domestic supply, (b) restricting geopolitical rivals, and (c) encouraging investment in locally based processing facilities. The shift is also apparent in current discussions around the need for a new paradigm of trade that can support the challenge of global economic integration and interdependence. A new three-fold strategy can be built around the need to prioritize reducing inequality, building resilience and accelerating the energy transition.

Regardless of whether the calls to reform international trade can be translated into a new regime of international economic governance, a significant reshaping of world trade is underway which includes a restructuring of global supply chains. Navigating this transformation poses major challenges to most developing economies at a time when their prospects for economic growth are deteriorating, the investment climate is worsening and financial stresses are mounting. Two risks can be already identified. First, many developing countries risk being caught in the crossfire of trade disputes or face growing pressure to take sides in economic conflicts they neither want nor need. Second, in large economies, the rise of protectionist unilateral trade measures and a wider use of industrial policies can adversely impact developing economies' exports and hinder their prospects for structural transformation.

At the same time, some developing countries may see gains from a restructuring of global supply chains in the near-term. A green investment boom in advanced economies might bring opportunities for some fortunately endowed countries, such as exporters of strategic minerals. However, sustainable developmental success will require parallel support to promote access to reliable (and cheaper) sources of finance, a rebalancing of trade rules and levelling the playing field.

Trade disputes and asymmetries

The twenty-first century has witnessed China displacing the United States as the world's leading exporter of manufactured goods. While a growing trade deficit with China provoked intermittent responses from legislatures in the United States, a more assertive stance only began in 2017, seen in progressive tariff increases on exports from China. These tariff increases resulted in significant trade diversion, mostly benefiting the main economic rivals to China, including Mexico and the European Union.

A paradox of the current trade dispute between the world's two largest economies is that total imports of goods to the United States from China have returned to their pre-COVID-19 peak. This is due to the sharp increase in products not subject to tariffs. Bilateral imports of goods and services from China to the United States reached the highest level ever recorded – $564 billion in 2022 – as services continued to expand. The United States remains the main destination for exports of merchandise from China. This is followed by Japan, the Republic of Korea, Viet Nam and India. At the same time, notwithstanding this recovery, the trade dispute has imposed costs on trading partners.

With regards to domestic supply concerns, current WTO rules allow for temporary export restrictions or prohibitions to prevent or relieve critical shortages of essential products. This is provided all measures are communicated, have phase-out timelines and are proportionate to the scale of the problem at hand. A key issue here is defining what is considered as "proportionate". In the early phases of the COVID-19 pandemic, over 80 countries resorted to banning exports of medical and personal protective goods. Similarly, following the outbreak of the war in Ukraine in early 2022, almost 100 export restrictions on essential agricultural commodities were identified to have been applied by 35 WTO members and observers.

Ultimately, such unilateral measures often do more harm than good, which begs the question of whether the international community should not come up with stricter rules, especially on essential goods such as medical products and food, to ensure that similar future practices are better controlled and do not result in a negative spiral that hampers the resilience of all. Discussions have been continuing for some time, yet no significant agreement has been reached and it is unlikely to emerge before the WTO 13th Ministerial Conference of February 2024.

The expansion of trade in the era of hyperglobalization has been closely tied to the spread of global value chains (GVCs) controlled by large firms that are primarily headquartered in advanced economies. In parallel, a growing number of developing countries have participated in the international division of labour by providing specific links in these chains, drawing on their abundance of unskilled labour. This mode of international integration was based on the promise that such fledgling manufacturing activities, through a mixture of upgrading and spillover effects, would quickly establish robust and inclusive growth paths aligned with their comparative advantage.

The success of this model has been neither uniform nor certain. This raises questions about the strong bets made in many developing economies on the spillovers expected from processing trade. Unless developing countries manage to capture part of the surplus created by these GVCs and reinvest it in productive capacities and infrastructure, immediate gains in output and employment are unlikely to translate into a dynamic move up the development ladder. In short, replicating the successes registered in several developing countries, mostly in East and South-East Asia, has proven difficult elsewhere.

"The rise in profits of large multinational enterprises, together with their growing concentration, is a driving force exacerbating income inequality."

Along with the rise of export market concentration, large firms have increased their ability to extract rents. Empirical evidence indicates that the rise in profits of large multinational enterprises, together with their growing concentration, is a driving force pushing down the global labour income share and exacerbating income inequality. This has also led to unequal trading relations, even as developing countries have deepened their participation in global trade. New data points to two main trends:

- Export concentrations appear to have strengthened in the majority of the observed developing countries between the pre-pandemic period and the COVID-19 years.

- Factor income distribution has continued to shift further in favour of capital owners during the COVID-19 pandemic years, with the profits of the largest 2,000 firms worldwide accounting for the bulk of this gain. This mirrored the continued decline of the labour income share globally.

A healthy trading system is crucial for meeting the 2030 Agenda. It remains unclear whether key trade partners have the political will to guide the system through its current difficulties. In 2023, the Group of 90 countries at WTO identified 10 specific multilateral trade agreements that would require revisions to allow more policy space for countries to be able to redesign their production, consumption and trading profiles to face contemporary global challenges. The Group of 90 proposal seeks to strengthen existing flexibilities for developing members, to make them more precise, effective and operational and to more effectively address members' development aims. Failure to address these concerns in a pro-development and cooperative approach may further exacerbate today's asymmetries. This will make it even more difficult for the world to deliver on the 2030 Agenda.

Trends in commodity markets

The aggregate Commodity Price Index registered a drop of more than 30 per cent in May 2023 compared to the previous year. The reduction in aggregate prices has primarily been driven by fuel commodities, which experienced a significant drop of over 40 per cent during this period. However, some product groupings in the UNCTAD Commodity Price Index registered more muted reductions during this period, to remain at historically high levels. The prices of minerals, ores and metals declined only 4 per cent, while food dropped by just 2 per cent.

Four factors explain the moderation of commodity prices. First, price surges in crude oil, natural gas and grains following the outbreak of the war in Ukraine eased from the middle of 2022. This was due to a reorientation of trade flows of key commodity exports from the Russian Federation and Ukraine, and the brokering of the Black Sea Initiative in July 2022 to enable the shipment of grains and other materials from strategically important Ukrainian ports. The second factor is the deteriorating outlook for global demand, compounded by monetary tightening across the globe. Third, restrictive monetary conditions and an accompanying uptick in international interest rates prompted investors to move financial investments away from commodities towards higher interest-bearing assets. Fourth, the slower than expected rebound in China following the reopening of its economy and the persistent weaknesses in its real estate sector also contributed to the loosening of broad commodity price indices after the peaks reached in 2022.

The commodity group where the impact of recent trends in international prices has been most detrimental for developing nations is that of food commodities. As noted by the United Nations Global Crisis Response Group, international food prices were already approaching historic highs even before the outbreak of the war in Ukraine, causing food import bills to rise dramatically. About two thirds of the increase of costs were concentrated in developing countries. The further climb in international food prices after February 2022 left many developing countries facing prohibitively high prices for many of their most basic staple food products. Moreover, the impact of the disruption in the supply and transport of grains, notably wheat, maize, and sunflower products from Ukraine and the Russian Federation proved particularly acute for African and Middle Eastern countries that rely on the flow of grains from these countries to meet their basic food needs.

The international prices of many of these food products have moderated over the 12 months to May 2023 – with prices of wheat, maize and sunflower oil dropping by 25, 21 and 51 per cent respectively – partly thanks to the Black Sea Initiative and to increased supplies from South America and other major producing countries.

Still, international food prices remain at historically high levels and the transmission of lower international prices to domestic prices has been weak. In several developing countries, the domestic prices of basic foods in June 2023 remained above their levels of the previous year and continue to impact food security. Relevant factors keeping domestic prices at elevated levels include high fertilizer costs, adverse weather, high distribution costs, strong indebtedness as well as domestic currency weaknesses. The financialization of food systems and the pricing behaviour of large commodity traders have also played a role in price and market volatility. As a result, almost 350 million people worldwide – including more than 100 million people in sub-Saharan Africa – are estimated to be food insecure in 2023, which is over double the number in 2020.

Global financial conditions and developing country vulnerabilities

On the eve of the COVID-19 shock, many developing countries already faced unsustainable debt burdens. Since then, compounding crises, along with the most aggressive monetary tightening in developed countries since the 1970s, have exacerbated this situation. While a systemic debt crisis – in which a growing number of developing countries move simultaneously from distress to default – has so far been kept at bay, a development crisis is already unfolding. External debt servicing is draining resources away from delivering on the 2030 Agenda and on the goals of the Paris Agreement.

One difference between the current and previous debt crises in the developing world is that emerging market economies, i.e. countries that were brought into international financial markets in earlier periods, are not at the forefront. This time around, it is generally low- or lower-middle-income developing countries that started to tap international capital markets. This mostly occurred during the capital flow boom after the global financial crisis and before COVID-19. These countries, referred to as "frontier market economies" (FMEs), have been the hardest hit. The recent rise in debt distress and related development setbacks in developing countries can be directly attributed to inherent structural weaknesses in the international financial system. The current structural paradigms are proving inadequate in facilitating access to reliable sources of external development finance in the required quantity, cost and maturity for these countries to meet their development needs.

Other factors contributing to the unfolding crisis of debt service include: insufficient official development assistance, a relative decline of official concessional financing (and the denial of access to some categories of developing countries for such schemes), decisions of credit rating agencies and an inadequate global financial safety net. Added to this is the significant presence of illicit financial flows (IFFs), which diminishes the scope for mobilizing domestic resources.

Given the magnitude of the debt challenges faced, a renewed sense of urgency to advance multilateral solutions is required. In the aftermath of the COVID-19 pandemic, the total world debt of both public and non-financial private sectors peaked at 257 per cent of world gross product in 2020, before receding 10 percentage points by the end of 2021. Within this broader context, developing countries are highly vulnerable. Their debts, both private and public, registered significant increases over the last decade. More specifically, private debt in a broad group of emerging markets and developing economies increased from 84 to 130 per cent of gross domestic product (GDP) between 2010 and 2021. Meanwhile, total public debt in these countries nearly doubled, reaching 64 per cent of GDP by 2022.

"Total public debt in emerging markets and developing countries has nearly doubled, reaching 64 per cent of GDP by 2022."

The rapid accumulation of non-concessional debt has caused a significant increase in interest payments. Since the ending of easy monetary policy in both developed and developing economies, these payments have reached new highs, with a double burden in countries that have seen their currencies depreciate against the dollar and euro. The number of countries where interest spending accounted for 10 per cent or more of public revenues increased from 29 in 2010 to 50 in 2022. Consequently, interest payments in many developing countries outpaced expenditures in critical sectors such as education, health, and public investment over the past decade. Currently, at least 3.3 billion people live in countries that spend more on interest than on either health or education. Most of these countries experienced declines in their Human Development Index in recent years. Carrying these greater debt burdens obstructs the mobilization of resources needed to achieve the goals of the 2030 Agenda.

"In the past decade, interest payments in many developing countries outpaced expenditures in critical sectors such as education, health, and public investment."

Within developing countries, frontier market economies require particular attention. Collectively, this subgroup of economies within developing countries registered the fastest growth of external public debt over the last decade. It is therefore not a coincidence that even if collectively, FMEs only represented 8 per cent of their GDP and 6 per cent of their total public debt in recent years, vis-à-vis the total of developing countries, they accounted for 20 per cent of developing countries' total external public debt. In other words, FMEs, and especially their public sector, are now particularly exposed to the asymmetries and shortcomings of the international financial architecture, particularly with respect to the consequences of debt distress.

"Currently, at least 3.3 billion people live in countries that spend more on interest than on either health or education."

The debt challenges faced by developing countries in general, and those of FMEs in particular, are set to increase as a large wave of bond repayments comes due in the next few years. FME bond repayments, including principal and coupon payments, will reach $13 billion in 2024 and continue to be high at least until the end of the decade. This raises concerns that more FMEs may default if their market access is not restored. Moreover, for emerging market economies and frontier market economies that have retained market access, new sovereign bond issuances will be costly given the higher interest rates in developed countries. Higher borrowing costs in a context of lower economic growth will undermine debt sustainability. Without measures to effectively address this dynamic, most countries are expected to prioritize fiscal consolidation to stabilize debt levels. Regrettably, this dynamic will place attaining the 2030 Agenda even further out of reach.

Food commodities, corporate profiteering and crises: Revisiting the international regulatory agenda

The last few years of commodity price volatility have coincided with a period of record profits for global energy and food traders. In food trading, the four companies that conservatively account for about 70 per cent of the global food market share registered a dramatic rise in profits during 2021–2022. The asymmetry between growing risks to food security of millions around the world and profiteering by a few corporations, became particularly stark during 2022–2023. In the highly concentrated commodity trading industry, the superprofits enjoyed by agripolies trickle down very slowly, if at all, to local farming communities.

Increasingly, warnings about this asymmetry come from market analysts, civil society, regulators and international organizations concerned with the lack of regulatory oversight of commodity trading. Yet opacity, cross-sector interconnections and intragroup corporate activity pose major hurdles in any effort to scope the problem, identify risks and workable solutions. This can explain why, despite growing public attention on the issue of market concentration and profiteering, current policy debate on possible multilateral solutions to the food systems crisis has not addressed this question in depth.

The current predicament has illuminated two key aspects of the status quo. First, there is ample evidence that banks, asset managers, hedge funds and other financial institutions continue to profit from the most recent bout of commodity market volatility. Second, by actively managing risk, commodity trading firms have assumed many financing, insurance and investment functions typically associated with the activity of banks. In this context, large international trading firms, or ABCD-type companies,[1] have come to occupy a privileged position in terms of setting prices, accessing financing and participating directly in the financial markets. This enables speculative trades in organized market platforms as well as in over-the-counter operations, over which most governments in advanced countries have no authority or control.

This Report presents results from UNCTAD research that studies patterns of profiteering in the global food trading sector. Analysis reveals that unregulated financial activities play a major role in the profit structure of global food traders. Relatedly, corporate profits from financial operations appear to be strongly linked with periods of excessive speculation in commodities markets and the growth of shadow banking.

Three specific findings follow from this analysis. First, food trading companies have come to rely on the use of financial instruments and engineering not simply to hedge their commercial positions, but to strategically ride the wave of market volatility. Second, market and price volatility appear to have a much more pronounced role in the sector's financial operations, in contrast to their core commercial activities. Third, financial instruments and techniques designed for hedging a range of commercial risks are being used by the sector for speculative purposes. This is enabled by the current regulatory architecture of commodity trading as a whole, which remains diluted and fragmented.

"Large grain processors with access to a wealth of information regarding food markets have a clear interest in using their hedging activities as a profit centre."

A key consequence of this regulatory fragmentation is the dichotomy between the regulatory treatment of commodity traders as manufacturing corporations on the one hand, and their increasingly more profitable (yet unregulated) activities in financial markets, on the other. The concept behind this distinction between commercial and financial market participants is that

---

[1] Large firms of a size and stature akin to the four big commodity traders, Archer Daniels Midland, Bunge, Cargill and Louis Dreyfus Company, known as "ABCD" because of the coincidence of their initials.

an industrial business should only look for security in prices, not betting for the sake of it. However, large grain processors with access to a wealth of information regarding food markets have a clear interest in using their hedging activities as a profit centre. In the process, they tend to change their business model and start operating like a financial actor, benefiting from exemptions designed for purely commercial hedgers.

In the case of major food giants, using hedging for purely speculative purposes appears to take place at the level of subsidiaries, and is often not reported at a consolidated level. Specifically, by using a series of subsidiaries located in appropriate jurisdictions, food monopolies have found a way to combine several advantages:

- A superior knowledge of the agricultural commodities markets (real-time supply and demand and prospective knowledge of how the markets will evolve);

- An ability to store agricultural commodities to harness price surges when they occur: ABCD invested heavily in infrastructure for storage and built significant grain reserves; but with no obligation to disclose their grain stocks;

- The secrecy of their operations and benefiting from derogations to the rules applicable to pure financial actors; ABCD have legally structured their operations using hundreds of subsidiaries incorporated to take advantage of the various menus of regulations (or lack thereof) offered by different jurisdictions, including secrecy jurisdictions, around the world.

Empirical analysis by UNCTAD indicates abnormal use of intragroup transfers within private corporate groups. Intragroup transfers are financial transactions between legally independent entities within a corporate group. The analysis led to three key findings:

- First, the cases showing growth in asset dominance are observed primarily at the subsidiary level within the group, indicating increased use of intragroup transfers.

- Second, this suggests that the amount of excess profits being made could be underestimated when only looking at public profit and loss reporting.

- Third, profiteering is not limited to a specific sector but is specific to individual firms. There are concerns that excess profits may be linked to market concentration, benefiting only a few global players in the commodity trading community. This reinforces the need to consider group membership and the evolving behaviour of major international players in the sector.

"Profiteering reinforces the need to consider corporate group membership and the behaviour of major players in the food trading sector."

These three issues crystallized in the commodities sector at the peak of the energy crisis in 2020–2021, when market volatility threatened the financial stability of clearing houses and required the support of public liquidity injections.

The growth of unregulated financial activities within today's food trading industry suggests that financial stability risks may evolve under the radar of regulators, while corporate influence over strategically significant markets continues to grow. This compounds the challenge of detecting and curbing excessive market speculation in commodity and food trading; it can add to risks of the shadow banking system and thus endanger financial stability. It also conceals IFF risks and exposures in the poorly regulated yet highly interconnected and systemically important food trading industry.

"The historical approach, which distinguishes between commercial and financial operators in agricultural commodity derivatives, is ill-suited to the current economic and legal structures of global trade in certain agricultural products and their associated derivatives."

Together, these developments warrant a revision to the existing regulatory architecture of commodity trading. The historical approach, which distinguishes between commercial and financial operators in agricultural commodity derivatives, is ill-suited to the current economic and legal structures of global trade in certain agricultural products and their associated derivatives. Possible solutions centre on three interrelated levels of policy reform that capture the connection between market practices and financial activities:

(a) Market-level reform: close loopholes, facilitate transparency;

(b) Systemic-level reform: recognize aspects of food traders' activities as financial institutions and extend relevant regulations;

(c) Global governance-level reform: extend monitoring and regulations to the level of corporate subsidiaries in the sector to address the problem of the origin of profits, enhance transparency and curb the risks of illicit financial flows.

Crucially, all three levels of necessary action require much more cooperation on data quality, disclosure and corporate transparency in the sector. At the same time, while data transparency is necessary, it is insufficient for market participants to discover prices. What is required is a process in which all market participants contribute daily price information, and which is accessible to all participants and regulators on a daily basis.

The role of monopolies on strategically important markets in times of crises and the complexity of global corporate and financial structures that enable speculation and profiteering not only require close attention, but also smart policies. Regulation of these interconnected problems needs to be targeted to the specific issues at hand, at a multilateral level. Crucially, reforms need to be conceived in an integrated way, targeting key priorities across the system. More specifically:

(a) The problem of excessive financial speculation in commodities markets needs to be addressed along with the problem of unregulated activities in the underregulated sector;

(b) The issue of corporate control over key markets cannot be resolved by antitrust measures alone but requires a coherent framework of national competition and industrial policies;

(c) International cooperation and commitment are critical in the effort to enhance data quality and transparency in commodity trading and curb the risks of financial instability and illicit finance.

Reforming the international financial architecture: The view from UNCTAD

The international financial architecture (IFA) is a framework of institutions, policies, rules and practices that govern the global financial system. Aimed at supporting international cooperation, IFA focuses on ensuring monetary and financial stability, international trade and investment and supporting the mobilization of financing required for sustainable development in the age of climate crises.

Recurring financial and debt crises, as well as the shortfall in required development and climate finance, highlight that the scope of today's financial, macroeconomic and development challenges stretch far beyond the IFA framework, the institutional core of which was created in the mid-twentieth century. And while many of today's problems are of a systemic nature, two aspects have been apparent from an early stage.

First, the framework of the IFA and its institutions are not set up to deliver the kind of financial support needed by developing countries to realize their growth and development ambitions in a rapidly changing global economy confronted with climate crises. Second, given that they often have sizable and lasting current account deficits, developing countries operate under conditions of asymmetrical access and restricted policy autonomy. This contributes to the accumulation of unsustainable external debt burdens.

The search for a desired change of direction requires these systemic challenges to be addressed comprehensively. However, both the required global agreement and the political will to take reforms forward have been lacking. Instead, a wide range of more piecemeal and ad hoc reforms have been pursued. A series of recent reform proposals (new institutions, new alliances between existing institutions, new policy instruments, and new systemic thinking), often initiated by developing countries, may be advanced into the basis for an alternative international financial architecture.

These proposed revisions are often contested, partly because they may appear incoherent both between themselves and with the current IFA. Yet, they are widening the scope for institutional experimentation and may eventually give rise to more participatory and sustainable global monetary and financial governance. UNCTAD promotes a systemic approach to finance, trade and development, and an insistence on structural transformation has put the institution ahead of the curve. Nevertheless, it is increasingly clear that a truly systemic approach goes beyond the interdependence of trade and finance. It must also incorporate the challenges that arise from environmental shocks and sustainability, most urgently linked to climate and biodiversity challenges, as well as geopolitical risks.

Chapters IV through VI of this Report analyse two sets of such challenges. The first involves promoting economic and financial stability in a world that is becoming increasingly financially fragile and vulnerable to cross-border spillovers. Timely and adequate liquidity support and an adequate financial safety net, combined with mechanisms to reduce trade imbalances and ensure capital for investment-led growth, have long been central to how UNCTAD would view an inclusive and sustainable international financial architecture.

The second set of challenges includes the need to secure vast financial resources to support economic, social, and human development; to make progress towards the Sustainable Development Goals; and to develop frameworks for the necessary cooperation to address complex problems in the global commons (e.g. global pandemics, climate change, forced displacement, tax avoidance, and cyberrelated risks).

Chapters IV to through VI of the *Trade and Development Report 2023* build on UNCTAD approaches to reforming the international financial architecture and advances proposals for a resilient, climate-oriented ecosystem of debt and financial governance.

Redesigning the global debt ecosystem to work for developing countries

A succession of recent crises and external shocks – often non-economic – has added to the burden of debt service across many developing countries. In parallel, the period of low growth globally and the effects of monetary tightening in core markets endanger pathways for export-driven recovery in developing countries. In these conditions, the historical narrative around the origins of and solutions to the sovereign debt problem is losing credibility.

Resolving sovereign debt burdens is made more complex due to deficiencies in IFA, which repeatedly falls short in providing timely and adequate support to countries in distress. The Common Framework for Debt Treatments beyond the Debt Service Suspension Initiative of the Group of 20, introduced during the COVID-19 pandemic, has proven sluggish and insufficient for effective debt restructuring. The hierarchical nature of the international financial system, marked by resource asymmetries, exacerbates these challenges and prompts many countries to accumulate more debt. These compounding problems demand a re-evaluation of how nations navigate the intricate landscape of sovereign debt across four key areas of global debt governance: transparency, sustainability tracking, debt resolution and restructuring.

The current debt landscape is both highly diverse and complex. Developing countries' sovereign debts surged to $11.4 trillion by the end of 2022, reflecting a 15.7 per cent increase since the onset of the COVID-19 pandemic. Recently, creditor composition has shifted too, with a significant rise in the share of private creditors. Private creditors' holdings almost doubled to 13 per cent in 2021 (up from 7 per cent in 2010), with bondholders' share reaching 4 per cent (from a share of 0 per cent in 2010).

The past three years have laid bare that an unforeseen shock can put many countries in a precarious position. The continual servicing of barely affordable debt places countries under a considerable burden and drains resources from development. On average, at the end of 2022, the debt service burden as a share of export revenues was 15.7 per cent for middle-income and low-income countries as a group, while it was 22.6 per cent for low-income countries as a group.

The historical mechanisms to resolve the problem of sovereign debt restructuring are ill-suited to respond to these changes. In approaching this problem, the international community has tended to engage in a practice of "muddling through", combining exchange offers with political pressure and an expansion of financial support instruments, particularly a proliferation of new funding instruments at IMF.

> *"The continual servicing of barely affordable debt places countries under a considerable burden and drains resources from development."*

Undergirding these efforts was the idea that austerity would re-establish creditor confidence, stabilize the fiscal position and trigger future growth in borrowing countries. On the downside, debt workouts continued to cause considerable damage to the economic and social stability of populations in borrowing countries, particularly among less affluent and more vulnerable groups. Human rights challenges to austerity succeeded in only a small number of cases. Some of the more successful cases of debt restructuring, such as in Barbados and Greece, featured the retroactive insertion of collective action clauses into domestic debt. Innovations in bond design, such as bonds linked to GDP, issued for example by Argentina and Greece, were meant to allow smoother recoveries. However, in the case of Argentina, this resulted in litigation over the method of calculating GDP.

The COVID-19 pandemic and concurrent ecological and geopolitical crises have underscored that a lack of government investment in health care might do more harm than good. At present, climate change and the need for a transition to clean energy follow a similar pattern, requiring upfront investment to mitigate longer-term consequences. Furthermore, inflationary pressures associated with value chain distortions and energy issues in the wake of the war in Ukraine have created adverse conditions for borrowing countries, putting many at risk of downgrading.

IMF has signed credit agreements with approximately 100 Governments since 2020; 13 countries have since defaulted: Argentina, Belarus, Belize, Chad, Ecuador, Ghana, Lebanon, Malawi, the Russian Federation, Sri Lanka, Suriname, Ukraine and Zambia. In addition, exposure of borrowers to new non-Paris Club creditors, such as China, has reached a crucial point, calling into question an institutional structure centred on the Paris Club and creating additional challenges for debt transparency. In this context, the sovereign debt debate has shifted towards global public policy instruments and away from overconfidence in markets or advanced countries.

To change this dysfunctional debt architecture, a new, development-centred ecosystem is needed. This requires a comprehensive re-evaluation of factors that contribute to unsustainable sovereign debt, such as climate change, demographics, health, global economic shifts, rising interest rates, geopolitical realignments, political instability and the implications of sovereign debt on industrial policies in debtor States. New creative thinking needs to be developed along the entire sovereign debt life cycle.

For debt workouts to be transformed in such a way that they contribute to sovereign resilience, multiple innovations both of a private (contractual) and a public (statutory) nature are required. These need to be coordinated rather than played out against each other. Improved sovereign debt restructuring requires substantive and institutional changes to the existing framework, potentially built around six key elements.

First, an automatic standstill for countries declaring distress is needed, to concentrate the minds of creditors on the workout process. This would prevent holdouts and encourage debtor countries to enter the distress stage before it is too late. Early declaration of distress and early resolution would prevent countries being locked out of markets for a prolonged period. To ensure creditor equity, a standstill might be a useful device to ensure inclusion of private creditors, as would principles on comparability of treatment and rules to prevent creditors from realizing collateral.

Second, a mechanism is needed to determine the perimeter of legitimate debt. This relates to rules regarding unconstitutional debt resulting from corruption, opacity and secrecy, flawed authorization and reckless creditor practices.

Third, at the country level, improved debt sustainability analysis needs to be available. Yet, it should not only reflect the need to achieve the Sustainable Development Goals and climate transition, including related investments and necessary industrial policies. Ideally, it should also empower country negotiators with improved data on their potential for growth and fiscal consolidation. This requires developing countries to have their own models, but it also requires greater transparency of the IMF debt sustainability analysis models and assumptions (and ideally, a willingness from IMF to modify them where necessary).

Fourth, country specifics need to be reflected in institutional flexibility and innovative approaches in macrofinancial policies. Discretion should be exercised over the use of various types of capital controls as part of the ordinary toolkit of developing countries. Improved innovative financial instruments are needed, such as debt-for-climate swaps or debt-for-nature swaps, that provide mechanisms to enhance fiscal space – albeit at the margins.

Fifth, the system needs an institutional framework that fosters resilience. Given the significant current ecological, social and geopolitical challenges, institutions charged with regulating sovereign debt need to bridge differences between constituencies and stakeholders. This speaks in favour of large, universal organizations, including the United Nations. Other actors, such as the Group of 20, might play a crucial role, particularly in ensuring the support of a wide range of capital-exporting States.

Sixth, a borrower's club needs to become part of global debt governance. Through a borrower's club, debtor countries could discuss technical issues and innovation, bond issuance experiences or novel debt instruments for sustainable development – and learn from each other's experiences. Debtor countries with recent experience could advise those facing debt distress on reducing their restructuring costs or building political relations between the debtor countries. This support could lead to a more stable and resilient global financial system, benefiting both borrowers and creditors.

Specific policy recommendations for a development-centred global debt architecture are to:

- Increase concessional finance through capitalization of multilateral and regional banks, and issuance of special drawing rights.

- Enhance transparency in financing terms and conditions, using the digitalization of loan contracts to improve accuracy.

- Revise the UNCTAD *Principles for Responsible Sovereign Lending and Borrowing* to motivate and underpin the importance of guiding principles throughout the stages of sovereign debt acquisition.

- Improve debt sustainability analysis and tracking to reflect the achievement of the Sustainable Development Goals and empower country negotiators with improved data on their potential for growth and fiscal consolidation.

- Enable countries to utilize innovative financial instruments such as sustainable development bonds and resilience bonds. Develop rules for automatic restructurings and guarantees.

- Enhance resilience during external crises, for example by implementing standstill rules on debtors' obligations in crises, and create a space to enable the avoidance of debt distress.

- Encourage borrowers to share information and experiences, drawing inspiration from private creditor coordination.

- Initiate work on a more robust debt workout mechanism and a global debt authority.

Financial reforms for climate-aligned development

The vulnerabilities in the current economic situation add tension to the intensifying debate on how to scale up finance and better guide it towards climate-aligned development. It is essential to reconcile ecological and developmental priorities and reflect this in the scale of finance available to developing countries and the terms on which it is offered.

The international financial system continues to deliver only a fraction of the financing needed – despite the relatively auspicious environment of a decade of record low interest rates and a slew of pledges from Governments, financial institutions and corporations. Now that lending conditions have changed, it is even more essential to address two major challenges that are the root cause of this. First, there is a need to reassess the role and optimal forms of participation of the public and the private sectors in financing economic transformation, which is marked by uncertainty, risk and redistribution. This is not a new story, but it is an urgent one. Second, continued patterns of public and private financing often lead to climate goals being undermined, directly and indirectly, and this is exacerbated by a lack of finance to cover the economic and social costs of transition. One example where finance flows are inconsistent with climate pledges includes the trillions of dollars still supporting fossil fuels.

"There is a need to reassess the role and optimal forms of participation of the public and the private sectors in financing economic transformation, which is marked by uncertainty, risk and redistribution."

The starting point of any reform should be the view that climate finance needs to be in addition and complementary to development finance. Current negotiations with respect to the climate agenda represent an important opportunity to align the two. The guiding principles to achieve this can draw on the lessons from the original New Deal of the 1930s and offer a means to tackle economic insecurity, long-standing infrastructure gaps and climate and finance inequalities.

From this view, one of the most obvious and elemental reforms would be to ensure that public funds pledged for development and climate action are indeed paid, as promised. In 2022, official development assistance was the equivalent of just 0.36 per cent of Development Assistance Committee donors' combined gross national income, much less than the 0.7 per cent pledged by these donors decades ago. Just 5 out of 32 of these donor countries meet their pledged target, meaning that tens of billions of dollars could be generated if the remaining members honoured their pledges.

In addition to the magnitude of finance available, what is also lacking is ease of access to finance for those who need it. One of the most effective ways to enable this would be to strengthen support to public development banks – of which there are more than 450, varying in size and scope, and with national, regional, or multilateral remits and ownership.

Public development banks have the mandate to follow social or economic imperatives beyond short-term profit maximization, meaning they are potentially able to lend for development and climate purposes that offer a social or ecological benefit and not necessarily a financial one. This objective, aligned with their capacity to create and leverage credit over and above the funds they receive, and the fact they can often access concessional finance for on-lending with other banks, including commercial ones, and private investors, means they can be an effective means of scaling up. Equally importantly, these banks also have the technical, managerial and operational skills necessary to utilize the finance effectively once it is raised. In addition to increasing banks' base capital, it is crucial to expand the lending headroom of development banks, widening out their lending activities to the poorest parts of the world, and enabling them to provide not only concessional loans and grants, but also loans in local currencies in collaboration with national development banks.

Central banks can also have a key role in shaping the national and international agenda for climate and development finance. Some central banks in both developed and developing countries are already implementing such policies, yet more could be done to enable these core institutions to play the market shaping roles of the not-so-distant past. Several central banks already have monetary policies and regulatory frameworks that aim to help realign finance with decarbonization targets. Several are incorporating climate risks and climate stress tests into their operations. More could be done to require these banks to report on financing related to Sustainable Development Goals, in addition to climate goals.

Some banks, including central banks and development banks, have set goals for divesting from coal, oil and gas. However, many more are continuing to lend to this sector and herein lies a major challenge for most countries and governments. The trillions of dollars' worth of lending for exploration and operation in this high-carbon sector, in addition to further trillions of dollars of subsidies to fossil fuel producers and consumers, is at odds with the ambition to reduce CO_2 emissions.

At the same time, for many developing countries, fossil fuels continue to be the most likely source of realizing basic electrification and development needs, in the short-term at least. Furthermore, fossil fuel subsidies are a blunt tool used to support low-income households. Principles of "common but differentiated responsibility and respective capabilities", "special and differential treatment" and "polluter pays" are well established in international law and provide a basis for articulating the respective obligations between richer and poorer countries. Much would need to change for this to be reflected in practice.

How can the record be changed? The COVID-19 pandemic has shown that when the will is there, Governments and their institutions can use their powers to mobilize vast amounts of capital for the welfare of their citizens, to restrict harmful activities and repurpose industries to achieve national goals.

This is not to say that all choices made during the time of the pandemic were perfect; but rather, it shows how it is possible to achieve rapid and profound change. One of the most effective ways to do this today needs to be addressing the continued dependence on fossil fuels head-on; to wind down the most problematic and polluting activities and shift to cleaner and renewable activities, while at the same time ensuring that development benefits are created and development needs are met. It means finding alternative long-term support for low-income countries and poor households and financing alternative paths for development. This is no simple matter, and would require a fundamental realignment of the financial system to orient finance towards supporting social and development needs, while respecting environmental limits.

Chapter I

Current Trends and Challenges in the Global Economy

Crisis averted?
How to future-proof against systemic shocks

Today's global economic landscape is characterized by growing inequalities and divergence of growth paths between key regions. The world economy is flying at "stall speed", with projections of a modest growth of 2.4 per cent in 2023, meeting the definition of a global recession. Cautiously, the outlook for 2024 suggests a modest growth improvement (2.5 per cent), contingent upon the euro area's recovery and the avoidance of adverse shocks by other leading economies.

While many economies will grapple with divergent recovery paths, deepening inequalities and mounting pressures of indebtedness, global growth is unlikely to rebound sufficiently to pre-pandemic trends. This means that urgent needs like food security, social protection, and climate adaptation risk not being addressed.

Compounding these issues is the absence of adequate multilateral responses and coordination mechanisms. Without decisive action, the fragility of the global economy and an array of diverse shocks risk evolving into systemic crises. Policymakers must navigate these challenges on multiple fronts to chart a more robust and resilient trajectory for the future.

To avert tomorrow's potential crises, this report urges policymakers to adopt a policy mix prioritizing the reduction of inequalities and the delivery of sustainable, investment-led growth and development.

Recommendations include

- Central banks must strengthen international coordination with a greater focus on long-term financial sustainability for the private and public sectors, and not just on price stability;

- Policymakers must enable advocate concerted increases of real wages and make concrete commitments towards comprehensive social protection;

- Investment in the energy transition process in developing countries must be actively pursued, by making technology and finance available and affordable, requiring stronger multilateral cooperation and appropriate agreements in the World Trade Organization (WTO), the International Monetary Fund (IMF) and the World Bank.

A. INTRODUCTION

The global economy is flying at "stall speed", with projected growth in 2023 of 2.4 per cent, meeting the conventional criteria for a global recession. The entire global economy, except East and Central Asia, has slowed since 2022. On a brighter note, inflation, while still above pre-pandemic years, is coming under control in many parts of the world. The banking crises that erupted in March 2023 did not lead to financial contagion, and commodity prices are down from their peaks in 2022. A small improvement in global growth is expected in 2024, contingent on the recovery in the euro area and other leading economies avoiding adverse shocks.

While there is a glimmer of hope on the horizon, celebrations of success would be inappropriate. Global growth, while showing some signs of improvement, has not sufficiently rebounded to pre-pandemic rates. This challenge compounds the difficulty of meeting critical needs such as food security, social protection, and climate adaptation, especially given the weakened foundation resulting from the global health pandemic.

Against this background, 2023 may turn out to be an inflection point in a fragile and uneven global recovery. Without adequate multilateral policy responses or coordination mechanisms, today's brittle economies and diverse shocks might evolve into tomorrow's systemic crises. This scenario is a threat to the multilateral system and global economic stability. Policymakers need to operate on multiple fronts to chart a stronger, more resilient trajectory for the future.

Analysis shows that three worrying trends are emerging in 2023:

- Divergent recovery paths in the context of slower growth across major regions;

- Deepening inequalities in income and wealth;

- Growing pressures of indebtedness and thinning policy autonomy in developing economies.

These three factors build onto an increasingly complex interplay between economic, climate and geopolitical risks. Growing inequalities within countries are a source of weak global demand and continue to hold back investment and growth. Divergence of low-growth trends between key regions, as well as within the Group of Seven and the initial BRICS countries (Brazil, the Russian Federation, India, China and South Africa), indicates that there is no clear driving force to propel the world economy onto a robust and sustainable recovery track.

"There is no clear driving force to propel the world economy onto a robust and sustainable recovery track."

Historically, growth divergence has led to uncoordinated domestic policy actions with negative global repercussions, especially for developing countries. Today, policy discussions in advanced economies often overlook systemic links and multilateral forums for policy coordination, such as the Group of 20 (G20), are not remedying the problem. This can hinder international cooperation and prevent the global economy from taking a sustainable recovery path.

The prospects for developing countries are especially concerning. Development requires a favourable external environment, characterized by strong global demand, stable exchange rates and affordable financing. Developing countries' ability to accelerate growth, strengthen productive capacities, decarbonize and meet their financial obligations is fundamentally dependent on steady and strong global demand. But international policy coordination centres on central banks that prioritize short-term monetary stability over long-term financial sustainability. This trend, together with inadequate regulation in commodity markets and continuous neglect for rising inequality are fracturing the world economy.

These threats are amplified by the uncertain impact of slower than expected growth in China and a deceleration of the economies in Europe, many of which have all but ground to a halt. They are particularly concerning given the present context, marked by a slowdown in the investment cycle, the impact of geopolitical conflicts on the structure of trade, food and energy security and the mounting costs of climate change and transition, all compounded by uncertainty in the outcome of the of the 2024 United States elections. Even if growing financial risks in the larger economies do not trigger sharper shocks, a development crisis is already unfolding, with countries across the global South facing increasing debt service obligations.

For people and planet, further rounds of monetary tightening to obtain quick disinflation in the advanced economies would mean more economic and social disruption at a time when recovery has stalled. An ongoing slowdown diminishes prospects for trade and investment, prompting a further loss of momentum, higher inequality and debt burdens expanding relative to gross domestic product (GDP).

Against this context, 2024 is unlikely to show substantial improvement. A strategy of growth in the global North becomes less feasible if high levels of debt (chapters II and V) and inadequate financial regulation threaten financial stability and food security (chapter III), and while income is increasingly retained by capital owners rather than workers (figure I.1). In the face of a crisis, previous coordination efforts have tended to ignore sectors or countries that are not considered systemically relevant, thus compounding the very crisis they sought to resolve. This mistake should be avoided at all costs.

"Monetary policy in advanced economies should take into account the damage that high interest rates can cause, in terms of structural change, climate adaptation and debt sustainability."

This Report presents an alternative response, in which the pace of disinflation takes into consideration the impact of high real interest rates not only on inflation indicators, but also on economic activity, employment, income inequality and fiscal stability. In an interconnected world in which developing countries are potential engines of economic growth, policymakers in advanced economies should take into account the damage that high interest rates can cause to long-term investment – both in terms of structural change and climate adaptation – as well as debt sustainability. In the current international financial architecture, policy space is easily curtailed by movements in financial markets, with heavy impacts on social policies, investment and employment generation.

To address these problems, this Report suggests that:

1.   Reducing inequality should be made a policy priority in developed and developing countries, keeping close watch on the labour share. This requires concerted increases of real wages and concrete commitments towards comprehensive social protection. Monetary policy is not to be used as a sole policy tool to alleviate inflationary pressures. With supply-side problems still unaddressed, a policy mix is needed to attain financial sustainability, help lower inequalities and deliver inclusive growth.

"A policy mix is needed to attain financial sustainability, help lower inequalities and deliver inclusive growth."

2.   In light of growing interdependencies in the global economy, central bankers should assume a wider stabilizing function, which would help balance the priorities of monetary stability with long-term financial sustainability.

3.   Internationally, a systemic approach to regulating commodity trading generally, and food trading in particular, needs to be developed within the framework of the global financial architecture.

4.   To help address the crushing burden of debt servicing and the threat of spreading debt crises, reforms are needed to the rules and practices of the global financial architecture. This architecture should ensure reliable access to international liquidity and a stable financial environment that promotes investment-led growth. Given the failure of the current architecture to facilitate the resilience and recovery of developing countries from debt stress, it is crucial to establish a mechanism to resolve sovereign debt workouts. This should be based on the participation of all developing countries and have agreed procedures, incentives and deterrents.

5.   Finally, the energy transition would require not only fiscal and monetary agreements among the G20, but also agreements within the WTO to implement technology transfer, and within the IMF and World Bank to provide reliable access to finance. Without eliminating the incentives and regulatory conduits that make cross-border speculative investment so profitable, private capital is unlikely to be channelled to measures to help adapt to climate change.

The chapter is structured as follows. Section B examines the emerging risks to post-COVID-19 growth trend at the global level. It finds that divergence within key regional blocks and between major economies clouds the fragile growth of 2023, with downside risks lingering into 2024. Section C analyses the sectoral contribution to global demand growth in G20 economies. Section D identifies some of the key dimensions of the asymmetry between growing corporate concentration on the one hand and thinning fiscal policy space on the other. Section E discusses credit, investment and the impact of monetary policy on income and wealth inequality. Section F explores inflation, distribution and the easing or persistence of inflationary trajectories. Section G looks at labour costs and inequality. Section H concludes.

B. GLOBAL GROWTH LANDSCAPE: DIVERGENCE UNDER THE CLOUDS OF UNCERTAINTY

The growth of the world economic output is expected to decelerate to 2.4 per cent in 2023, before registering a small uptick to 2.5 per cent in 2024. (table I.1). These are among the lowest growth rates of the last four decades, outside of crisis years. Moreover, the figure for 2023 is below the conventional threshold of 2.5 per cent which marks recession in the global economy. These projections are subject to downside risks which have increased in recent months.

All regions, except for East and Central Asia, are expected to post slower growth this year than in 2022, with the largest drop (2.3 points) occurring in Europe. Likewise, among G20 countries, only Brazil, China, Japan, Mexico and the Russian Federation are expected to see a growth improvement, with considerable variation. Of particular concern, given the ambitious development and climate targets set by the international community with a 2030 delivery date, growth in 2023 and 2024 is also set to fall below the average for the five-year period before the pandemic, in all regions. Latin America is the exception, where growth in the earlier period was particularly weak (ECLAC, 2023).

In 2023, global growth showed uneven deceleration. Larger emerging economies are unlikely to provide a robust offset to slower growth in advanced economies. With tighter monetary policy, low investment (figure I.1), and limited government spending, the world economy is experiencing a lacklustre recovery reminiscent of the aftermath of the 2008–2009 financial crisis.

Figure I.1 Private investment is slowing down sharply again
Growth of private investment
(Percentage change)

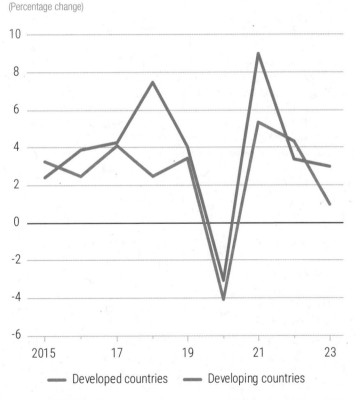

— Developed countries — Developing countries

Source: UNCTAD calculations based on the United Nations Global Policy Model and database.
Note: GDP at constant 2015 prices, PPP.

Table I.1 World output growth, 1991–2024

(Annual percentage change)

Country groups	1991–1999[a]	2000–2009[a]	2010–2014[a]	2015–2019[a]	2019	2020	2021	2022	2023[b]	2024[b]	Revision for 2023[c]
World	2.9	3.3	3.2	3.0	2.5	-3.2	6.1	3.0	2.4	2.5	+0.3
Africa	2.4	5.5	2.7	3.0	2.6	-2.4	4.5	3.1	2.7	3.0	+0.2
North Africa (incl. South Sudan)	2.7	5.3	-1.9	4.1	2.3	-3.3	4.8	1.9	2.9	3.0	+0.1
South Africa	2.7	4.0	2.5	1.0	0.3	-6.0	4.7	2.0	0.0	1.0	+0.3
Sub-Saharan Africa (excl. South Africa and South Sudan)	2.0	6.4	6.3	2.9	3.4	-0.9	4.2	4.0	3.2	3.4	+0.2
America	3.4	2.5	2.4	1.9	1.7	-3.8	6.0	2.5	2.0	1.8	+0.9
Latin America and the Caribbean	3.2	3.5	3.4	0.1	-0.3	-7.1	6.7	3.9	2.3	1.8	+1.0
Central America (excl. Mexico) and the Caribbean	2.8	4.4	3.6	3.0	2.2	-8.6	8.2	4.8	2.9	2.9	+0.4
Mexico	3.0	1.9	3.2	2.1	-0.2	-8.0	4.7	3.0	3.2	2.1	+1.4
South America	3.4	3.9	3.4	-0.9	-0.7	-6.6	7.2	4.0	1.9	1.6	+0.9
Argentina	4.6	3.8	2.7	-0.3	-2.0	-9.9	10.4	5.0	-2.4	-0.6	-1.9
Brazil	2.9	3.6	3.2	-0.4	1.2	-3.3	5.0	2.9	3.3	2.3	+2.4
North America	3.4	2.3	2.1	2.3	2.3	-3.0	5.9	2.2	1.9	1.8	+0.9
Canada	2.8	2.3	2.6	2.0	1.9	-5.1	5.0	3.4	1.3	1.0	-0.8
United States	3.5	2.3	2.1	2.3	2.3	-2.8	6.0	2.1	2.0	1.9	+1.1
Asia (excl. Cyprus)	4.3	5.6	5.7	4.8	3.7	-0.9	6.5	3.6	3.9	3.9	-0.0
Central Asia	-4.4	8.3	6.8	3.4	3.8	-1.2	5.3	4.5	4.5	3.8	+0.1
East Asia	4.4	5.6	5.8	4.8	4.0	0.4	6.7	2.4	3.8	3.8	-0.1
China	11.0	10.6	8.6	6.8	6.0	2.2	8.4	3.0	4.6	4.8	-0.2
Japan	1.2	0.9	1.4	0.9	-0.4	-4.3	2.2	1.0	2.3	0.9	+0.7
Republic of Korea	6.8	4.9	3.6	2.9	2.2	-0.7	4.2	2.6	0.9	2.1	-1.0
South Asia	4.7	6.3	5.4	6.0	3.7	-3.8	7.7	5.8	5.2	5.2	+0.1
India	5.9	7.2	6.6	7.0	4.6	-6.0	8.9	6.7	6.6	6.2	+0.6
South-East Asia	5.3	5.4	5.6	5.0	4.3	-3.9	4.0	5.4	3.9	4.2	-0.1
Indonesia	4.8	5.2	5.8	5.1	5.0	-2.1	3.7	5.2	4.2	4.1	-0.4
Western Asia (excl. Cyprus)	4.1	5.0	5.5	2.9	1.4	-3.2	6.3	6.6	3.3	2.7	+0.2
Saudi Arabia	1.7	4.0	5.8	1.9	0.8	-4.3	3.9	8.7	2.5	2.9	-1.0
Türkiye	3.9	5.0	7.6	4.3	0.8	1.9	11.4	5.6	3.7	1.9	+1.1
Europe (incl. Cyprus)	1.3	2.2	1.2	2.1	1.8	-6.0	5.8	2.9	0.6	1.2	+0.1
European Union (27 Members)	1.9	1.8	0.8	2.2	1.8	-5.7	5.6	3.4	0.4	1.2	-0.3
Euro area	1.9	1.6	0.6	2.0	1.6	-6.1	5.4	3.4	0.4	1.2	-0.3
France	1.8	1.6	1.1	1.7	1.8	-7.8	6.8	2.5	0.9	1.2	-0.1
Germany	1.6	1.0	2.0	1.8	1.1	-3.7	2.6	1.8	-0.6	1.1	-0.6
Italy	1.5	0.7	-0.8	1.1	0.5	-9.0	7.0	3.7	0.6	0.8	-0.1
Russian Federation	-5.9	6.2	3.1	1.2	2.2	-2.7	5.6	-2.1	2.2	1.9	+3.6
United Kingdom	2.3	2.0	1.8	2.1	1.6	-11.0	7.6	4.1	0.4	0.4	+0.4
Oceania	3.7	3.2	2.8	2.7	2.1	-1.8	5.1	3.5	1.8	1.5	-0.1
Australia	3.7	3.3	2.8	2.5	1.9	-1.8	5.2	3.7	1.9	1.5	+0.0
Memorandum items:											
Developed countries	2.3	2.2	1.7	2.1	1.8	-4.2	5.4	2.4	1.4	1.5	+0.4
Developing countries	4.9	6.4	5.8	4.4	3.6	-1.6	7.1	3.9	3.9	4.0	+0.1

Source: UNCTAD calculations, based on United Nations Global Policy Model; United Nations, Department of Economic and Social Affairs, National Accounts Main Aggregates database, and *World Economic Situation and Prospects* (WESP): Update as of Jun-2023; ECLAC, 2023; Organisation for Economic Co-operation and Development (OECD), 2023; International Monetary Fund (IMF), *World Economic Outlook*, spring 2023; Economist Intelligence Unit, EIU CountryData database; JP Morgan, Global Data Watch; and national sources.

Note: The composition of the five geographical regions follows the M49 standard of the United Nations Statistics Division. The distinction between developed and developing countries is based on the updated M49 classification of May 2022. Calculations for country aggregates are based on GDP at constant 2015 dollars.

[a] Average.
[b] Forecasts.
[c] Revisions relate to comparisons with forecasts presented in April 2023 in an UNCTAD *Trade and Development Report* update.

So far in 2023, four main factors have shaped the global outlook. Each introduces considerable uncertainty into near-term projections:

1. International prices of oil, gas and food have returned to late 2021 levels eliminating a powerful driver of inflation. However, retail prices in many countries remain higher than pre-pandemic averages, putting pressure on household budgets. While relief from major supply-side drivers of inflation would allow governments to address profiteering domestically, most major central banks continue to signal the likelihood of ongoing elevated interest rates.

2. The United States, comprising a quarter of the world economy, has displayed resilience throughout two years of rising consumer price inflation (April 2020–June 2022), despite a year of blanket disinflation policies (11 interest rate hikes in 18 months) and sporadic financial market disruptions. Key parts of the economy, buoyed by employment and nominal wage growth, have sustained consumption and spending. While unemployment has reached historic lows, the employment rate remains at recession levels, standing at 58 per cent of the population. Additionally, weakness in the manufacturing sector and recent aggregate figures[1] have heightened the risk of a sharper slowdown in the latter half of 2023.

3. In China, lifting of the remaining COVID-19-related restrictions has helped sustain the recovery which began in 2022 and which enabled a revamp of industrial production. The country's economic growth relies less on exports than in the past (table I.2) and the government continues to enjoy considerable fiscal space. However, persistent weaknesses in the real estate sector pose challenges, including potential financial stress, reduced job creation, constrained consumer spending and delayed investments. Additionally, escalating geopolitical tensions are disrupting how China dominates key global value chains, clouding prospects in some of its frontier technology sectors, at least in the short-term. Authorities in China have responded to slower-than-expected growth with a mix of monetary expansion, supply-side incentives and regulatory tightening. The overall impact of these measures as well as their spillover effects, particularly on neighbouring economies, remains uncertain.

4. Concern over growth prospects in China risks overshadowing the deteriorating economic health of the European economy. While growth in China has now decreased approximately 30 per cent compared to the pre-COVID-19 average of 2015–2019, growth in Europe has decreased approximately 70 per cent. With a share of the global economy similar to that of China (approximately 18 per cent in purchasing power parity, higher at current exchange rates), the global consequences of the slowdown in Europe are at least twice as heavy as those of the slowdown in China. Continuing monetary tightening in the euro area risks tipping the region into recession in 2024.

"Post-pandemic growth performance in the leading developed and emerging economies over the past three years points to divergent recovery pathways."

Post-pandemic growth performance in the leading developed and emerging economies over the past three years points to divergent recovery pathways. On the one hand, differences reflect country positions in the international monetary and financial hierarchy, which defines the scope of autonomy policymakers enjoy when formulating macroeconomic responses to shocks. The favourable position of developed countries in this hierarchy helped them to manage a swift turnaround from the initial shock of the pandemic.

However, these routes depend on governments' willingness to deploy policies for longer-term growth plans. Advanced economies, aside from the United States and Japan, struggled to maintain a steady recovery after the 2020 pandemic shock. The United States stabilized through an aggressive use of industrial policy, widening the gap with other developed countries. Austerity-constrained Europe lagged behind (figure I.2.A). Among developing countries, China and India saw strong recoveries, while other BRICS members benefitted from favourable export conditions. South Africa stands out as an exception (figure I.2.B).

---

[1] Data released during the summer of 2023.

Table I.2 Developing countries have been generating critical global demand

Growth of demand stance of institutional sectors, G20 countries, 2022

(Annual percentage change)

	GNI	Private	Government	External
Developed countries				
Australia	3.6	2.8	0.7	0.0
Canada	3.2	0.0	0.8	2.4
France	2.2	0.8	-0.3	1.7
Germany	2.1	0.0	0.0	2.1
Italy	3.3	0.7	-0.4	3.0
Japan	2.1	-0.4	-1.8	4.3
Republic of Korea	2.7	-0.4	0.6	2.5
Russian Federation	-1.8	-0.2	2.4	-4.0
United Kingdom	3.8	2.2	-1.6	3.2
United States	2.0	0.8	0.1	1.1
Developing countries				
Argentina	5.3	1.9	2.5	1.0
Brazil	2.9	0.1	0.6	2.2
China	3.3	1.3	2.0	0.0
India	6.7	3.5	1.7	1.5
Indonesia	4.7	-1.3	0.4	5.6
Mexico	2.7	0.3	-0.1	2.5
Saudi Arabia	8.2	-1.8	1.8	8.2
South Africa	2.2	2.6	1.9	-2.3
Türkiye	6.1	5.3	0.8	0.0

Source: UNCTAD calculations based on the United Nations Global Policy Model and database.
  Note: GNI: gross national income.

Figure I.2 Real GDP levels recovering separately

(Index numbers, third quarter of 2019=100)

A. G7 countries

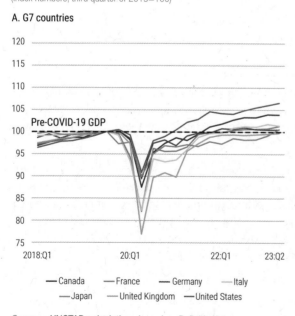

B. Selected developing countries

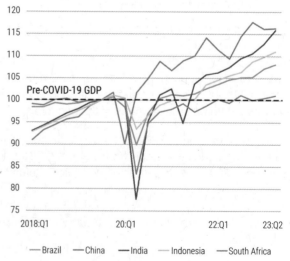

Source: UNCTAD calculations based on Refinitiv data.
  Note: Data is seasonally adjusted.

C. LEADING ECONOMIES IN AN INTERDEPENDENT WORLD

To further assess the outlook for global growth, table I.2 illustrates the sectoral contribution to global demand growth in G20 economies. It shows that export sectors in developed countries are growth drivers in those countries. They tap global demand rather than generate demand for developing countries. At the same time, many developing economies positively contribute to global demand by importing more than they export. South Africa is an extreme case, with substantial growth in private sector demand. However, the external sector has absorbed a substantial part of that demand, partly due to a 20-year depreciation of the rand, which has made import costs higher.

As a guide to understanding how different sectors affect domestic growth prospects, table I.2 distinguishes the private sector (households and businesses) from the government and the external sector (the rest of the world). Numbers indicate the portion of economic growth generated by each sector, considering the positive effect of its spending and the negative effect (on growth) of its saving. The advantage of this approach lies in its straightforward rearrangement of national accounts data. It adheres to the accounting convention that fully distributes value added in production as income to workers, businesses, and the government.

Looking ahead, a "soft landing" for the **United States** economy still seems possible. This would imply that GDP growth is already close to hitting its low point (sparing the country a recession, conventionally defined as two consecutive quarters of negative growth), along with a small uptick of unemployment and moderate disinflation. In fact, disinflation has largely happened with the rate of annual price increases coming down two thirds from 8.9 per cent in June 2022 to 3.0 per cent in June 2023. This is bound to drive up the real cost of capital, which remained negative until early 2023. GDP growth in the United States is expected to slow from 2.1 per cent last year, to 2.0 per cent in 2023 and 2024.

The slowdown has been mainly policy-induced, owing to the combination of monetary tightening and a neutral fiscal policy. Recent signals from the Federal Reserve suggest interest rates will remain high for the remainder of the year, with further rises not ruled out. The fiscal stance is expected to turn recessionary next year in line with the latest congressional agreement on the Federal debt ceiling, pushing growth lower in 2024.

Uncertain developments in several specific domestic factors in the United States economy will have a bearing on prospects for the global economy. A drop in key asset prices is a worrying sign that financial markets may not be able to withstand higher interest rates much longer. Bank shares have been sliding since earlier this year, a movement that preceded both the global financial crisis and the sovereign debt crisis in Europe, as have the values of 10-, 15-, and 20-year treasuries compared to early 2020. Over this period, holders of 20-year treasuries have borne a 17 per cent loss. Given their ubiquity in structured financial asset portfolios, large write-downs of treasuries would likely be destabilizing.

"Uncertain developments in several specific domestic factors in the United States economy will have a bearing on prospects for the global economy."

On the other hand, the policy interest rate (Federal Funds Rate) may fall in 2024. Nevertheless, small rate cuts are not effective at reversing growth deceleration and a large cut would run counter to the stated objective of monetary policy normalization (Federal Reserve Board, 2022). If unemployment begins to increase and real wages stagnate, the growth rate of consumption would likely slow, blocking any quick response of residential investment to reductions in interest rates.

The rest of North America is expected to follow the business cycle of the United States, with differences in outcome largely due to national policies. In **Canada**, more aggressive monetary policy and ongoing withdrawal of COVID-19 stimulus spending have led to a downward correction of 2023 growth projections. In **Mexico**, prospects have improved as the economy has benefited from less aggressive monetary tightening and an inflow of new investment to establish new manufacturing capacity, triggered by the bottlenecks that emerged in East Asia in 2021 and 2022.

In South America, Argentina and Brazil (which together account for almost 70 per cent of the region's output) are experiencing different developments. In **Brazil**, booming commodity exports and bumper harvests are driving an uptick in growth, from 2.9 per cent in 2022 to 3.3 per cent in 2023. However, negative demand forces are weighing on growth. These include the delayed impacts of monetary tightening, which started at the end of 2021, and which pushed the Brazilian real short-term interest rate to 9 per cent by the beginning of this year. This is in addition to growing private debt, especially by households, during the COVID-19 crisis. Significant fiscal expansion in 2023 should offset these recessive forces, but the fiscal impulse for 2024, although still subject to political negotiations, is expected to turn negative, reducing GDP growth below 3 per cent.

Argentina is experiencing both a recession and accelerating inflation. On the real side, a severe drought has raised the price of food and power, driving up an already high inflation rate, with significant negative effects on the purchasing power of households, especially among the poorest segments of the population. On the monetary side, the rise in inflation has triggered a run on foreign currency and currency depreciation. Fiscal policy turned contractionary because high inflation erodes real spending faster than it erodes tax revenues, but the induced fiscal tightening has not been sufficient to control inflation.

In this outlook, the darkest clouds hover over **Europe**, where the sharp rise in energy costs through most of 2022 and early 2023, as well as stubborn food price inflation and reduced household purchasing power are exerting downward pressure on consumption. Some governments partially absorbed the energy price increases but are now reducing fiscal spending to offset deficit pressures. While the euro area is still expected to experience marginal positive growth in 2023, it is on a knife edge.

The second quarter of 2023 saw the euro area narrowly avoid recession, in no small part due to an unexpected investment surge, which was more statistical artefact than renewed productive capacity: a reflection of the acquisition of intellectual property rights by a number of multinationals in Ireland (Bank of Italy, 2023; Arnold, 2023). The decision of the European Central Bank (ECB) to raise interest rates by the end of September is already casting a shadow over prospects for the fourth quarter, increasing the risk of tipping the euro area into a recession.

Overall, the largest economies in Europe, with the exception of Germany, are still projected to continue growing, primarily driven by exports. This highlights their market power vis-à-vis their trading partners in the face of price increases. Growth will, to a lesser extent, also be driven by private consumption and investment. Germany, France, Italy and the United Kingdom, are on a path of slowing demand growth. **Germany** experienced three quarters of negative growth in the last year and, in 2022, a record fall of real wages. But both the private sector and the government recorded a small surplus, spending less than their incomes and overall subtracting approximately 4 per cent from the country's economic growth. The export sector more than made up for this, bringing total growth barely into positive territory. This has not continued in 2023. **France** also "exported" its way out of a recession in 2022, but its private sector was a net contributor to aggregate demand. The government engineered a contraction of its net demand, continuing to reduce its net borrowing after the peak of 2020, while the external sector contributed almost 80 per cent of the country's growth.

Italy followed a similar pattern but with a less pronounced impact of reduced government net borrowing and an external sector that contributed approximately 90 per cent of growth. The labour share recovered somewhat in 2022 but not as result of improving workers' compensation. Rather, real wages fell, but productivity fell more, leaving the labour income share at a record low level and the profit share at a record high level. In the **United Kingdom**, the labour share fell drastically in 2021 and this continued in 2022, losing approximately 3 per cent of GDP to profits. Government net borrowing was also cut substantially, which led the government sector to subtract from aggregate demand rather than contribute to it. However, private sector spending, financed increasingly with debt accumulation and sustained by a resurgence in household consumption of services, along with support from the external sector, kept the economy out of a recession, albeit barely. Tentative data suggests that this might not be the case in the second half of 2023.

In the **Russian Federation**, economic growth has been slowed by a large reduction of net external demand, likely related to the economic response to the war in Ukraine. The overall volume of oil and gas exports, the country's main source of foreign currency, has not changed dramatically: exports of natural gas reportedly fell by 32 per cent in 2022, mainly as a result of shifting demand from Europe, which imported less piped gas and more liquified gas via tankers. However, oil exports, amounting to the majority of energy exports (75 per cent), remained mostly stable at 3 million barrels per day. Small volume changes notwithstanding, the revenue from oil and gas exports dropped by nearly half (47 per cent) in the first half of 2023 following the decrease of international prices, a trend that the Russian Federation responded to by cutting production. Whether this will yield the desired result remains to be seen. Meanwhile, the currency has posed another challenge. The rouble remained mostly stable through 2022, thanks to effective capital controls, but it has since depreciated sharply, compounding the problem posed by falling oil prices and further hindering the country's ability to purchase foreign commodities and manufactures. So far, the government has been able to pick up the slack in demand by increasing its net borrowing, in no small part thanks to a comfortably low sovereign debt ratio (23 per cent of GDP), but financial pressures are likely to intensify towards the end of the year. Based on all these factors, GDP growth is projected to be 2.2 and 2 per cent in 2023 and 2024, respectively.

Energy price and currency woes have affected **Türkiye**, too. The country was hit hard by high energy prices in 2022 but retained strong domestic demand throughout the first half of 2023 thanks to strong fiscal support, an effective programme of transfers to households, and a 10-point cut of the policy interest rate. However, while the latter provided stimulus to domestic demand, it placed pressure on the currency. The lira has been depreciating since before the pandemic, with a severe loss of value occurring earlier in the second quarter of 2023. Overall, projections for the country's economy are growth at 3.7 per cent in 2023, decelerating to 1.9 per cent in 2024.

In **Japan**, economic growth was driven last year by a surge in external demand, caused in large part by the pent-up global demand for automobiles and by a weaker yen. At the same time, government spending on goods, services and transfers fell, turning the public sector into a net saver. This year the currency has appreciated vis-à-vis the dollar and depreciated vis-à-vis the renminbi, leading to weaker net exports. External demand has continued to be strong while moderate inflation and a national agreement on wage growth have reinvigorated consumer demand. On the other hand, the contractionary stance of fiscal policy has continued, leading to a projected growth of 2.3 per cent this year and of 1.2 per cent in 2024. With sustained external demand and strong domestic demand, the main risks to the outlook come from the policy mix, notably a faster reduction of the fiscal deficit and a possible tightening of monetary policy.

In **China**, government net demand has remained the main driver of economic growth, while the external sector has exercised a drag on demand, contrary to frequent portrayals of the world's largest developing economy as purely export-driven. But it must also be noted that recently, the private sector in China has played a less relevant role as a driver of growth than it did it even in the aftermath of the global financial crisis. The relative weakness of the private sector to generate growth points to the ongoing challenge of establishing a deeper domestic market, which has left China more dependent today on fiscal expansion than it was a decade ago. The weakness in private sector demand in China is a source of uncertainty for global economic prospects. A deflating real estate bubble and a chain of financial crises among large developers, which started even before the pandemic struck, have caused significant losses in the construction sector and for owners of real estate and other affected assets. The government has responded with a series of measures aimed at reducing leverage in real estate finance (a major incubator of financial risk) and, more recently, cutting interest rates to stimulate aggregate demand. Meanwhile, domestic demand remains stable and key financial indicators have not yet exhibited concerning swings: bank share prices have decreased moderately (less than in the United States or Europe), demand for sovereign bonds has remained buoyant, and the renminbi has appreciated compared to other leading currencies in the region (although it has depreciated against the United States dollar). These factors together suggest GDP growth of 4.6 per cent in 2023 and 4.8 per cent in 2024. This is somewhat below the government target of 5 per cent, but still well above the average figure in advanced economies.

In **India**, the external sector – alongside the private and government sector – has contributed to domestic growth, partly helped by many countries redirecting trade flows away from the Russian Federation, with which India maintains a direct relationship. Growth in 2022 moved back in line with pre-pandemic rates and is expected to continue into next year. However, other indicators still suggest caution: with rates of unemployment still standing at 8.5 per cent in June 2023, employment remains disappointingly low by historical standards. Inequality has also significantly increased – as suggested by data on real wages and the labour share – which could hinder growth.

Indonesia has recently exhibited a shift from growth driven by private sector demand to a more export-oriented pattern, facilitated by the recent commodity boom, including for nickel. Robust growth this year is expected to continue into 2024. The government has been reducing its net borrowing since 2020 and its net claims on income are now absorbing aggregate demand rather than contributing to it. Investment and employment creation have also slowed, in a concerning sign for an economy whose growth has begun to be driven by commodities.

D. CORPORATE CAPTURE AND THE DEMISE OF FISCAL POLICY

"A functioning international financial architecture would isolate governments from these pressures and nudge them to adopt policies that favour growth, development and the necessary structural investments."

In 2010, this Report warned that fiscal retrenchment – the rapid rolling back of emergency support during the global financial crisis – would backfire. A few years later, economists from several international financial institutions expressed a mea culpa for advocating (premature) fiscal austerity (Blanchard and Leigh, 2013). After the devastating pandemic in 2020 and 2021, growth in most G20 countries is still much lower than it was in the 2010s, but primary fiscal balances (i.e., the balances that exclude interest payments, therefore the more easily controllable parts of governments' budgets) have quickly turned positive (figure I.3). This largely results from the high pressure faced by governments to reduce deficits to continue to have access to international credit markets. A functioning international financial architecture would isolate governments from these pressures and nudge them to adopt policies that favour growth, development and the necessary structural investments.

Figure I.3 illustrates how fiscal policy is considered at best, a shock absorber, subject to limited and temporary action (Bernanke, 2008) before a return to austerity. This approach has been proven to exacerbate boom–bust cycles and diminish the desired impact from emergency measures, including corporate capture as a contributing factor (Crouch, 2009; Costantini, 2020; TDR, 2021, 2022). In turn, this represents a reduction in States' ambition to strategically shape the economic trajectory and comprehensively address heightened inequalities.

This problem has played out differently in developed and developing countries. Driven by inflationary fears, developed countries with sufficient fiscal space have tended to limit themselves to smoothing out the cycle, on both its downswings and upswings, around a mediocre normal. For most countries, this fiscal framework tends to drive up debt-to-income ratios, due to subdued growth and costly emergency spending. Meanwhile, the growing concentration of market power by large corporations and the influence of high net worth individuals reduce the ability to raise tax revenues (figure I.4). In an era of compounding crises that increasingly require public resources to address systemic disruptions, the asymmetry between growing corporate consolidation and the thinning fiscal space need to be addressed by revisiting dominant economic paradigms and, critically, the policy decisions based on them.

"The asymmetry between growing corporate consolidation and the thinning fiscal space needs to be addressed by revisiting dominant economic paradigms and, critically, the policy decisions based on them."

Figure I.3 Rushed withdrawal of fiscal support: Post-2008 and post-2020

Real GDP growth and government primary net lending as a share of GDP, selected countries
(Percentage)

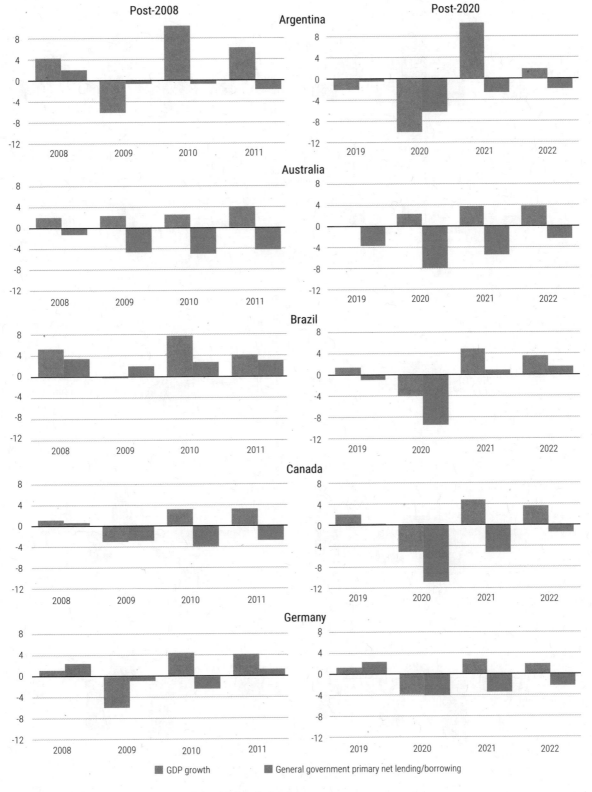

Source: UNCTAD calculations based on IMF World Economic Database.

Figure I.3 Rushed withdrawal of fiscal support: Post-2008 and post-2020 *(cont.)*
Real GDP growth and government primary net lending as a share of GDP, selected countries
(Percentage)

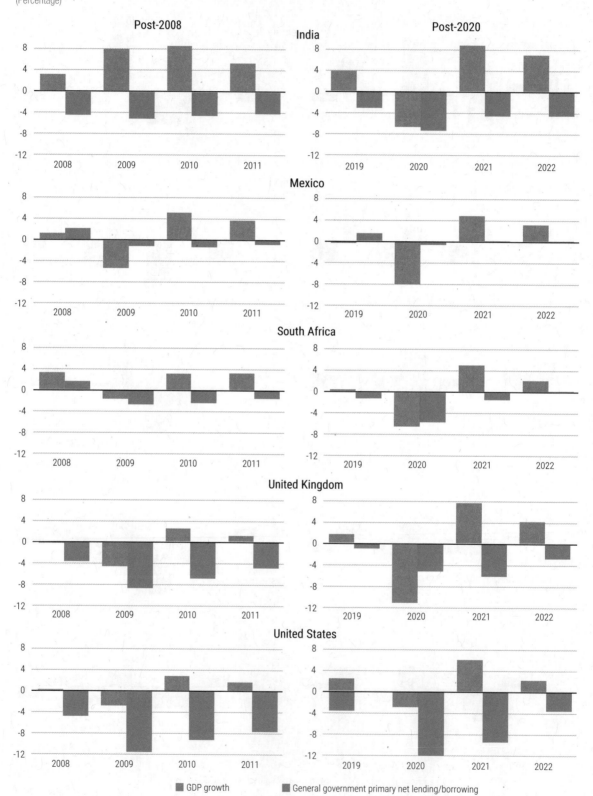

Source: UNCTAD calculations based on IMF World Economic Database.

Figure I.4 Globally: Rising profit share, shrinking fiscal space

Shares of operating profits and indirect taxes (net of subsidies)

(Percentage of GDP)

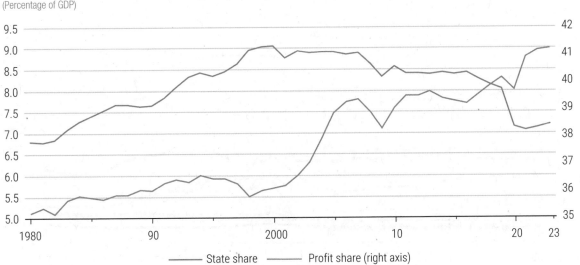

Source: UNCTAD calculations based on the United Nations Global Policy Model and database.
Note: GDP at constant 2015 prices, PPP.

E. CREDIT, INVESTMENT AND THE ROLE OF MONETARY POLICY

From 2010–2021, with inflation subdued and often below target (see box I.2) and investment remaining stagnant, quantitative easing and record low interest rates were the policies of choice for many central banks, including in developing countries (TDR 2022: chapter III). While this central bank activism, which included regular purchases of bonds and assets of private corporations, contributed to a period of relative financial stability even during the shock of the pandemic, it did so by inflating asset prices and financial profits, which drove up inequality further. Meanwhile, fiscal austerity and low wages discouraged private investments and hampered productivity growth.

When inflation finally picked up in late 2021, central banks began "normalizing" their policies, scaling back their balance sheets (i.e., selling assets on the open market) and raising interest rates. But these moves were immediately met with sell-offs in several markets, prompting many central banks to adopt a slow pace of balance sheet reduction and, in some cases, to quickly resume asset purchases (figure I.5). Also, interest rate increases have been met with less opposition overall, partly because after their initial declines, stocks have rebounded markedly. In this context, it is also worth noting the actions of the United States Federal Reserve, which has recently experimented a hybrid policy of quantitative easing alongside interest rate hikes, suggesting that if a conflict arises between the priorities of price stability and financial market buoyancy, the latter is likely to prevail.

But more importantly, private credit creation – which is driven by financial sector profits and perceived risks, not policy priorities – has not followed the descending pattern of central bank credit. Where private credit has contracted, it has mostly done so much less than central bank credit. As a result, real interest rates are still close to zero in the United States and at or near record lows in many other developed countries (figure I.6). On the other hand, developing countries do not appear to benefit from this aspect of financialization, as they are experiencing markedly higher real interest rates.

Figure I.5 Central banks have only partly retrenched from the pandemic expansion

Monetary base to GDP

(Percentage)

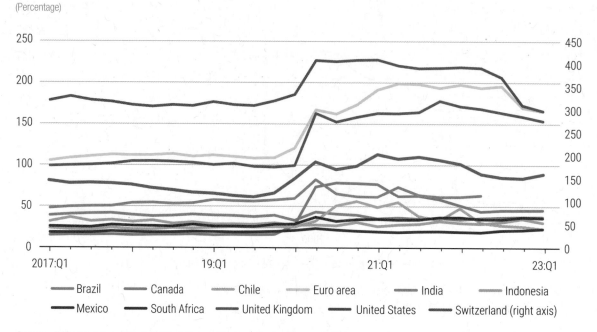

Source: IMF International Financial Statistics and Federal Reserve Economic Data.
Note: Q1: first quarter.

Figure I.6 Though real rates have rebounded they remain low in some developed countries... but credit conditions are considerably less favourable in developing countries

Consumer price index deflated policy rates, selected developed and developing countries

(Percentage)

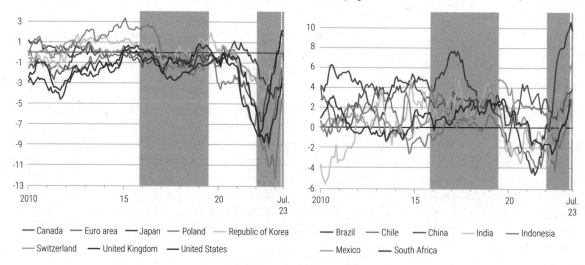

Source: UNCTAD calculations based on data from Bank of International Settlements.
Note: Grey areas refer to periods during which the policy rates were rising in the United States.

In fact, the interest rate hikes by central banks in developed countries may have limited effects domestically, but they wreak havoc in developing countries. Especially for countries with weaker currencies, higher interest rates in advanced economies can easily cause significant capital outflows, which puts more pressure on the currency, drives up inflation and can easily cripple the productive system.

"Interest rate hikes by central banks in developed countries have limited effects domestically, but wreak havoc in developing countries."

This in turn, exacerbates inequality and compromises livelihoods. Developing countries are then under strong pressure to raise their own interest rates, sacrificing their financial stability to defend their monetary stability – an impossible choice in the best of times. With a muted fiscal policy, increased cost of credit affects the most fragile sectors and regions of the world economy, leading to reduced investment, stagnant wages, limited employment growth and liquidity stress. The hardest hit are the unemployed and low-to-medium earners, as well as firms and governments with high external debt in developing countries (chapter II).

The unbound response of private credit explains the divergence of total credit from investment (figure I.7), as pointed out in previous editions of the *Trade and Development Report*. In leading developed and developing economies, bumper credit creation in the early 2000s did not trigger fast investment demand, nor did it do so during the pandemic years. Some localized increase in capital formation may well be due more to inflation itself, which encourages the accumulation of inventories (not picked up in the charts below). Clearly, credit has continued to be channelled more towards financial assets rather than real investment.

The decoupling of investment and credit and the persistence of low real interest rates in key economies indicate that the immediate effect of monetary tightening is a worsening of income and wealth distribution, with only an indirect impact on economic growth.

"... the immediate effect of monetary tightening is a worsening of income and wealth distribution, with only an indirect impact on economic growth."

Of course, a hierarchy of safety applies to the different public and private means of money creation. As financial stability is the main concern of monetary institutions, their approach is a pragmatic one, with activity focused on markets that appear to be systemically relevant. As a result, liquidity is not guaranteed everywhere, and pockets of gluts and scarcity persist. The distribution of liquidity creation typically exhibits a North–South divide, although at times speculative inflows of capital are invested in developing regions (chapters II and V). In 2023, as the market for high yield corporate bonds in developed countries has become less attractive due to the rising costs of credit, high yield seekers have focused on developing countries with market access. Meanwhile, in the United States, corporate bankruptcies have picked up, a concerning trend that has likely contributed to the decision by the Federal Reserve to increase purchases again (figure I.5).

Recent developments in monetary policy clearly confirm that financial markets can, for long periods of time, remain largely detached from the performance of the rest of the economy and be sustained by prevailing conventional expectations. They can thrive when the rest of the economy is struggling and investment is down – as in 2020 – but if they do freeze up, the rest of the economy is hit hard, as in 2008. Therefore, the massive expansion and appreciation of financial assets, as has been observed in recent years, creates huge risk, with negligible benefits for many non-financial businesses

"... if the desired outcome is to create a sound macroeconomic environment that promotes capital formation and employment creation in leading sectors, then monetary policy cannot play the lead role."

(particularly smaller companies), and the vast majority of workers. In terms of policy design, monetary policy does have a large, if underappreciated, impact on income and wealth inequality. However, if the desired outcome is to create a sound macroeconomic environment that promotes capital formation and employment creation in leading sectors, then monetary policy cannot play the lead role. Fiscal and industrial policies remain the protagonists.

Figure I.7 Investment and credit remain decoupled

Stocks of fixed capital and domestic credit

(Percentage of GDP)

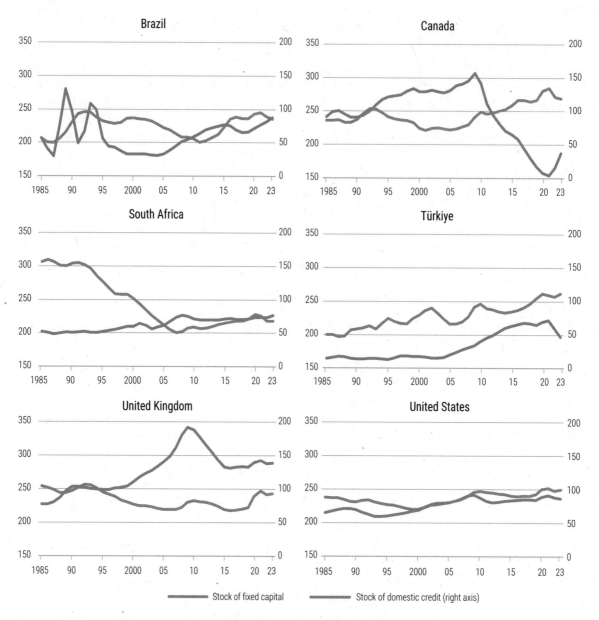

Stock of fixed capital   Stock of domestic credit (right axis)

Source: UNCTAD calculations based on the United Nations Global Policy Model and database.
Note: GDP at constant 2015 prices, PPP.

F. INFLATION AND DISTRIBUTION

After 2020, inflation accelerated along similar trajectories in most countries, but in 2023, as inflation began to decrease, the paths diverged.

Signs of an inflation pick-up began to appear in the United States in the early months of 2021. Various temporary and lasting triggers contributed to this. These include four main factors: (a) changes to global trade patterns that impacted import costs; (b) a surge in consumption expenditure by the wealthy, who benefited from the stock market gains fuelled by extra-loose monetary policy; (c) small increases in the real wages of the lowest paid occupations; and (d) the ability of producers and retailers to raise prices in order to recoup cost increases and increase profit margins (Bivens, 2022; Konczal and Lusiani, 2022; Hayes and Jung, 2022; Schnabel, 2022; Storm, 2022; Weber and Wasner, 2023).

Concerns that inflation was extending beyond the expected transitory period that would normally accompany recovery from a deep economic shock only began towards the end of 2021, as an initial easing of rising prices was reversed. Failure to distribute effective vaccines worldwide prolonged the pandemic, causing temporary factors to linger on, eventually interacting with a largely anticipated initial increase in commodity prices. Then, as the war in Ukraine began, some commodity prices spiked, raising inflation rates further, especially in the European Union (see TDR, 2022 for a discussion). Despite the supply-side origins of this new round of inflationary pressure, leading central banks, beginning with the United States Federal Reserve, embarked on monetary tightening sooner than had been previously signalled.

Figure I.8 Inflation rates have remained in line with historical standards in most developing countries

Monthly consumer price index growth, selected developing countries

(Year-on-year percentage change)

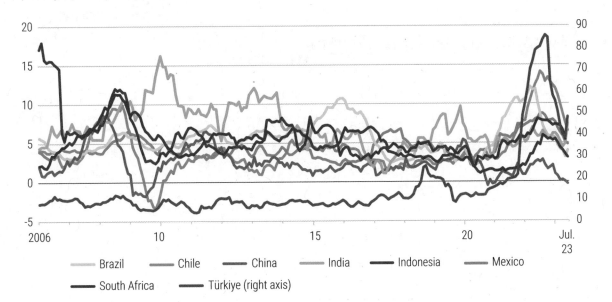

Source: OECD Statistics and national sources.

While inflation has been driven by the movements in the international prices of key energy and food commodities, beginning in late 2021 and early 2022, national outcomes differed depending on market structure and the capacity (and willingness) of their governments to offset the transmission to consumer prices. Furthermore, as the Federal Reserve began to raise interest rates, the dollar appreciated against other currencies, further intensifying import price inflation, especially for net importers of energy and food. This was particularly the case in countries which have liberalized the wholesale and retail energy sectors, such as the European Union, resulting in a swift transmission of international price changes to domestic consumers (TDR, 2022). It was also the case in many developing countries, where previous financial vulnerabilities and weak currencies left them doubly exposed.

As of mid-2023, as prices of key commodities eased, inflation around the globe has followed, albeit at an uneven pace (table I.3). In some cases, core inflation remains persistent and above the recent historical average, showing an ongoing persistence of rising corporate markups and localized exposure to supply chain disruptions. Among developed economies, the euro area has followed a markedly different path compared to Japan and the United States (figure 1.9).

Figure I.9 Inflation rates are down in developed countries and some prices are falling
Monthly consumer price index growth, selected developed countries
(Year-on-year percentage change)

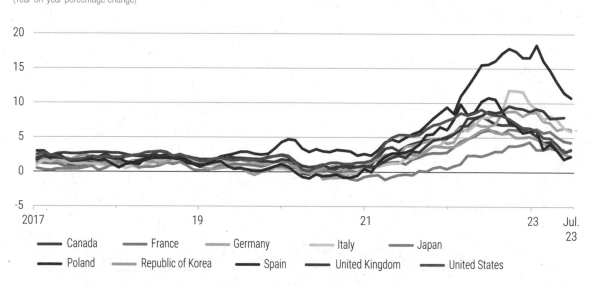

Source: OECD Statistics and national sources.

Table I.3 Inflation eases at different rates across countries, due to their economic structures

Consumer Price Index (CPI) inflation and contributions of food and energy, selected countries, January 2022–June 2023

(Year-on-year percentage change and shares)

Chile

	Yearly	Quarterly	Monthly			Weight
	2022	First quarter 2023	April 2023	May 2023	June 2023	
Annual CPI inflation	11.6	11.8	9.9	8.7	7.6	
Contribution to total inflation						
Food	29.4	34.1	28.8	28.1	30.1	19.3
Energy	13.5	8.6	6.2	5.0	2.1	7.5
Non-food	56.2	56.0	64.0	65.9	67.1	73.2

Germany

	Yearly	Quarterly	Monthly			Weight
	2022	First quarter 2023	April 2023	May 2023	June 2023	
Annual CPI inflation	6.9	8.2	7.2	6.1	6.4	
Contribution to total inflation						
Food	21.8	29.5	27.9	28.2	25.0	11.9
Energy	32.6	14.2	8.3	4.5	4.4	7.4
Non-food	46.1	56.4	64.3	68.2	71.4	80.7

South Africa

	Yearly	Quarterly	Monthly			Weight
	2022	First quarter 2023	April 2023	May 2023	June 2023	
Annual CPI inflation	7.0	7.3	7.1	6.6	5.4	
Contribution to total inflation						
Food	22.6	32.4	33.6	30.8		17.1
Energy	28.6	11.2	7.6	7.0		8.5
Non-food	48.1	56.3	58.7	61.9		74.3

United Kingdom

	Yearly	Quarterly	Monthly			Weight
	2022	First quarter 2023	April 2023	May 2023	June 2023	
Annual CPI inflation	10.9	18.1	7.8	7.9	8.0	
Contribution to total inflation						
Food	13.1	19.1	23.3	22.1		9.5
Energy	38.9	33.3	8.8	6.7		6.5
Non-food	56.4	52.3	66.8	69.1		84

France

	Yearly	Quarterly	Monthly			Weight
	2022	First quarter 2023	April 2023	May 2023	June 2023	
Annual CPI inflation	5.2	6.0	5.9	5.1	4.5	
Contribution to total inflation						
Food	20.1	37.7	38.6	42.2	30.1	14.4
Energy	40.4	17.3	10.9	3.8	2.1	8.9
Non-food	40.8	44.8	50.7	54.6	67.1	76.6

Mexico

	Yearly	Quarterly	Monthly			Weight
	2022	First quarter 2023	April 2023	May 2023	June 2023	
Annual CPI inflation	7.9	7.5	6.3	5.8	5.1	
Contribution to total inflation						
Food	43.3	34.1	28.8	28.1	30.1	25.8
Energy	6.7	8.6	6.2	5.0	2.1	10.0
Non-food	48.8	56.0	64.0	65.9	67.1	64.2

Türkiye

	Yearly	Quarterly	Monthly			Weight
	2022	First quarter 2023	April 2023	May 2023	June 2023	
Annual CPI inflation	72.3	54.3	43.7	39.6	38.2	
Contribution to total inflation						
Food	30.1	32.5	31.4	33.7		25.4
Energy	21.2	8.5	3.6	-5.6		12.1
Non-food	50.6	59.1	65.7	72.9		62.5

United States

	Yearly	Quarterly	Monthly			Weight
	2022	First quarter 2023	April 2023	May 2023	June 2023	
Annual CPI inflation	8.0	5.8	4.9	4.0	3.0	
Contribution to total inflation						
Food	11.8	14.2	11.8	11.6	12.8	8.3
Energy	25.8	3.0	-8.4	-23.7	-46.3	8.2
Non-food	64.2	80.1	93.5	110.0	135.8	83.5

Source: UNCTAD calculations based on OECD Statistics data and national sources.

Note: "Weights" are percentages of the national total CPI; 2022 weights are used for 2023 contributions.

Three factors need to be considered to fully understand recent price dynamics.

1.   As the cost of key inputs accelerates, several circumstances allow firms to gain higher profits by setting their prices following the general increasing trend, even if the goods were produced when inputs were cheaper. Oligopolies and vertically integrated firms in particular were in a privileged position and have taken advantage of the general inflation to increase their profit margins. For them, the increased cost of credit has had a very limited impact, as the growth of their revenues has more than kept up with it (figure I.10).

2.   Second, falling energy and food prices in international markets may well reduce inflation, but this does not signal a decrease in the price of most retail goods and services: at best these will remain stable at their elevated levels. Furthermore, depending on market power and regulation, domestic prices of food and energy will keep increasing even if the international prices of the commodities they use as key inputs decrease. This means that wages will have to increase to regain the real purchasing power lost with inflation. Whether current policies are consistent with this scenario is doubtful (see section E above). Policymakers should consider how to tackle income inequality while also addressing the unchecked capacity of businesses in critical sectors of the economy to pass higher labour costs through to increased prices.

"Food prices remain well above pre-pandemic averages: an unsustainable level for many households, especially in developing countries that are net importers of food."

3.   Third, key factors of uncertainty and instability in international markets have not been addressed. The emergence of new players in commodities trade, such as the United States, now a net exporter of oil and gas, and of new restrictions to manufacturing trade, such as those relating to chips and semiconductors, evidently matter. But the structural problem relates to the organization of markets and trade, which are heavily exposed to asymmetric regulations and profiteering (chapters II and III, also TDR, 2022). Food prices, for instance, remain well above pre-pandemic averages: a largely unsustainable level for many households, especially in developing countries that are net importers of food.

"Policymakers should consider how to tackle income inequality while addressing the unchecked capacity of businesses to translate higher labour costs into increased prices."

Figure I.10 Profit shares have increased above their long-term rising trends

Income from profits and rents

(Percentage of GDP)

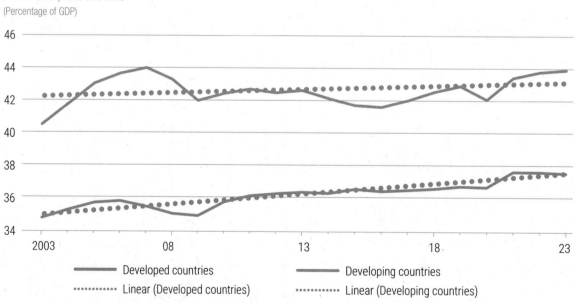

Source: UNCTAD calculations based on the United Nations Global Policy Model and database.
Note: GDP at constant 2015 prices, PPP.

G. LABOUR COSTS AND INEQUALITY

During the past six years, wage growth has lagged behind price inflation in most economies, causing substantial decreases of real wages (figure 1.11). By contrast, markups and profits have more than kept up, with significant sectoral differences, reflecting a number of factors, most significantly, market power.[2]

In the European Union, high coverage of collective bargaining has delayed wage claims longer than elsewhere after the rise of inflation. Most contracts were signed in 2021 and did not anticipate the subsequent price changes. But contracts signed in 2022 were not "revised up" to include the full increase in inflation. In addition, governments have sometimes opted for one-off tax breaks on compensation rather than let real wages grow (Bank of Italy, 2022). This clearly derails any prospects that this period of inflation can lead to a rebalancing of income distribution. Only in France and in the Kingdom of the Netherlands has the trend been somewhat more favourable to workers, due to more frequent bargaining. Moreover, in France, the minimum wage is indexed to inflation.[3] Overall, in Europe, hourly wages have mostly been on a declining trend, at least since 2018. This fact is hidden in annual wage statistics, which only report negative growth in 2022. This shift is largely due to the substantial increase in worked hours after 2020, which impacted annual wage statistics.

In the United States, the Employment Cost Index shows that the pandemic interrupted a positive trend in real total compensation. This trend had been particularly favourable for workers in the retail, trade, food and accommodation industries. Inflation induced a plunge across industries. Only as inflation started slowing in the third quarter of 2022 did real wages and salaries begin to recover, although remaining far below previous levels. Typically, low wage sectors and lower wage occupations have seen their real compensation fall less quickly and have recovered faster than others, pointing to a closer link with subsistence levels. These lower wage sectors remain far below the previous rising trend (figure I.12).

Figure I.11 Wages have not kept up with inflation

Change in real hourly wages by quarter

(Number of surveyed countries)

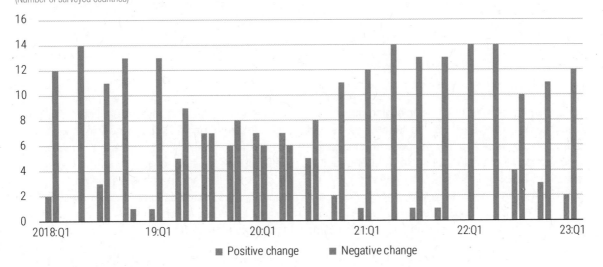

Source: UNCTAD calculations based on ILO and BIS data.

Note: The sample is limited to 14 countries: Brazil, Chile, France, Germany, India, Ireland, Italy, Japan, Mexico, Poland, South Africa, Spain, Switzerland, United States.

---

[2] The interpretation of inflationary pressures as a manifestation of cost-push inflation, driven by energy commodities and imports in general, which then was amplified by firms' price setting behaviour was advanced by a number of scholars (Bivens, 2022; Konczal and Lusiani, 2022; Storm, 2022; Schnabel, 2022; Hayes and Jung, 2022; Weber and Wasner, 2023) as well as TDR 2021 and 2022, but was originally opposed by many commentators. Today, it is widely acknowledged, including by the Federal Reserve and the ECB, that rising average markups, which account for the largest part of profit share increases, contribute to the price dynamics.

[3] See the 2022 Annual Report (Relazione Annuale) of the Bank of Italy for a detailed account of different collective bargaining practices in the euro area.

Figure I.12 Post-pandemic, real compensation in the United States still has to recover

Quarterly total compensation of workers in the United States, by industry

(Index numbers, average 2006=100)

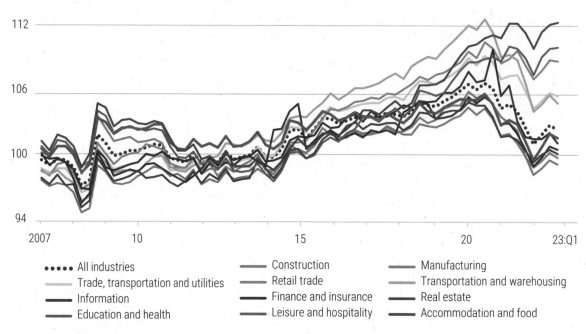

Source: United States Bureau of Labor Statistics.

Recent debates on inflation should serve as a reminder that inflation in developing countries is generally higher than in developed ones (figure I.8). This often results from the process of structural transformation rather than a destabilizing excess of income, demand or money creation. For example, when new manufacturing sectors emerge, they often offer higher wages to attract workers from established sectors. This spurs the development of new market segments that cater to higher earning consumers. Historically, inflation rates of up to 20–30 per cent have often accompanied steady growth and development (Bruno and Easterly, 1996; Epstein, 2003; Chowdhury and Sundaram, 2023).

For most developing countries, inflationary pressures are not simply the outcome of internal growth dynamics but of their asymmetric and unstable integration in the global economy (Toye and Toye, 2004; Fontaine, 2021). A concern is how to deal with the current domestic economic structure, namely with an inefficient agricultural sector, small markets, a low tax base and inadequate infrastructure. These factors impede the reallocation of resources to the industrial sector and obstruct prospects for more sustained growth. In this regard, the literature has long established the need to look at a series of rigidities and bottlenecks which, combined with distributional conflicts, could trigger inflationary pressures. These rigidities cannot be addressed by a programme of public expenditure cuts, wage repression and market deregulation, as such measures typically bring down inflation at a very high cost in terms of lost output investment and jobs.

The international financial landscape, marked by strong instability and compounded by the problems arising from flexible exchange rates, presents a formidable challenge to low- and middle-income countries. Exposure to boom–bust cycles and to precarious integration into a highly fragmented global value chain with no significant technology transfers and a race to the bottom in wage setting, has been a crucial factor in the ensuing de-industrialization (TDR, 2019; Storm, 2017). The latter has been reinforced by technology-driven transformations of the economy and services, as well as the rise of intangible assets in value chains.

In these circumstances, a spike in inflation can signal a weakness bearing serious consequences, both economic and in terms of the legitimacy of the institutions involved. It may be the result of a drastic deterioration of the value of a currency, which pushes import prices up, or it reflects volatility in some key input prices, such as energy. These pressures cannot be absorbed by a quick adjustment in production or wage growth.

In such cases, the increase in costs corresponds to a transfer of financial resources from one institutional sector, typically workers, to producers and importers, without a corresponding increase in the quantity supplied. While some of these financial resources may well leak straight abroad, high domestic markups also frequently occur, being both the cause and consequence of rising inflation. In fact, since production takes time, the price of the final product can be higher than it would have been when inputs were purchased. This gap is exacerbated by concentrated corporate control over markets and the lack of appropriate regulations. Chapter II examines this problem in the case of export concentration in developing countries. Workers, on the other hand, end up seeing any contractual adjustment to the cost of living eroded and sometimes surpassed by further rounds of inflation. In contrast with the first example of virtuous inflation, however, this process is not conducive to more production and job opportunities.

This kind of inflation has a clear asymmetric impact on different social groups, as the current inflationary event has shown. When public institutions try to respond without acknowledging this asymmetry, their actions often act to deepen it, provoking a stronger sense of injustice in the majority of the population. Interest rate increases, which are in themselves an aggravation of costs, also apply to those families who do not benefit from inflation. In fact, they apply especially to families, as well as to smaller and younger businesses that lack well-established relations with banks.

Throughout history, significant increases in the cost of living have often triggered protests. In some cases, these led to progress in the organization of labour, production, and society in general. In such instances, a growing government bureaucracy stepped up to guarantee economic stability, monitoring, and then regulating the decisions of companies and even individual managers to enhance stability (Costantini, 2018).

"There is a need to reorganize global value chains to make the economic structure more resilient and governable and reduce its unfair consequences on wage rates and the global South."

These examples point to the need to reorganize global value chains to make the economic structure more resilient and governable and reduce its unfair consequences on wage rates and the global South. But this also requires sharing technologies to globally coordinate this transition, without wasting resources and with the avoidance of local crises. Price volatility in key commodities needs to be addressed, tackling the opaque financialized system that fuels and feeds off it (chapter III). As seen in recent years, re-shoring attempts (chapter II) and a revival of industrial and protectionist policies in some countries can lead to price frictions and temporary inflationary tensions.

H. CONCLUSION

Since the last Report was published in October 2022, global growth has slowed against a backdrop of price deceleration. Recovery patterns across regions have varied considerably, and the lack of policy action accompanies talk of a "soft landing" for the global economy. A misplaced emphasis on demand-side inflationary pressure has been met with textbook interest rate hikes by central banks. Fiscal and supply-side measures have been more the exception than the rule (e.g., using Strategic Petroleum Reserve in the United States and ensuring food and fertilizer shipments through the Black Sea Initiative). The result has been a slowdown in global growth, persistently lower employment rates in many countries compared to pre-COVID-19 levels, and an exacerbation of income inequality, further shifting from wages to rents and profits, which had already been skewed prior to the pandemic.

Developing countries, and some developed ones are more exposed than ever to financial stress arising from high indebtedness and environmental shocks that are met with an uncoordinated response across the global economy. With monetary policy geared towards preserving financial market stability, even the possibility of using inflation as an instrument to reduce real debt burdens and redress income and wealth inequalities appears to be off limits.

More generally, lack of policy coordination and weakened multilateral cooperation have betrayed the promise of "building back better", constraining recent policy shifts that hold out the possibility of a more balanced recovery beyond this year (box I.2).

Box I.1 Is a just transition possible in a low growth environment?

With appropriate international policy coordination, a period of low growth in developed countries can be an opportunity. It eases resource pressure, giving developing countries room for the industrial transition needed for a fast decarbonization. This would require fiscal and monetary agreements among the G20, WTO deals for technology transfer and collaboration with IMF and World Bank to provide access to finance. Energy efficiency has lagged in both developed and developing economies, with the latter needing more time due to lower incomes and limited policies. The former need to progress beyond the reliance on market-based mechanisms, as these are insufficient for the scale of the challenge.

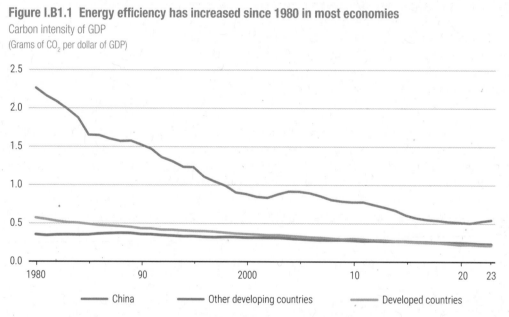

Figure I.B1.1 Energy efficiency has increased since 1980 in most economies
Carbon intensity of GDP
(Grams of CO_2 per dollar of GDP)

Source: UNCTAD calculations based on the United Nations Global Policy Model and database.
Note: GDP at constant 2015 prices, PPP.

Market-based emission reduction strategies, such as carbon taxation, aim to promote renewables and fund the transition. However, these plans face practical hurdles. Energy spending, including fuels and power, typically accounts for less than 10 per cent of GDP in most economies (table I.B1.1). This poses challenges for shifting from fossil fuels to renewables. Carbon tax proposals depend on revenue redistribution to households and businesses or investments in the renewable transition. Realistic tax rates, coupled with energy spending below 10 per cent of GDP, result in relatively small transfers compared to other income flows driving demand. This underscores the need for industrial policy and direct interventions to effectively guide energy production.

Table I.B1.1 Spending on energy is a small fraction of total spending in most countries

Spending on primary energy as percentage of GDP, current prices, 2022
(Percentage)

	Primary energy expenditure (Percentage of GDP)
Russian Federation	21.4
Saudi Arabia	13.8
Indonesia	11.8
India	11.4
Australia	7.3
Canada	6.0
Brazil	5.7
Republic of Korea	5.6
Mexico	5.4
Argentina	5.0
Türkiye	4.7
South Africa	3.5
United States	3.4
China	3.3
Japan	3.2
Italy	2.7
France	2.5
Germany	2.4
United Kingdom	1.8

Source: UNCTAD calculations based on the United Nations Global Policy Model and database.

1. The effects of anti-inflation policies in advanced economies have been skewed, with the benefits accruing mostly to owners of financial assets and the costs mostly borne by wage earners and recipients of transfers everywhere, especially in developing countries. Aggressive monetary tightening threatens to hold back productive investment and restrain productivity growth for years to come. Moreover, focusing on containing wage growth, a minor player in the recent flare-up of inflation, has effectively put the burden of defending the real value of wealth on working people in both developed and developing countries. The focus on inflation reduction could have been on controlling prices that played a major role, such as energy prices, food and retail prices and exchange rates. The unchecked capacity of large firms to pass higher costs through to higher prices, while discussions on international taxation of profit move slowly, continues to compromise livelihoods worldwide.

2. Prioritizing private returns over social needs was demonstrated during the distribution of vaccines during the pandemic and the related protection of intellectual property rights, even when mass casualties have been the price to pay. This, together with the trade tensions described in chapter II, leads to deferral of critical decisions and commitments by technologically advanced countries, and sets a worrying precedent for the rest of the world as global temperatures and climate shocks intensify.

3. The return of industrial policy, most visibly in a series of legislative initiatives in the United States, while signalling a welcome break with the old Washington Consensus, is being shaped by geopolitical tensions and a retreat from multilateralism.

"Achieving a post-pandemic recovery that reduces inequalities and averts a climate catastrophe, requires substantial changes to rules and practices of the global economy."

There is an urgent need to change course. Real wages need to start growing again in most leading economies and sustain their growth over a long period of time in order to effectively reduce inequality. Doing so will provide an incentive for capital formation and productivity growth. Instead, most leading central banks have continued to raise interest rates throughout 2023, sometimes with the explicit intention of impeding wage growth. An alternative growth trajectory requires employment to expand, which, with the limited time left to respond to the climate challenge, must be efficiently directed to the right sectors and technologies. For developing countries, sufficient policy and fiscal space will be essential to better manage international resources which have been left to market forces.

However, as discussed in Part II of this Report, achieving a post-pandemic recovery that reduces inequalities and averts a climate catastrophe, requires substantial changes to rules and practices of the global economy.

Box I.2 Inflation targeting: the history of the 2-per cent target

Inflation targeting involves announcing inflation targets and a "credible and accountable" strategy to achieve them (Bernanke et al., 1999; Setterfield, 2006). The strategy reaffirms the prominent role of central banks setting interest rates, and on the fiscal authorities' commitment to frugality (avoiding fiscal dominance).

Theoretically, central banks could pick any target inflation rate and adjust the nominal rate accordingly. But in the 1990s, the 2-per cent inflation target – a figure arbitrarily set by the central bank of New Zealand in 1990 – became widely adopted and justified by a series of assumptions about wage rigidity and product differentiation (Akerlof et al., 1996).

The main academic tenets of this approach continue to be put forward to this day, but after the Global Financial Crisis of 2008, the case for a higher inflation target gained force. It was based on the argument that, in a recession, when inflation falls, the nominal interest rate that equals the natural rate that can stimulate the recovery may well fall close to or below the zero lower bound. A higher inflation target in normal times would imply higher average nominal interest rates and provide more room for monetary policy to decrease interest rates when needed (Blanchard, 2022).

"The 2-per cent inflation target – a figure arbitrarily set by the central bank of New Zealand in 1990 – became widely adopted and justified by a series of assumptions about wage rigidity and product differentiation."

To update the theoretical framework, two ideas emerged: first, a Phillips curve with a broad flat section (Yellen, 2019; Seccareccia and Khan, 2019; Ratner and Sim, 2022) suggesting that disinflationary policies have become more costly in terms of employment. Indeed, "among the greatest disappointments for proponents of inflation targeting has been its apparent inability to reduce the so-called sacrifice ratio, the unemployment costs of fighting inflation" (Epstein, 2003: 2), Bernanke and co-authors concluded that the sacrifice ratio is often higher after adoption of an inflation-targeting regime (Bernanke et al., 1999). Second, the concept of a secular fall in the natural interest rate due to aging and automation (Eggertsson et al., 2019) is contradicted by the data (Taylor, 2017).

At the end of 2022, there were calls for a new monetary normal around a higher inflation target. Some observers suggested a 3 per cent figure (Blanchard, 2022) while others proposed a more flexible target varying between 2 and 4 per cent (Stiglitz, 2023). But should there be a target at all for monetary policy?

Researchers have found that the policy record experience of the inflation-focused approach has been rather disappointing, even disastrous for many countries (Epstein, 2003; Ball and Sheridan, 2004; Roger and Stone, 2005). "On average, there is no evidence that inflation targeting improves performance as measured by the behaviour of inflation, output or interest rates" (Ball and Sheridan, 2004; 250). Often, the rate of inflation has been decreasing independently of whether these countries adopted an inflation target or not, while employment gains have generally not materialized.

Figure I.B2.1 Inflation targeting is complicated by the difficulty of making correct projections

Projections of the European Central Bank and actual Harmonized Index of Consumer Prices inflation rate

(Percentage)

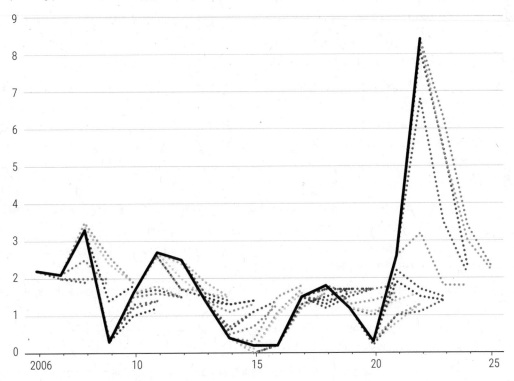

Source: European Central Bank Macroeconomic Projection Database.
Note: Each coloured dotted line reflects a given projection at a certain moment in time.

REFERENCES

Akerlof GA, Dickens WT, Perry GL, Gordon RJ and Mankiw NG (1996). The macroeconomics of low inflation. *Brookings Papers on Economic Activity*. (1):1–76.

Arnold M (2023). Ireland's wild data is leaving economists stumped. *The Irish Times*. 23 August.

Ball L (1994). What determines the sacrifice ratio? In: Mankiw NG, ed. *Monetary Policy*. The University of Chicago Press. Cambridge MA:155–193.

Ball LM and Sheridan N (2004). Does inflation targeting matter? In: Bernanke B and Woodford M, eds. *The Inflation-Targeting Debate*. University of Chicago Press. Chicago, Il: 249–282.

Bank of Italy (2023). *Relazione Annuale Anno 2022*. Rome.

Bernanke BS, Laubach T, Mishkin FS and Posen AS (1999). *Inflation Targeting: Lessons from the International Experience*. Princeton University Press. Princeton, NJ.

Bivens J (2022). Corporate profits have contributed disproportionately to inflation. How should policymakers respond? Working Economics Blog of the Economic Policy Institute.

Blanchard O (2022). It is time to revisit the 2% inflation target. *Financial Times*. 28 November.

Blanchard O and Leigh D (2013). Growth forecast errors and fiscal multipliers. IMF Working Papers. 13/143. International Monetary Fund. Washington, DC.

Bruno M and Easterly W (1996). Inflation and growth: In search of a stable relationship. *Review*. 78(3).

Chowdhury A and Sundaram JK (2023). Inflation phobia myths and dogma exacerbate policy responses. *Review of Keynesian Economics*. 11(2):147–171.

Costantini O (2018). Invented in America: Birth and evolution of the cyclically adjusted budget rule, 1933–61. *History of Political Economy*. 50(1):83–117.

Costantini O (2020). Eurozone as a trap and a hostage: Obstacles and prospects of the debate on European fiscal rules. *Intereconomics*. 55(5):284–291.

Crouch C (2009). Privatized Keynesianism: An unacknowledged policy regime. *British Journal of Politics and International Relations*. 11(3):382–399.

Eggertsson GB, Lancastre M and Summers LH (2019). Aging output per capita and secular stagnation. *American Economic Review: Insights*. 1(3):325–342.

Epstein GA (2003). Alternatives to inflation targeting monetary policy for stable and egalitarian growth: A brief research summary. PERI Working Paper. 62.

Epstein GA and Yeldan AE (2009). *Beyond Inflation Targeting: Assessing the Impacts and Policy Alternatives*. Edward Elgar Publishing Limited. Glos.

Federal Reserve Board (2022). History of the FOMC's Policy Normalization Discussions and Communications. Available at: https://www.federalreserve.gov/monetarypolicy/policy-normalization-discussions-communications-history.htm (accessed 29 August 2023).

Hayes C and Jung C (2022). *Prices and Profits after the Pandemic*. Institute for Public Policy Research. London.

Schnabel I (2022). The globalisation of inflation. Speech at a conference organized by the *Österreichische Vereinigung für Finanzanalyse und Asset Management*. 11 May. Available at: https://www.ecb.europa.eu/press/key/date/2022/html/ecb.sp220511_1~e9ba02e127.en.html (accessed 31 July 2023).

Konczal M and Lusiani N (2022). Prices profits and power: An analysis of 2021 firm-level markups. Roosevelt Institute Working papers. New York, NY.

Levrero ES (2021). Estimates of the natural rate of interest and the stance of monetary policies: A critical assessment. *International Journal of Political Economy*. 50(1):5–27.

Ratner D and Sim J (2022). Who killed the Phillips curve? A murder mystery. FEDS Working Paper. 2022–28.

Roger S and Stone MR (2005). On target? The international experience with achieving inflation targets. IMF Working Papers 163. International Monetary Fund. Washington, DC.

Seccareccia M (2017). Which vested interests do central banks really serve? Understanding central bank policy since the global financial crisis. *Journal of Economic Issues*. 51(2):341–350.

Seccareccia M and Khan N (2019). The illusion of inflation targeting: Have central banks figured out what they are actually doing since the global financial crisis? An alternative to the mainstream perspective. *International Journal of Political Economy*. 48(4):364–380.

Setterfield M (2006). Is inflation targeting compatible with post Keynesian economics? *Journal of Post Keynesian Economics*. 28(4):653–671.

Stiglitz JE (2023). How not to fight inflation. *Project Syndicate*. 26 January

Storm S (2017). The political economy of industrialization. *Development and Change.* (Virtual Issue):1–19.

Storm S (2022). Inflation in the time of corona and war: The plight of the developing economies. Working Paper Series 192. Institute for New Economic Thinking. New York, NY.

Taylor L (1988). *Varieties of Stabilization Experience: Towards Sensible Macroeconomics in the Third World.* Clarendon Press. Oxford.

Taylor L (2017). The "natural" interest rate and secular stagnation: Loanable funds macro models don't fit today's institutions or data. *Challenge*. 60(1):27–39.

UNCTAD (TDR, 2009). *Trade and Development Report 2009: Responding to the Global Crisis*. (United Nations Publication. Sales No. E.09.II.D.16. New York and Geneva).

UNCTAD (TDR, 2019). *Trade and Development Report 2019: Financing a Global Green New Deal* (United Nations publication, Sales No. E.19.II.D.15. Geneva).

UNCTAD (TDR, 2021). *Trade and Development Report 2021: From Recovery to Resilience – The Development Dimension*. (United Nations Publication. Sales No. E.22.II.D.1. Geneva).

UNCTAD (TDR, 2022). *Trade and Development Report 2022: Development Prospects in a Fractured World: Global Disorder and Regional Responses*. (United Nations Publication. Sales No. E.22.II.D.44. Geneva).

Weber IM and Wasner E (2023). Sellers' inflation profits and conflict: Why can large firms hike prices in an emergency? *Review of Keynesian Economics*. 11(2):183–213.

Wessel D (2018). Alternatives to the Fed's 2 per cent inflation target. Rethinking the Fed's 2 per cent inflation target. *Brookings Institutions Working Papers*. Washington DC.

Yellen J (2019). Former Fed Chair Janet Yellen on why the answer to the inflation puzzle matters. Remark delivered at a public event "What's (not) up with inflation?" hosted by the Hutchins Center on Fiscal & Monetary Policy at Brookings. 3 October. Available at: https://www.brookings.edu/articles/former-fed-chair-janet-yellen-on-why-the-answer-to-the-inflation-puzzle-matters/ (accessed 31 July 2023).

Chapter II

International Markets:
Trade, Capital Flows,
Commodities

From a fractured international architecture to a sustainable new global order

The current wrong-footed international financial architecture and global trading system undermines the pursuit of the harmonious and stable order required to meet the goals of the 2030 Agenda for Sustainable Development or the Paris Agreement targets. More concretely, UNCTAD analysis finds that after the COVID-19 shock:

- International trade and its related power asymmetries have contributed to further worsening global labour income share. In addition, unilateral shifts in industrial policies in developed economies are generating tensions among trading partners, hampering prospects for structural transformation in developing countries.

- Elevated commodity prices persist globally, harming the most vulnerable and creating food insecurity for 350 million people worldwide.

- Global financial conditions are markedly deteriorating, placing almost one third of frontier market economies on the precipice of debt distress. This follows the deepening of their financial integration into international capital markets over the last decade.

In envisioning a hopeful future, a new paradigm is needed, one that goes beyond the traditional boundaries of globalization and trade liberalization. This new global order would require a comprehensive approach and a concerted effort to transform aspirations into a resilient, multifaceted system capable of meeting the intricate demands of an interconnected world. The imperative is clear: escalate the search for effective governance measures to rectify the imbalances and vulnerabilities inherent in the current global economic and financial architecture.

In light of these dynamics, UNCTAD proposes

- Building a new consensus for international trade that can better accommodate policy priorities such as building resilient supply chains, achieving a just energy transition, delivering decent jobs, tackling corruption and corporate tax avoidance, and developing a secure digital infrastructure.

- Revisiting existing international trade agreements to create policy space for countries to redesign their production, consumption and trading profiles to face contemporary global challenges.

- Strengthening South–South trade cooperation, for instance by revitalizing the Global System of Trade Preferences (GSTP).

- Establishing effective mechanisms for debt restructuring and relief based on the participation of all developing countries with agreed procedures, incentives and deterrents.

A. INTRODUCTION

Two key sets of factors have shaped the recent evolution in international markets. On the one hand, the year 2022 marked the culmination of the pandemic recovery. In this sense – and considering the risks to global growth discussed in chapter I – the world economy now begins a post-COVID-19 pandemic period conditioned by a few decisive elements whose overall impact is difficult to predict. These include a tighter monetary stance by central banks in advanced countries; a more geostrategic policy approach to international economic relations; the growing influence of industrial policy on trade strategies of major economies; and multiple geoeconomic uncertainties.

On the other hand, the post-pandemic cycle reveals trends that build upon pre-existing structural weaknesses in the global economy, which pre-date the COVID-19 shock. These are particularly onerous for developing countries and relate to:

- The growing concentration of export markets and related asymmetry of income distribution;

- A slowdown in investment and an unsustainable burden of debt;

- A widening technological divide;

- The mounting costs of the climate crisis and related challenges around the energy transition.

The intertwining of conjunctural and structural concerns poses governance challenges for today's highly interdependent global economy. In addition to the gaps in the international financial architecture analysed in Part II of this Report, there are serious concerns about the rule-based multilateral trading system given the diminishing prospects of achieving the kind of harmonious and stable order required to meet the goals of the 2030 Agenda and the targets set by the Paris Agreement.

If, and how, policymakers will meet these governance challenges over the coming months will determine whether the world avoids a global recession in 2024; whether developing countries avoid a "lost decade", and whether the currently fractured multilateral system ends the decade in more robust health.

Finding the right response will require policymakers to adopt a long-term perspective and a holistic approach. Many longstanding concerns of developing countries regarding the international trading system, including distorted agricultural markets, food insecurity, premature de-industrialization and restrictive business practices, have never been adequately addressed, often leading to winner-takes-most outcomes rather than the win-win results envisaged in canonical trade models.

This chapter addresses these dilemmas, surveying recent developments in international trade (section B), commodity markets (section C) and international capital markets (section D), with the aim of identifying priority areas that require multilateral attention.

B. TRADE

"Global trade is forecast to grow about 1 per cent in 2023, significantly below world economic output growth, with merchandise trade hovering in negative territory."

After experiencing a rollercoaster ride in 2020–2022, global trade in goods and services is forecast to grow about 1 per cent in 2023, significantly below world economic output growth (chapter I). It is also lower than the average growth registered during the last decade, itself the slowest average growth period for global trade since the end of the Second World War. In the medium term, trade is heading back to its subdued pre-crisis trend; in the near term, it will stand even below this figure. This is because the growth of merchandise trade has hovered around negative territory in 2023, despite global trade in services showing resilience.

Behind these observations lie deeper shifts in the structure of global trade and a transformation of the political readings of the role of international trade today. Many of these changes concern the governance system that emerged with the conclusion of the Uruguay Round in 1994 and the creation of the World Trade Organization (WTO).

If the 1980s and the 1990s are commonly described as the period of trade liberalization, the past three decades were marked not so much by reducing trade tariffs and barriers to investment but by changes to domestic regulatory standards and norms within national jurisdictions. The global regulatory architecture that emerged as a result of these reforms has benefited the interests of big business, such as international banks and other multinational enterprises (MNEs), above all else (Rodrik, 2023). As many developing countries were on the receiving end of these reforms, their policy space has been progressively diminished by the recent crises.

The asymmetry of gains from the international trading system, apparent in both the advanced and developing countries, has been building into a backlash against the rules of global governance and, increasingly, the very idea of free trade. This backlash is prompting policymakers to reassess their strategic prioritization of the role of trade. In the unfolding policy debate on the regulatory architecture of global trade, the potential costs of deeper trade relations are no longer seen as marginal. Similarly, the notion that the benefits from deregulation reforms – to developed and developing countries alike – would flow automatically has never been challenged so strongly and so widely. Instead, managing trade increasingly turns on harnessing strategic interests with the support of State actors, much more willing to intervene in the workings of markets, both domestic and international (Sullivan, 2023; Hudson, 2022).

> *"The asymmetry of gains from the international trading system, apparent in both advanced and developing countries, has been building into a backlash against the rules of global governance and the very idea of free trade."*

A new lexicography of trade reflects these ongoing shifts, with a series of buzzwords, such as "fragmentation", "deglobalization", "slowbalization", "reshoring", "nearshoring", "friendshoring", "de-risking", "decoupling", "open strategic autonomy" and "new industrial policy" peppering current discussions around trade policy. The turning tide is also visible in an emergent new paradigm of trade that approaches the challenge of global economic interdependence from a more strategic standpoint that can better accommodate new policy priorities, such as reducing inequality, building resilience, and accelerating the energy transition (Rodrik, 2023).

The question to what extent the emergent consensus on the need to reform international trade can be translated into a new regime of international trade remains open. What is already apparent is that a significant reshaping of world trade, including the restructuring of global supply chains, is under way. Navigating this transformation poses major challenges to most developing economies at a time when their prospects for economic growth are deteriorating, the investment climate is worsening, and financial stresses are mounting (see chapter I and section D below).

> *"A significant reshaping of world trade is under way. Navigating this transformation poses major challenges to most developing economies."*

If history is any guide, as national security and geopolitical considerations move to the centre of the policy stage, not only will multilateral options struggle for attention, but many developing countries risk being caught in the crossfire of trade disputes or face growing pressure to take sides in economic conflicts they neither want nor need. Furthermore, the rise of protectionist unilateral trade measures and the more widespread use of industrial policies in large economies can adversely impact developing economies' exports and hinder their prospects for structural transformation.

Some developing countries may see gains from a restructuring of global supply chains in the near-term. Similarly, a green investment boom in advanced economies might bring opportunities for some fortunately endowed countries, such as exporters of strategic minerals. Yet, sustainable developmental success will require parallel support to promote access to reliable (and cheaper) sources of finance, a rebalancing of trade rules and levelling the playing field.

This, in turn, includes policies that facilitate technology transfer and reduce the market power of large MNEs, as well as enabling developing countries to add more value domestically to their exports, including through greater processing of raw materials. What is more, an analysis of several key indicators relating to income distribution and power asymmetry confirms that development cannot be reduced to increased trade flows, and that achieving the Sustainable Development Goals (SDGs) requires a set of proactive policy strategies and institutions that reflect economic, social and environmental priorities of the developing countries.

1. Review of recent cyclical developments in international trade

Recent trends in international trade provide a mix of good and bad news, with the balance tipping to the negative side, especially when looking beyond conjunctural indicators and considering some recent developments relating to trade policy (subsection 2) and the distributional impact of trade (subsection 3).

"The normalization of cyclical trade indicators should not mask the ongoing tectonic shifts that are taking place in international trade policy settings."

On the positive front, several indicators suggest a return to some form of normalcy after the collapse and recovery that followed the COVID-19 outbreak, with the major supply-chain disruptions that took place between 2020 and 2022 coming to an end (figure II.1). Altogether, this is expected to ease pressures on prices owing to the end of the lockdowns in China, the normalization of trade composition after the COVID-19 boom in demand for manufactured goods, the stabilization of transport logistics for goods in several developed countries, and adjustments to the effects of the war in Ukraine and the economic sanctions that followed.

The trend towards normalization is also reflected in the sharp drop of international maritime freight rates for container and dry bulk during the second half of 2022, after a surge to historical highs in the aftermath of the COVID-19 outbreak (figure II.2).

Figure II.1 The sharp swing of supply chain pressures after their COVID-19 highs

Global supply chain pressure index

(Standard deviations from average value)

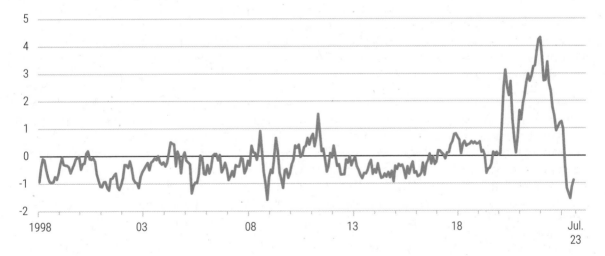

Source: Benigno et al. (2023).
Note: The Global Supply Chain Pressure Index (GSCPI) integrates transportation cost data and manufacturing indicators to provide a gauge of global supply chain conditions, by considering a number of metrics with the aim of providing a comprehensive summary of potential supply chain disruptions. For global transportation costs, it includes data from the Baltic Dry Index and the Harpex index, as well as airfreight cost indices from the United States Bureau of Labor Statistics. GSCPI also uses several supply chain-related components from Purchasing Managers' Index (PMI) surveys, focusing on manufacturing firms. The index is normalized such that a zero indicates the index is at its average value, with positive values representing how many standard deviations the index is above this average value (and negative values representing the opposite).

Figure II.2 Maritime freight rates have returned close to their 2010s average

Monthly rates, dry bulk and containers

(Index numbers, average 2015=100)

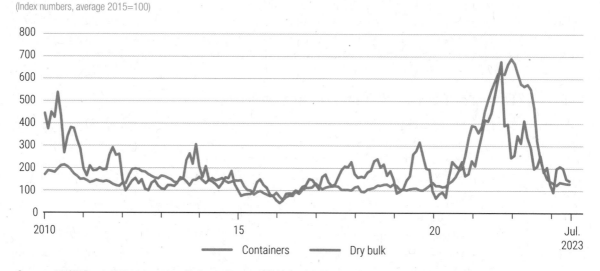

Source: UNCTAD calculations based on Clarksons Research Shipping Intelligence Network database.

Note: "Dry bulk" relates to the Baltic Exchange Dry Index and "containers" to the Shanghai Containerized Freight Index (SCFI) Comprehensive index.

Furthermore – and relevant for trade in services as it relates to both international transport and tourism, two of its main components – the recovery in international air traffic has continued after the sector was hit hard by the pandemic. Global air revenue-passenger kilometres (RPKs) – which indicates the number of kilometres travelled by paying passengers – was only 9 per cent below pre-pandemic levels in May 2023. This followed an expansion of almost 50 per cent year on year, owing partly to China reopening its international markets, which resulted in an almost threefold annual increase for Asia–Pacific carriers (figure II.3).

All the above positive trends pushed international trade, when measured in current dollars, to an all-time high of around $32 trillion in 2022, an increase of 13 per cent compared to 2021 and a rise of 25 per cent from the pre-COVID-19 levels of 2019. However, a pertinent factor behind this result relates to the *sharp price increases in some heavily traded commodities*, especially energy and to a lesser extent agri-food, metals and minerals. When measured in constant prices, international trade, both goods and services, recorded an increase of about 3.5 per cent in 2022.

Under a more granular examination, quarterly data shows that merchandise trade peaked during the second or third quarters of 2022 – depending on whether figures are looked at in constant (volumes) or current prices (values) (figure II.4). Over the subsequent quarters, declines set in, albeit more slowly when controlling for the negative price effects (dashed line). This was unexpected to most observers, who had anticipated a significant rebound owing to a normalization of the inventory cycle and a relaxing of the pandemic restrictions in China. Preliminary estimates for the second and third quarters of 2023 confirm the downward trend as the post-lockdown rebound has waned and expectations about international merchandise trade prospects have deteriorated (*Financial Times*, 2023a).

Regarding trade in services, this subaggregate component also receded during the second half of 2022, while estimates for 2023 show resumed growth during the first half of 2023. This highlights the overall resilience of some of the services sectors, even if the overall growth over the last five quarters has been weak.

As a result, the annual growth of international trade in goods and services is expected to decelerate to about 1 per cent in real terms in 2023, less than half the already subdued growth of global economic activity (chapter I). Moreover, multiple downside risks remain, which could further impact the trade outlook. These include, inter alia, ongoing trade tensions between major economies, the weakening of global demand and growing geopolitical uncertainties.

Figure II.3 International air passengers flying high: But Asia still not at cruising altitude

International revenue passenger kilometres, year-on-year change compared to 2019

(Percentage)

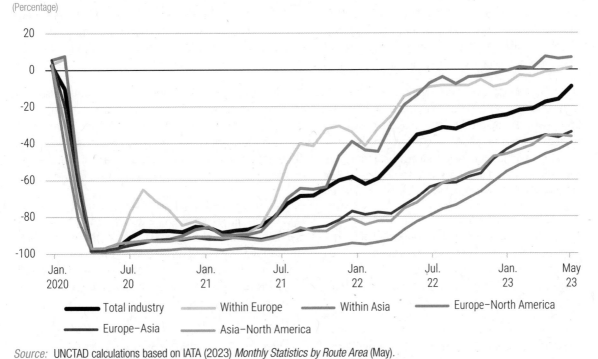

Source: UNCTAD calculations based on IATA (2023) *Monthly Statistics by Route Area* (May).

Note: The figure depicts the top five route areas in 2019, ranked by performed traffic level. RPKs corresponds to the sum of the products obtained by multiplying the number of revenue passengers by the flight stage distance (one RPK means that one passenger is carried on one kilometre).

Figure II.4 Global trade: Merchandise is declining while services appear more resilient

Quarterly world trade, merchandise (in values and volumes) and services (in values)

(Index numbers, first quarter of 2015=100)

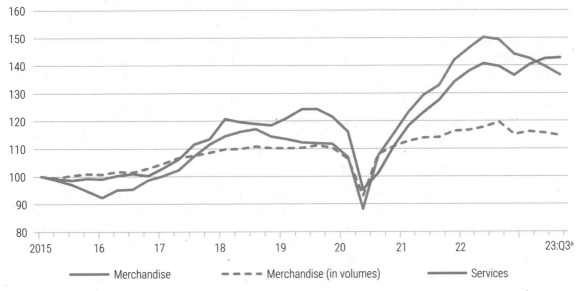

Source: UNCTAD calculations based on UNCTADstat database.

Note: All series are seasonally adjusted.

  [a] Estimates from UNCTAD nowcasts for the second and third quarters of 2023.

2. A new paradigm of international trade?

The subdued trade outlook coincides with a renewed focus on policy matters. For much of the post-World War II era, policy decisions on trade were built on a relatively straightforward set of assumptions. A general commitment to openness tempered by abiding sectoral priorities and security concerns, combined with a recognition that the places where goods were made largely coincided with where jobs were created and profits registered (and reinvested).

While the connections were never perfect, particularly in developing countries, international trade was seen, both academically and politically, as an important lubricant that could help support a virtuous circle connecting jobs, investment, productivity, and incomes. Even where the required international linkages were weak, broken, or missing altogether, the "permissive international trade regime" embedded in the post-war global economic architecture gave governments the policy space and tools to repair or replace them. It also allowed governments to "create social and economic institutions that suited their individual preferences and needs" (Rodrik, 2023). That stopped being the case a while ago.

The evolution of global value chains, the financialization of corporate structures, the adoption of one-size-fits-all policy programmes and the squeezing of national fiscal autonomy have narrowed the room for policymakers aiming to align their efforts at integrating into the global economy with national and local priorities. For many developing countries, this challenge has coincided with uneven growth spurts coexisting with weak job creation (at least in the formal economy), structural regression towards less diversified economies, including through "premature de-industrialization", increased commodity dependence and widening social divisions.

The limits of the labour-intensive trade-led growth model and the unequal benefits from trade integration became a growing concern before the pandemic (e.g., World Bank, 2020). During the past two years, this concern further transformed into a set of moves that point to a new political economy of trade governance. In the emergent "new consensus", globalization in general, and trade liberalization specifically, are secondary to the goals of building resilient supply chains, supporting a just energy transition, delivering decent jobs, tackling corruption and corporate tax avoidance, and developing a secure digital infrastructure (Luce, 2023).

In a candid statement, the National Security Adviser to the President of the United States, argued that, not only did meeting these goals move trade policy beyond a simple call to reduce tariffs, it also abandoned the assumption that "trade-enabled growth would be inclusive growth, that the gains of trade would end up getting broadly shared within nations" and rather took the view that a more integrated policy approach was required, built around a dedicated industrial strategy and new international partnerships (Sullivan, 2023).

These are laudable aims, long advocated by UNCTAD and previous editions of this report (e.g., TDR 1997, 2018). But without adequate policy coordination at all levels of policymaking, the move towards a new set of priorities for international trade governance can generate tensions among trading partners. It also can raise serious concerns, particularly for developing countries with no fiscal space, if the approach is adopted unilaterally and without careful consideration of the implications for established multilateral practices and procedures. Some aspects of these tensions, current and potential, are examined below.

a. The trade dispute between China and the United States

This century has seen the United States displaced by China as the world's leading exporter of manufactured goods (chapter I). While a growing trade deficit with China provoked intermittent responses from legislatures in the United States (Siripurapu and Berman, 2022), a more assertive stance began only in 2017, with progressive increases in tariff on exports from China. This has resulted in significant trade diversion, mostly to the benefit of main economic rivals to China, including Mexico and the European Union (Moody's Analytics, 2020), though some policy details have also created worries, and at times outright disapproval, among these beneficiaries.

A paradox of the current trade dispute between the world's two largest economies is that total imports of goods to the United States from China have returned to their pre-COVID-19 peak. This is due to the sharp increase in products not subject to tariffs (figure II.5). Bilateral imports of both goods and services from China to the United States reached the highest level ever recorded, at $564 billion in 2022, as services continue to expand. The United States remains by far the main destination for exports of merchandise from China; followed by Japan, Republic of Korea, Viet Nam and India.

Figure II.5 The paradox of United States-China trade decoupling
The merchandise imports by the United States from China that were subject to increased tariffs have followed a divergent trend. The rest of the bilateral imports continued to rise until mid-2022, resulting in the total bilateral import bill of 2022 nearly matching its record high of 2018

Goods imports of the United States from China and the rest of world by tariff list
(Index numbers, June 2018=100)

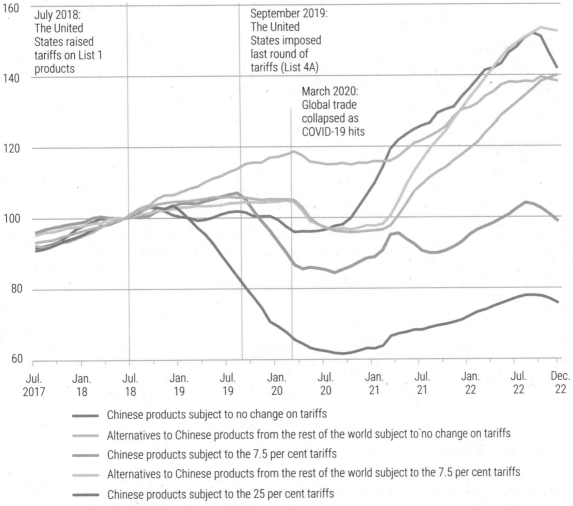

Source: Bown (2023) based on United States imports data from the United States Census Bureau and the Bureau of Economic Analysis.

Notes: Lighter lines refer to imports from the rest of the world, which have therefore not been subject to increased tariffs by the United States. All series refer to 12-month trailing sums of not seasonally adjusted import data. A "list" refers to the group of products subject to the United States tariffs imposed on imports from China under Section 301 of the Trade Act of 1974. "Chinese products subject to the 25 per cent tariffs" relates to goods appearing in lists 1, 2 or 3. "Chinese products subject to the 7.5 per cent tariffs" relates to goods appearing in list 4A.

At the same time, notwithstanding this recovery, the trade dispute has imposed costs on the trading partners. A large body of research shows that real incomes have been adversely affected in both countries due to the tariffs, with consumers of imported goods shouldering the burden through increased prices (e.g., Amiti et al., 2019; Cavallo et al., 2021; Fajgelbaum and Khandelwal, 2022). Fajgelbaum et al. (2023) find that it also opened new trade opportunities for "bystander" countries rather than just causing shifts among existing trade partners.

While the precise trigger of the process is yet to be ascertained, this may be explained by the fact that countries that became the beneficiaries of the trade war (e.g. Czechia, Malaysia and Mexico, according to Fajgelbaum et al., 2023) might have viewed it as an opportunity to invest in new facilities, trade infrastructure, or trade and investment facilitation, or alternatively, because these countries might have enjoyed better credit reallocation conditions (Hassan et al. 2020). Alternatively, they might have already been well integrated into global trade, allowing them to seize new exporting opportunities across various sectors. Importantly, the significant diversity of the benefiting economies (not the sectors) suggests that country-specific reforms and institutions can be key determinants in driving how countries' exports respond in this new era of post-pandemic globalization.

b. The rise of export controls

New export controls have been another manifestation of the shifting sentiment around trade policy across the globe. These have mostly covered three types of non-mutually exclusive objectives: (i) securing domestic supply, (ii) restricting geopolitical rivals, and (iii) encouraging investment in locally based processing facilities.

(i) Securing domestic supply

With regards to domestic supply concerns, the current WTO rules allow for temporary export restrictions or prohibitions to prevent or relieve critical shortages of essential products, provided all measures are communicated, have phase-out timelines and are proportionate to the scale of the problem at hand.

A key issue here is to define what can be considered as proportionate. During COVID-19, for instance, over 80 countries resorted to banning exports of medical and personal protective goods in the early phases of the pandemic (UNCTAD, 2021a). Similarly, following the outbreak of the war in Ukraine in early 2022, almost 100 export restrictions on essential agricultural commodities were identified to have been applied by 35 WTO members or observers (WTO, 2023).

Overall, such unilateral measures often do more harm than good, which begs the question of whether the international community should not come up with stricter rules, especially on essential goods such as medicinal products or food, to ensure that similar future practices are better controlled and do not result in a negative spiral that ultimately hampers the resilience of all. Discussions have been continuing for some time, yet no significant agreement has been reached and it is unlikely to emerge before the WTO Thirteenth Ministerial Conference of February 2024, at best.

(ii) Constraining geopolitical rivals

A plethora of additional geopolitical-related export restrictions – such as non-automatic licensing, incomplete rebate of value added tax (VAT) on exports or even outright bans – have also emerged in recent years. Under Article XXI of the General Agreement on Tariffs and Trade (GATT), "national security" has long provided an umbrella for derogation of international trade rules. The war in Ukraine, along with concerns about potential future military conflicts, has only strengthened that position. As a result, the supply of different raw materials critical for the green transition or for food or industrial production has been affected after several exporters implemented such measures (OECD, 2022).

In other cases, these curbs have related to high-technology components, for example the overseas sales of chip-making technology, as well as sales of advanced chips to some countries including, China, by the United

States in October 2022. This was later followed by Japan and the Kingdom of the Netherlands. Other similar interventions relate to the efforts of the United States to exclude Chinese companies from participating in the development of global digital infrastructure for security concerns such as the development of the global submarine cable market (*Financial Times*, 2023b). Elsewhere, Poland, Slovakia, Hungary and Romania have imposed a ban on the import of Ukrainian grain, even as the European Union discontinued its own ban in September 2023 (AP News, 2023).

(iii) Encouraging investment in locally based processing facilities

Export restrictions aimed at boosting value addition domestically and building forward linkages within the country are, from a developmental perspective, becoming an objective for some commodity exporting countries. In this vein, Indonesia has encouraged investment in locally based processing facilities relating to the global energy transition by limiting its nickel exports through successive policies since 2009. This culminated in a complete ban on nickel ore exports in 2014 (UNCTAD, 2017).

The European Union disputed this policy at the WTO, and in November 2022, a Panel recommended that Indonesia brings its measures into conformity with its obligations under the GATT 1994. Indonesia subsequently appealed that decision, and as of now, the case is pending due to the current non-operational status of the Appellate Body.[1] More recently, Zimbabwe, in December 2022, and Namibia, in June 2023, also announced the ban of exports of unprocessed critical minerals including rare earths and lithium to try to build more of the supply chain for processing raw materials domestically (Africanews, 2022; Reuters, 2023).

In this instance, and notwithstanding the specific aspects of each commodity and situation, UNCTAD has long maintained that effectiveness of such types of trade policy depends on the non-substitutability of the commodity in question. If ready substitutes for the product are available in international markets, other exporters are likely to benefit from these export bans.

"One metric to gauge the adequacy of export restrictions of raw materials to promote domestic processing facilities by developing countries should be how well a policy can promote economic diversification and advancement."

The trade-off between national policy autonomy and global and regional economic integration is difficult to manoeuvre for most developing countries. Insufficient policy space can prevent governments from addressing local needs, ultimately undermining the effectiveness and trust in global regulations. One metric for assessing the appropriate balance of policies for a country's needs can be the effectiveness of a policy in promoting economic diversification and advancement. This is provided there is no superior alternative option for achieving the same objective for all parties involved.

c. The growing use of subsidies and other trade instruments by developed countries to foster the green transition

The growing use of subsidies – sometimes discriminatory – has emerged, notably in developed countries that have rediscovered a more active role for industrial policies to promote investment and jobs at home and facilitate the transition to green practices. In the United States, there have been a series of interrelated legislative initiatives – the Inflation Reduction Act (IRA), the Creating Helpful Incentives to Produce Semiconductors (CHIPS) and the Infrastructure Investment and Jobs Act (IIJA) – which promote new spending and tax credits aimed, inter alia, at supporting key sectors of the economy – electric vehicles, green manufacturing, the semiconductor industry, and renewable energy production – as well as addressing regional divergence, labour market inequalities, and national security issues.

In the European Union, under the banner "open strategic autonomy", the main relevant frameworks are the Green Deal Industrial Plan (GDIP) and its Net-Zero Industry Act (NZIA). GDIP will include multiple funding approaches and places an emphasis on workforce training, aiming to equip European workers with the

---

[1] For more details, see https://www.wto.org/english/tratop_e/dispu_e/cases_e/ds592_e.htm.

necessary skills to maximize their employability during the energy transition. NZIA will ease the regulations on state aid regarding allowable domestic subsidies, to cover more types of clean energy projects. Also, the European Union intends to extend its support to domestic manufacturing through the implementation of the European Sovereignty Fund, offering subsidies for select industries. However, unlike the initiatives in the United States, there are no clear budget lines attached to these proposals, with some countries arguing that it is simply a way to allocate unused funds from the Recovery and Resilience Facility of the European Union as well as other existing funding programmes (such as InvestEU, REPowerEU, and Innovation funds).

Though they stand outside the subsidy provision, when it comes to trade, two parts of the overarching GDIP are particularly pertinent: the carbon border adjustment mechanism (CBAM) and the Deforestation Regulation (EUDR). CBAM is scheduled to start in October 2023, while the EUDR entered into force in June 2023.[2]

These initiatives have raised concerns around the world, especially among developing countries (e.g., UNCTAD, 2021b). Several countries, including China, are expected to challenge it at WTO, partly because the introduction of distinct carbon pricing certificates based on a product's country of origin might infringe upon the WTO "most favoured nation" (MFN) principle (Garg, 2022). Moreover, they risk unfairly penalizing the exports of developing countries because these economies have often less capacity to adapt to new specific standards. Furthermore, by imposing equal carbon taxes on developed and developing nations, the proposed CBAM would also violate the Paris Agreement principle of "common but differentiated responsibilities" (CBDR). With respect to EUDR, exporting countries are concerned that the traceability requirement will be impractical and could constitute a *de facto* import ban.

"The fact that recent initiatives were not discussed multilaterally, even though developing countries will bear a significant part of the consequences, is problematic."

In other words, it is important for every nation to acknowledge its role in addressing a common global challenge like climate change or deforestation. However, it is unfair to place equal demands on less affluent countries, compared to wealthier ones. Historically, wealthier countries have generated a greater amount of carbon emissions over time – and continue to do so. Many of them have also carried out significant levels of deforestation. This calls for better alignment between the non-discrimination and the CBDR principles, for which the coherence between special and differential treatment provisions (SDT) and CBDR could offer a starting point for understanding a development-sensitive approach to the trade-climate nexus.

Also, the fact that these recent initiatives were not discussed multilaterally, even though developing countries will bear part, and most likely a significant part (TDR, 2022), of the consequences, is problematic (Rajan, 2023). Weighing the advantages of domestic climate-oriented industrial policies against their adverse impacts on trade relations will likely require an independent assessment, including a revamping of some WTO agreements, notably to ensure that (green) technology is adequately shared with the developing world. This is a pressing concern because as green industrial policy strengthens, trade policies and environmental goals are now interacting much more closely.

3. Revisiting the distributional impacts of trade

That increased trade flows have not always been accompanied by considerable progress in terms of development outcomes is a longstanding concern of UNCTAD since its creation in 1964. While the trading system has undergone significant changes in the intervening years – particularly since the implementation of

---

[2] Under CBAM, importers in the European Union buy carbon certificates corresponding to the carbon price that would have been paid, had the goods been produced under the carbon pricing rules of the European Union. It is a policy tool to reduce the risk of carbon leakage, i.e., preventing the importers of the European Union from diverting purchases to foreign goods that may be cheaper than the equivalent of the European Union but more carbon-emitting. Yet, the measure may be perceived as an additional tariff on a specific import, the rate of which corresponds to the carbon price of the European Union (European Commission, 2021). EUDR requires foreign exporters to the European Union of commodities like soybeans, beef, palm oil, wood, cocoa, coffee, rubber and some of their derived products to prove that products do not originate from recently deforested land or have contributed to forest degradation.

the Uruguay Round agreement – insufficient attention to their distributive impact explains, in part, why many developing countries, and more recently some constituencies in developed economies, have expressed their discontent towards the current rules and practices of the international trading system (Davies et al., 2021; Levell and Dorn, 2022; Rodrik, 2022).

The expansion of trade in the era of hyperglobalization has been closely tied to the spread of global value chains (GVCs) controlled by lead firms, primarily headquartered in advanced economies (TDR, 2018: chap. II). In parallel, more developing countries have participated in the international division of labour by providing specific links in these chains, drawing on their abundance of unskilled labour. The promise was that such fledgling manufacturing activities, through a mixture of upgrading and spillover effects, would quickly establish robust and inclusive growth paths aligned with their comparative advantage.

The success of this model has been neither uniform nor certain (cf. World Bank, 2020). This raises questions about the strong bets made in many developing economies on the spillovers expected from processing trade, because unless developing countries manage to capture part of the surplus created by these GVCs and reinvest it in productive capacities and infrastructure, immediate gains in output and employment are unlikely to translate into a dynamic move up the development ladder. In short, replicating the successes that have been registered in several developing countries, mostly in East and South-East Asia, has proven difficult elsewhere.

Moreover, along with the rise of export market concentration, large firms have increased their ability to extract rents. Empirical evidence suggests that part of the surge in the profitability of top MNEs – a proxy for the very large firms dominating international trade and finance – together with their growing

"The rise in big profits for MNEs, together with their growing concentration, is pushing down the global labour income share, exacerbating income inequality."

concentration, has acted as a major force pushing down the global labour income share, thus exacerbating personal income inequality. It has also led to unequal trading relations even as developing countries have deepened their participation in global trade. Chapter III examines the problems of market concentration in the global food trading sector in detail.

Assessing distributional concerns, both within and across countries, usually comes with delays due to difficulties in data availability and measurement. To help address these difficulties, the empirical analysis proposed below builds on TDR (2018: chap. II). More concretely, this subsection provides an update of previous findings in two areas: (a) the concentration of exports among firms within developing countries, and (b) the evolution of labour and capital income shares, especially for the top 2,000 largest firms in the world.

While a fully-fledged analysis is beyond the scope of this chapter, this update gives an indication of the role trade has played vis-à-vis these metrics during the COVID-19 pandemic years, with new data supporting two main findings:

- Export concentrations appear to have strengthened in the majority of the observed developing countries between the pre-pandemic period and the COVID-19 years.

- Factor income distribution has continued to shift further in favour of capital-owners during the COVID-19 pandemic years, with the profits of the largest 2,000 firms worldwide accounting for the bulk of this gain. This mirrored the continued decline of the labour income share globally.

The details of these findings are further discussed in the remaining part of this subsection.

a. Concentration in export markets has strengthened in recent years

International trade has long been dominated by large MNEs that trade and invest abroad. This greater market access has often led to unequal gains, and these gains disproportionately benefit a minority of economic entities. This finding is also valid in developing countries.

The recent update of the *Exporter Dynamics Database* by Fernandes et al. (forthcoming) – which provides aggregated firm-level data on goods exports (excluding the oil sector, as well as services) for 30 developing countries for the period of 2020–2022 – confirms this stylized fact. Data show that within each country the top 1-per cent largest exporting firms altogether received between 40–90 per cent of the total export revenues of the entire country (figure II.6).

Figure II.6 During the pandemic, export concentration strengthened further in more than half of surveyed developing countries

A. Changes in countries' exports shares of the top 1-per cent exporting firms by types of export specialization: 2015–2019 vs. 2020–2022
(Percentage points)

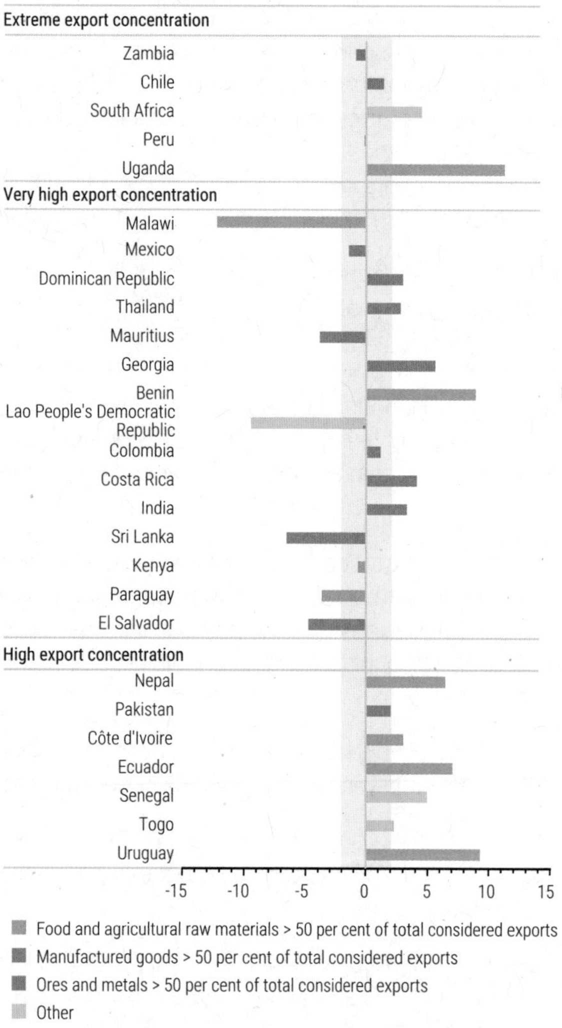

B. Shares in a country's exports by its largest exporting firms, 2020–2022
(Percentage)

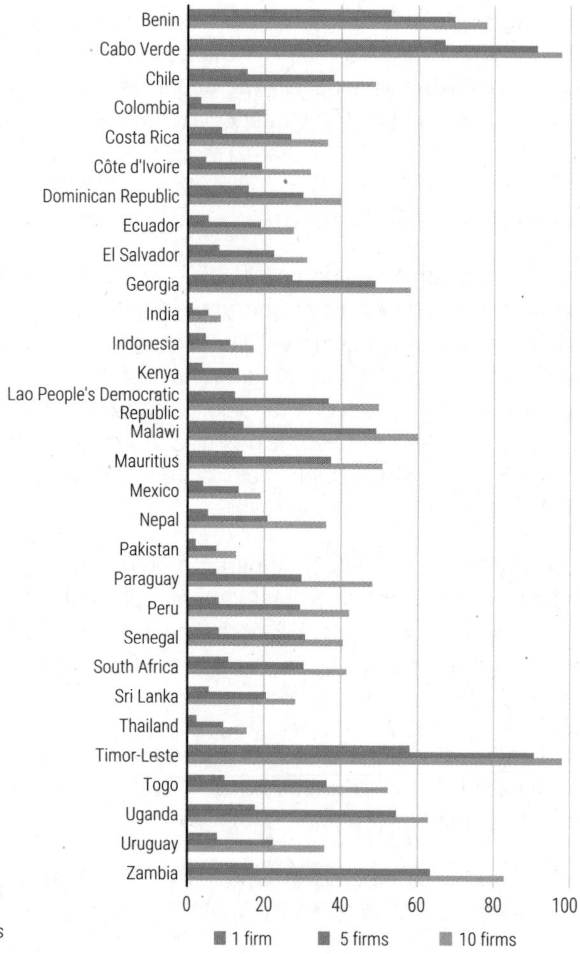

- Food and agricultural raw materials > 50 per cent of total considered exports
- Manufactured goods > 50 per cent of total considered exports
- Ores and metals > 50 per cent of total considered exports
- Other

■ 1 firm   ■ 5 firms   ■ 10 firms

Source: UNCTAD based on the 2023 release of the Exporter Dynamics Database described in Fernandes et al., 2016.
Notes: The current version of the database includes 30 developing countries with data for 2020–2022, of which only 27 economies also have data for 2015–2019. The database reports aggregated firm-level data on goods exports (excluding the oil sector and services) within the very restricted circle of exporting firms. In panel A, countries are sorted in a descending order of their export concentration. Moreover, "extreme" export concentration designates countries where the top 1-per cent firms accounted for more than 70 per cent of total exports in 2015-2019. Similarly, "very high" and "high" export concentration designate countries where the top 1-per cent firms accounted for between 50 and 70 per cent, and between 36 and 49 per cent, respectively.

What is more telling still, is that this indicator of export concentration has increased in recent years in more than half of the developing countries included in the database. The statement is based on a comparison between the average export shares that accrue to the top 1-per cent exporting firms in each country during the 2015–2019 period versus the one that was registered during the 2020–2022 pandemic years.

These results presented in figure II.6.A show a trend towards further export concentration after COVID-19. More precisely, out of 27 countries for which sufficient data exist, the aggregated share in total exports of the top 1-per cent largest exporters had increased by at least 2 percentage points in 14 cases. The average increase for this group of 14 countries was almost 6 percentage points.

Notably, as figure II.6.A shows, it is mostly countries specialized in food and agricultural raw materials or manufactured goods (5 jurisdictions each) that accounted for the bulk of these increases. Figure II.6.A also points to the fact that in the 7 countries with the lowest export concentration in the 2015–2019 period (ranging between 36–50 per cent), the share of exports accruing to their top 1-per cent firms increased in all these jurisdictions by an average of 5 percentage points within this relatively short time span.

By contrast, export concentration had significantly diminished (i.e., a decline of at least 2 percentage points) in only 6 countries out of 27. For those economies, the average decline was less than 3 percentage points. Meanwhile, export concentration had remained rather constant (i.e., an absolute change of less than 2 percentage points) in the 7 remaining countries. Out of these 7 cases, 3 jurisdictions are considered as ores and metals exporters. Their exports were already extremely concentrated on the eve of the COVID-19 shock, in the sense that each country's top 1-per cent exporting firms accounted in aggregate for more than 70 per cent of the total country exports in 2015–2019.

Focusing further on the top firms, this time in absolute numbers, not in relative terms, figure II.6.B shows that foreign trade is often dominated by just a handful of firms. For instance, when the sample is restricted to the largest exporting firm(s) – unlike above, the number of entities, not the top percentage(s) of firms – within each country, data show that for the period 2020–2022, the share of total exports can sometimes exceed 50 per cent for one single firm. Moreover, except for a few outliers in the database, there is only a handful of countries where the share of the 10 largest firms represents less than 20 per cent of the total exports. In general, the value is much higher. For instance, the median is about 40 per cent, and it is common to see figures above 50 per cent. One outlier is India, which records the smallest figure in the database. Its 10 largest firms account for 8 per cent of its total exports, although the total number of exporting firms exceeded 123,000 in 2021.

To sum up, recently released data confirm that the levels of export concentrations among large MNEs are elevated across the board and that this tendency has strengthened during the pandemic years. These findings raise concerns about market control and the distribution of the gains from trade. This topic is addressed below by looking at the evolution of the factor income and the role played by MNEs worldwide in contributing to income inequality.

b. Asymmetry of world income distribution deepens

Another metric to examine when analysing how the activities of large firms affect income distribution globally is the evolution of labour and capital incomes shares, and especially the role played by the largest 2,000 MNEs worldwide.

Figure II.7 updates previous analyses on functional incomes at the level of the world economy until 2022, splitting the capital incomes share into two components. One relating to the net income (i.e., profits) of the 2,000 largest firms globally, and a residual that can be interpreted as the remaining capital income outside the profits of these large enterprises worldwide.[3]

---

[3] For more details about the methodology and a further discussion on the relevance of the use of this metrics for international trade, both in goods and services, see TDR, 2018:56–57.

Figure II.7 Increasing asymmetries of trade benefits: After the COVID-19 shock, profits of top 2,000 multinational enterprises further increased while the global labour income share continued to shrink

A. Global functional income distribution

B. Evolution compared to 2002

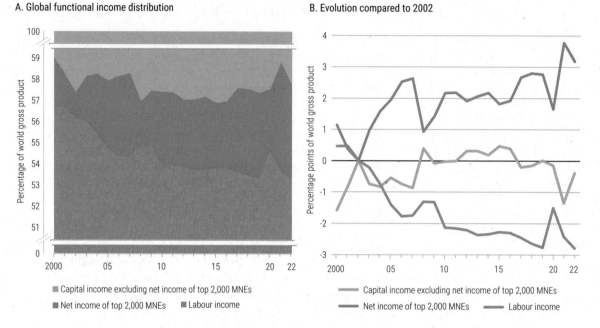

■ Capital income excluding net income of top 2,000 MNEs
■ Net income of top 2,000 MNEs   ■ Labour income

―― Capital income excluding net income of top 2,000 MNEs
―― Net income of top 2,000 MNEs   ―― Labour income

Source: UNCTAD calculations based on the Refinitiv Eikon database and the United Nations Global Policy Model.
Notes: The selection of the top 2,000 firms is based on their market capitalization. Thus, it excludes non-listed firms. In panel A, the net income of the top 2,000 MNEs (derived from the financial statement of listed firms) and the capital income excluding net income of top 2,000 MNEs add up to the world capital income (derived from national accounts data) even though methodologies differ in several regards across both sets of accounts.

While the share of capital income other than profits accruing to the top 2,000 MNEs has remained relatively flat over the last two decades, the profits of top MNEs have registered a gradual increase over this period, only interrupted temporarily at times of major turmoil such as the global financial crisis (GFC) in 2008 and the COVID-19 shock in 2020. Mirroring this evolution, global labour income share has registered a decline of 3 percentage points from almost 57 per cent in 2000 to slightly more than 53 per cent in 2022. The declining labour share and the rising profits of MNEs point to the key role of large corporations dominating international activities – partly though by no means exclusively through their organization of production and trade – in driving up global functional income inequality.[4]

"While the costs and risks of asymmetric structure of global trade are more readily acknowledged, the search for governance solutions to address these issues has barely begun."

More broadly, the trends of growing income inequality and continuing concentration of market power press the need to find more equitable policy solutions. Here, while the costs and risks of asymmetric structure of global trade are now more readily acknowledged, the search for governance solutions to address these issues has barely begun. In the meantime, increasingly complex crises and compounding risks further magnify the structural asymmetries of the global economy.

---

[4] The critical role of control of intellectual property in the inequality story has been examined elsewhere, see TDR 2017 and Baker 2018.

4. Conclusion

A healthy trading system is crucial for meeting the 2030 Agenda. Unfortunately, it remains unclear whether there is the political will among key trade partners to guide it through its current difficulties. For the future outcome to be positive, policymakers will need a bold pro-developmental and cooperative approach to address the fault lines in the international trading system, both old and new. The ideal response is neither to double down on free trade nor to return to the situations in place prior to the COVID-19 shock.

Building such an adequate answer requires revisiting existing agreements at the bilateral, regional and multilateral levels to create policy space for all countries to redesign their production, consumption and trading profiles to face contemporary global challenges.

"There is a need to revisit existing agreements at the bilateral, regional and multilateral levels to create policy space for all countries to redesign their production, consumption and trading profiles to face contemporary global challenges."

Ten specific multilateral trade agreements have, for example, been identified by the Group of 90 (G90) developing countries at the WTO (G90, 2023), which include the Agreement on Subsidies and Countervailing Measures (ASCM), Agreement on Trade-Related Investment Measures (TRIMS), and Trade-Related Aspects of Intellectual Property Rights (TRIPS). The G90 proposal seeks to strengthen existing flexibilities for developing members to make them more precise, effective and operational so that they may more effectively address development aims of members. Failure to address these concerns may result in growing asymmetries, which will make it even more difficult for the world to deliver on its 2030 Agenda.

Ideally, such reforms should build upon some of the core General and Special Principles (GSP) that Member States agreed upon at the creation of UNCTAD in 1964. These remain relevant to the governance of international trade relations and trade policies in support of development, namely "policy space", "special and differential treatment" and "voice and solidarity" (Davies et al., 2021).

Given the new industrial policy initiatives being adopted in advanced countries (as discussed in subsection B.2.C above), which may shorten their existing supply chains, developing countries will need to look for new outlets to diversify their export markets. In this context, regional trade as well as South–South trade can provide a significant opportunity. Since 1995, South–South merchandise trade has grown faster than global trade and faster than North–South trade. In 2022, South–South trade accounted for around 54 per cent of South's total trade. South–South trade has also grown steadily in food, fuel, ores and metals, and fertilizers, with many developing countries, including Brazil, China, India, Indonesia and Thailand playing major roles.

"Since 1995, South–South merchandise trade has grown faster than global trade and faster than North–South trade. In 2022, South–South trade accounted for around 54 per cent of the South's total trade."

While South–South trade should not be seen as an alternative to North–South trade, it can provide an opportunity for developing countries to diversify their production and export basket. In the same vein, regional integration programmes – such as the African Continental Free Trade Area (AfCFTA) – to the extent they support diversification and the benefits are broadly shared, can also mitigate the negative effects of the current situation, including with respect to climate change and food insecurity.

To further boost South–South trade, the Global System of Trade Preferences (GSTP) initiative of UNCTAD can play a critical role by providing an opportunity to negotiate inter alia tariff reductions among developing countries in products based on mutual preferences (box II.1). GSTP can also support a just green transition in the developing countries by focussing on green products and facilitating green technology transfers. Doing so will, however, need a more integrated policy nexus of financial-investment-industrial-technology-trade cooperation among developing countries (TDR, 2022; UNCTAD, 2023a).

Box II.1 South–South trade cooperation: recent developments around the BRICS and the Global System of Trade Preferences initiative

Emerging economies' rapidly increasing economic prominence in international trade has become more pronounced in recent years. The expansion of the five-member group of the BRICS (Brazil, the Russian Federation, India, China, and South Africa) with six more members (Argentina, Egypt, Ethiopia, the Islamic Republic of Iran, Saudi Arabia and the United Arab Emirates), as announced in August 2023, suggests a potential new economic block that accounts for 30 per cent of current global GDP, with a growing population that already stands as 46 per cent the world population.

The XV BRICS Ministerial Declaration confirms the members' commitment to "the open, fair, predictable, inclusive, equitable non-discriminatory and rules-based multilateral trading system with WTO". While there appears to be advancements in finance and investment cooperation, trade among BRICS has yet to fully exploit the South–South trade potential: current trade flows mainly take place between China and the other members, with relatively little bilateral trade among Brazil, India and South Africa for instance.

GSTP is another older initiative aiming at strengthening South–South trade cooperation. GSTP is an agile partnership framework that allows its members to take a variety of cooperative actions in the area of tariffs, para-tariffs, non-tariff measures, direct trade measures and sectoral arrangements.

The conceptual basis of GSTP was provided in 1976 by the Group of 77 (G77). GSTP was accepted in the multilateral trading system, under paragraph 2(c) of the Decision of 28 November 1979: "Differential and More Favourable Treatment, Reciprocity and Fuller Participation of Developing Countries", generally referred to as the "Enabling Clause" of the GATT. During the subsequent three decades, GSTP has had its ups and downs.

A new impetus occurred in December 2010 in Brazil with the conclusion of the third round of negotiations. This culminated in the adoption of the São Paulo Round Protocol by eight participants (counting Mercosur as one): Cuba, Egypt, India, Indonesia, Malaysia, Morocco, the Republic of Korea and Mercosur (i.e., Argentina, Brazil, Paraguay and Uruguay).

Though the São Paulo Round Protocol has still to enter into force, the ratification by Brazil at the end of 2022 created a significant step forward in this direction, which could help the 11 current signatories reap up to $14 billion of shared welfare gains (UNCTAD, 2019). Furthermore, such a framework can be an effective tool for accelerating the Goals by fostering knowledge sharing on best practices in trade, investment, capacity–building and technology transfer, including in new areas for cooperation such as energy transition and food security.

C. COMMODITY MARKETS

The notable recent upward trajectory in commodity prices – brought on by the pandemic and, in some cases, exacerbated by the outbreak of the war in Ukraine – has given way to a moderation in these prices starting in mid-2022 and continuing into 2023. Yet, many commodity prices have not returned to their pre-pandemic levels. Still, the aggregate commodity price index registered a drop of more than 30 per cent in May 2023 compared to a year earlier (figure II.8). The reduction in aggregate prices has been primarily driven by fuel commodities, which experienced a significant drop of over 40 per cent during this period. However, some product groupings in the UNCTAD price index registered more muted reductions during this period to remain at historically high levels. Notably the prices of minerals, ores and metals declined only 4 per cent, while food dropped by just 2 per cent.

Figure II.8 Commodity prices have moderated since 2022, but many products remain at historical levels

Commodity price indices, selected commodity groups and products

(Index numbers, average 2015=100)

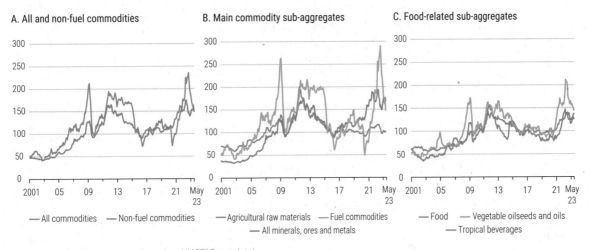

A. All and non-fuel commodities   B. Main commodity sub-aggregates   C. Food-related sub-aggregates

— All commodities   — Non-fuel commodities   — Agricultural raw materials   — Fuel commodities   — Food   — Vegetable oilseeds and oils

— All minerals, ores and metals   — Tropical beverages

Source: UNCTAD calculations based on UNCTADstat database.

Note: Index numbers are based on prices in current dollars.

A key factor in the moderation observed in commodity prices since the middle of last year has been the deteriorating outlook for global demand, compounded by the sharper than anticipated tightening of monetary policy by central banks across the globe. This current round of global monetary tightening has been both more rapid and synchronized than the previous bout of tightening just prior to the GFC. The application of this more restrictive monetary stance has dampened expectations for global economic growth. Meanwhile, the heightening of financial market stress – with the failure of several banks in the United States and the exposed fragility of large banking institutions elsewhere during the first half of 2023 – has added further gloom to the global economic outlook, resulting in a softening in the global demand for raw materials. Similarly, the more restrictive monetary conditions and accompanying uptick in international interest rates has also prompted investors to move financial investments away from commodities towards higher interest-bearing assets (chapter III). Lastly, the slower than expected rebound in China following the reopening of its economy and the persistent weaknesses in its real estate sector have also contributed to the slackening in broad commodity price indices after they peaked in the course of 2022.

"Although commodity prices have moderated since mid-2022, they remain above their pre-pandemic levels."

For its part, the surge in the prices of commodities – most notably crude oil, natural gas and grains – following the outbreak of the war in Ukraine eased from the middle of 2022 thanks in large part to a reorientation of trade flows of key commodity exports from the Russian Federation and Ukraine, as well as the brokering of the Black Sea Initiative agreement in July 2022 to enable the shipment of grains and other materials from strategically important Ukrainian ports (UNCTAD, 2022a).

1. Oil and natural gas

Fuel commodities is the group that initially showed the sharpest decline after mid-2022, with prices of crude oil and natural gas falling by 33 per cent and 67 per cent, respectively, over the 12 months to May 2023. Though the oil price has since rebounded somewhat to over $90 per barrel, the initial drastic drop corresponded to the outsized impact of the global factors outlined above in the energy sector, together with a range of factors specific to the energy industry. Moreover, despite the announced rounds of production cuts by OPEC+ countries in April 2023 – representing a reduction of over 1 million barrels per day – a significant increase in oil production from non-OPEC+ countries as well as a substantial release of strategic petroleum reserves by OECD member countries have more than offset the agreed OPEC+ cuts. For its part, Western economic sanctions on Russian crude oil exports have mostly resulted in redirecting these flows to countries such as China and India at a discounted price, meaning that their impact on global oil supplies has been minimal while also having a downward influence on global crude prices.

The precipitous fall in natural gas prices from the unprecedented highs registered last year – in the wake of the restrictions imposed by European importers of Russian natural gas and the intermittent shutting down of gas pipelines to Europe by the Russian authorities – is principally due to the reshuffling of export and import markets in this sector. European countries have successfully re-oriented their natural gas imports towards liquefied natural gas (LNG) purchases, particularly from the United States, alleviating, to a significant degree, the upward price pressures in the region's natural gas markets. The longer-term reorientation of European natural gas imports towards LNG is reflected in the much milder downturn in global LNG prices during the last year (15 per cent). This re-orientation by European gas importers is not without its negative consequences: various developing countries, such as Bangladesh and Pakistan, have seen a tightening and redirecting of the global supply of LNG shipments on which their economies depend. Similarly, while the prices of both crude oil and natural gas have fallen significantly from the highs observed in the middle of 2022, they still lie significantly above the average levels registered during the five years prior to the pandemic, posing a significant challenge for developing countries dependent on the import of these products to meet their energy needs.

2. Minerals and metals

The expected bump in demand for various commodities due to the relaxing of COVID-19 restrictions and reopening of the economy in China in December 2022 has proven to be far less pronounced than anticipated. This outcome has been particularly relevant for the minerals and metals commodity group for which Chinese demand represents about half of total global demand. Specifically, the reduction in metals prices observed over the 12 months to May 2023 is to a large degree due to the continuing financial challenges faced by the Chinese real estate sector, which accounts for a significant share of global demand for industrial metals. Partially offsetting this comparative shortfall in demand has been strong State spending on infrastructure projects by the Chinese authorities. This has helped to sustain the demand for products such as copper and iron ore whose downward price movement of 12 and 20 per cent, respectively, would have been far more pronounced without the bump to global demand provided by this spending.

3. Food

The commodity group where the impact of recent trends in international prices has been most detrimental for developing nations is that of food commodities. As the Global Crisis Response Group of the United Nations noted, international food prices were already approaching historic highs even before the conflict broke out, causing food import bills to rise dramatically, with about two thirds of the increase of costs concentrated in developing countries (United Nations, 2022). The further climb in international food prices in the wake of the outbreak of the war in Ukraine left many developing countries faced with prohibitively high prices for many of their most basic staple food products. Moreover, the impact of the disruption in the supply and transport of grains, notably wheat, maize, and sunflower products, from Ukraine and the Russian Federation, proved particularly acute for African and Middle Eastern countries that rely on the flow of grains from these countries to meet their basic food needs (UNCTAD, 2022b).

The international prices of many of these food products have moderated over the 12 months to May 2023 – with prices of wheat, maize and sunflower oil dropping by 25, 21 and 51 per cent respectively – partly thanks to the Black Sea Initiative and to increased supplies from South America and other major producing countries. Still, international food prices remain at historically high levels, and the pass-through of lower international prices to domestic prices has proven to be weak. In fact, in several developing countries, the domestic prices of basic foods in June 2023 remained above their levels of the previous year and continue to weigh on food security. Relevant factors which have kept domestic prices at elevated levels include high fertilizer costs, adverse weather, high distribution costs, strong indebtedness as well as domestic currency weaknesses (UNCTAD, 2023b; FAO, 2023). As discussed further in chapter III, the financialization of food markets and the pricing behaviour of large commodity traders have been other contributing factors. As a result, almost 350 million people worldwide – including more than 100 million people in sub-Saharan Africa – are projected to be food insecure in 2023, which is over double the number in 2020 (WFP, 2023).

For its part, higher food prices also impact income distribution within countries. Where the production is more capital-intensive, as happens in larger farms and where land is more concentrated, higher food prices generate rents that favour the richest individuals and large landowners (Mohtadi and Castells-Quintana, 2021). Moreover, where food supply chains are highly concentrated and small farmers have no bargaining power, at the global level food price increases may be fully captured by big corporations controlling food trade, storage, processing and retail (Hansen, 2013; Deconinck, 2021).

Using data covering 126 countries (82 developing and 44 developed) for the period 1990–2020, an empirical analysis shows that rising food prices are associated with increased inequality in developing countries, while the impact in the developed countries was found to be statistically insignificant (UNCTAD, 2023c). This highlights the importance of the role played by government policies to provide safety nets to both producers and the consumers of food. For example, the United States implements the Supplemental Nutrition Assistance Program (SNAP) earlier known as the Food Stamp Program to protect consumers, and the Federal Crop Insurance Program buffers farmers' incomes from losses due to disasters or low prices.

While COVID-19 and the war in Ukraine have accelerated food price volatility, and thus raised global food insecurity, data show that after decades of improvements, the number of people in hunger started to rise around 2014, some years before the emergence of these two events (Saccone, 2021). Along with local conflicts and national economic crises, a main driver for this increase has unequivocally been identified as climate change (FAO et al., 2020; Ray et al., 2019; Mirzabaev et al., 2023). More generally, the rapidly changing climate, political turmoil, and macroeconomic shocks, combined with the speculative behaviour of commodity traders, have introduced further instability and uncertainty in food markets (IPES-Food, 2022; Rabbi et al., 2023), which call for specific policies that address food insecurity. Part of these requires to improve the integration of small farmers into the domestic and international markets, raising their bargaining power, and making the gains from trade reach the poorest farmer. This requires addressing the high concentration of food markets and discouraging speculative behaviour with adequate regulations. Breaking the food monopolies is critical for progressing towards global food security. These issues are dealt with in more detail in chapter III.

D. GLOBAL FINANCIAL CONDITIONS AND DEVELOPING COUNTRY VULNERABILITIES

On the eve of the COVID-19 shock, many developing countries already faced unsustainable debt burdens (TDR, 2019). Since then, compounding crises – the pandemic, the war in Ukraine, the deepening climate crisis and the cost-of-living crisis – along with the most aggressive monetary tightening in developed countries since the 1970s, have exacerbated this situation (chapter I). While a systemic debt crisis – in which a growing number of developing countries move simultaneously from distress to default – has so far been kept at bay, a development crisis is already unfolding, with external debt service draining resources away from delivering the 2030 Agenda and the goals of the Paris Agreement (UNCTAD, 2023c).

One difference between the current and previous debt crises in the developing world is that emerging market economies (EMEs) – i.e., countries that were brought into international financial markets in earlier periods – are not at the forefront. This time around, it is mostly low- or lower-middle-income developing countries that started to tap international capital markets. This mostly occurred during the capital flow boom after the global financial crisis and before COVID-19. These countries, hereafter referred to as "frontier market economies" (FMEs), have been the hardest hit (see special section in this chapter (p. 66) for the list of countries considered as FMEs in this Report).

The staggered integration of EMEs and FMEs into international capital markets has meant that while both groups are vulnerable to changes in global financial conditions and changes in the risk perceptions of global investors, they have experienced different degrees of external financial vulnerability since COVID-19. However, without a concerted effort from the international community, the slowdown of the global economy in 2023, and the danger that things could worsen in 2024, raises serious concerns across the developing world. As a result, an increasing number of developing countries, financially exhausted from years of treading water, may begin to sink under the growing weight of unpayable debts.

This section provides an overview of the recent evolution of capital flows and debt vulnerabilities in developing countries, with a particular focus on FMEs.

1. Capital flows to developing countries: Recent developments

Cross-border financial transactions involving developing countries have experienced significant shocks in recent years. With the onset of the COVID-19 pandemic, net capital inflows to low- and middle-income developing countries (excluding China) came to a sudden halt during the first quarter of 2020. This scenario repeated itself during the third quarter of 2020 when additional pandemic-related measures were put in place as the second wave of COVID-19 hit. These two quarterly figures contrast markedly with the lower bound of about $50 billion of net quarterly capital inflows that these countries, in aggregate, typically received between 2010 and 2019 (figure II.9).

The second half of 2021 and the first half of 2022 also marked abnormal times for capital flows, albeit in the upper end of the distribution this time around. Net foreign direct investments (FDI) and other investment inflows reached record levels in three quarters, partly due to the cyclical rebound of the global economy and, in the case of other investments, to the new allocation of special drawing rights (SDRs) during the third quarter of 2021. Meanwhile, net portfolio inflows turned strongly negative for four quarters in a row, as the policy stance by the central banks of developed countries was to raise policy rates to contain and attenuate inflationary pressures (TDR, 2022).

Since mid-2022, sharp portfolio outflows have ceased, while net foreign direct investments and other investments, in aggregate, have receded from their previous highs, leaving the sum of the three main components of the financial account slightly above the $50 billion mark per quarter.

Figure II.9 Capital flows to developing countries have been very volatile in recent years, with portfolio investments turning highly negative in late-2021 and early-2022

Net capital inflows to low- and middle-income developing countries, excluding China

(Billions of dollars)

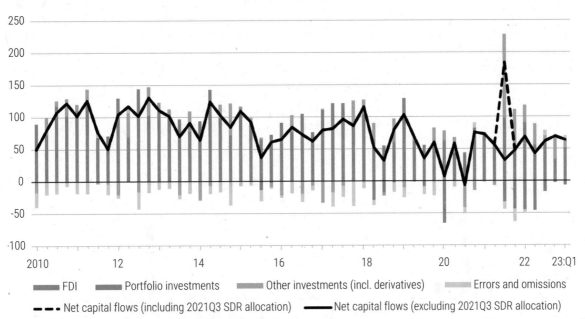

Source: UNCTAD calculations based on IMF Balance of Payments Statistics.

Notes: The two "net capital flows" series exclude the transactions of the monetary authorities registered under Reserves in the balance of payments statistics. Because SDR allocations (unlike SDR holdings, which are included in Reserves) are registered under "Other investments" in the financial account, the "Net capital flows (excluding 2021Q3 SDR allocation)" series aims at neutralizing the SDR allocation of the third quarter of 2021 worth about $650 billion, of which it is estimated that about 20 per cent was shared among the countries considered in this figure. All series refer to net non-resident inflows minus net resident outflows. Thus, positive values correspond to net inflows to this group of countries. Each component reflects the aggregation of the net figures of all available low-income and middle-income developing countries in the database. The balance of net derivatives, which is relatively small, was merged with other investments.

However, the aggregates mask significant differences between countries and regions. For example, FDI flows to Latin America and the Caribbean – typically the most stable source of foreign capital for developing countries – experienced a significant increase in 2022 (UNCTAD, 2023c). By contrast, FDI flows to least developed countries (LDCs) fell by 16 per cent to $22 billion in 2022, with the top five recipients of this group – Ethiopia, Cambodia, Bangladesh, Senegal, and Mozambique, in that order – accounting for about 70 per cent of this figure. Turning to portfolio flows, significant differences exist between its equity and debt subcomponents, including external versus domestic sovereign bonds. During the third quarter of 2021, non-resident outflows totalling $28.5 billion mostly affected equity flows. Leaving aside the special case of the first quarter of 2020, when COVID-19 hit, the withdrawal of debt investments by non-residents reached a record of almost $25 billion during the first quarter of 2022. And while equity investment by non-residents started to bounce back earlier, the debt investment counterparts have remained in negative territory up to the fourth quarter of 2022 at least.[5]

For more recent trends relating to EMEs, due to the lag in the publication of balance of payments data for many of these countries, it is necessary to rely on proxy indicators which are only available for a limited number of countries. One source is the weekly release of *JP Morgan EM Flows*, which focuses on a subset of portfolio

---

[5] At the time of going to press, data for the first quarter of 2023 remained incomplete to have a final assessment of the aggregate for this group of countries.

investments. According to these data, figure II.10.A shows that during the first seven months of 2023, total investor fund flows were positive, in aggregate, due to a rebound of its equity subcomponent, though this total figure conceals different developments across the types of capital flows and country groups in recent months.

Equity fund flows experienced a robust rebound in the first quarter of 2023, primarily attracted by low valuations in EMEs following the selloffs of 2022 (figure II.10.B). These flows have since declined sharply. Meanwhile, hard currency bond flows increased significantly in January 2023 followed thereafter by five consecutive months of outflows, which were particularly large between March and April 2023. Local currency net bond flows have so far hovered around zero throughout this year, owing to large outflows from the Chinese domestic bond market, which offset inflows into other EME local bonds.

Figure II.10 Equity fund flows to emerging market economies rebounded in early 2023

Emerging markets fund flows, bond and equity
(Billions of dollars)

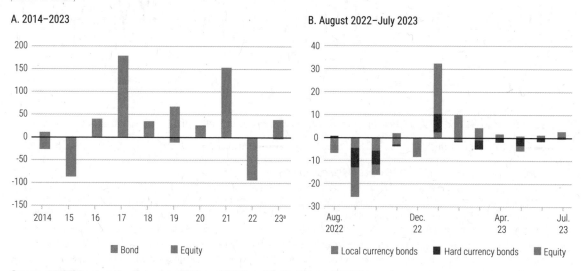

A. 2014–2023

B. August 2022–July 2023

Bond · Equity

Local currency bonds · Hard currency bonds · Equity

Source: UNCTAD calculations based on JP Morgan EM Flows Weekly (4 August 2023).
  [a] The figure for 2023 includes data until July.

Figure II.11 Significant appreciations of several emerging market currencies in the first half of 2023

Change in the value of the domestic currency vis-à-vis the dollar, selected economies
(Percentage)

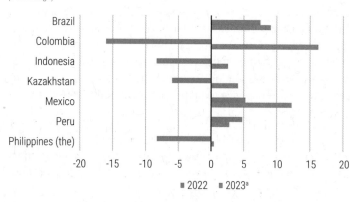

Brazil
Colombia
Indonesia
Kazakhstan
Mexico
Peru
Philippines (the)

-20   -15   -10   -5   0   5   10   15   20

■ 2022   ■ 2023[a]

Source: UNCTAD calculations based on Refinitiv data.
  Note: Positive value indicates currency appreciation.
  [a] The figure for 2023 includes data until 31 July 2023.

Altogether, these net inflows have triggered appreciations of at least 14 EME currencies, most of them in Asia and Latin America, making local bonds even more profitable for global investors (figure II.11).

Overall, these patterns suggest that spillovers from bank distress in March 2023 have been milder on larger EMEs (IMF, 2023). As many EME central banks sharply hiked their interest rate before the Federal Reserve started tightening its interest rates, many of these economies have become increasingly attractive to hot capital flows seeking higher yields (UNCTAD, 2023c). By contrast, debt problems appear more acute in several FMEs.

2. Debt and development distress in developing countries: Insights from the frontier market economies

The recent rise in debt distress and related development setbacks in developing countries can be directly attributed to inherent structural weaknesses in the international financial system. It has proven inadequate in facilitating access to reliable sources of external development finance in the required quantity, cost and maturity, for these countries to meet their development needs.

Other related factors have also played a role as further explained below. These include: (i) the insufficient official development assistance (ODA) (box II.2); (ii) a relative decline of official concessional financing (and the denial of access to some categories of developing countries for such schemes); (iii) decisions of credit rating agencies (CRAs); and (iv) an inadequate global financial safety net (GFSN). Added to this is the significant presence of illicit financial flows (IFFs), which diminish government revenues and drain resources away from development (UNCTAD, 2023e).

On the back of these developments, developing countries have become increasingly reliant on global financial markets to meet their funding requirements. Moreover, for most of the last decade, these private actors have provided access to capital for countries that were previously excluded from financial markets, albeit at an elevated cost even during relatively stable times. However, the strongly cyclical nature of these flows and the compounding crises of recent years have exposed the limitations of the system in dealing, in an equitable and timely manner, with debt distress and its subsequent impact on development.

"Frontier market economies are currently experiencing severe financial vulnerabilities after deepening their integration into international capital markets over the last decade."

A renewed sense of urgency to advance multilateral solutions is required, given the magnitude of the debt challenges faced. In the aftermath of the COVID-19 pandemic, the total world debt of both public and non-financial private sectors peaked at 257 per cent of world gross product in 2020, before receding 10 percentage points by the end of 2021. Within this broader context, developing countries are highly vulnerable, as their debts, private and public, registered significant increases over the last decade. More specifically, private debt in a broad group of emerging markets and developing economies increased from 84 to 130 per cent of GDP between 2010 and 2021.[6] Meanwhile, total public debt in these countries nearly doubled, reaching 64 per cent of GDP by 2022.

The rapid accumulation of non-concessional debt has caused a significant increase in interest payments. Since the ending of easy monetary policy in both developed and developing economies, these payments have reached new highs, with a double burden in countries that have also seen their currencies depreciating against the dollar and euro. The number of countries where interest spending accounted for 10 per cent or more of public revenues increased from 29 countries in 2010 to 50 countries in 2022. Consequently, interest payments in many developing countries outpaced expenditures in critical sectors such as education, health, and public investment over the past decade. Currently, at least 3.3 billion people live in countries that spend more on interest than on either health or education (United Nations, 2023). Most of these countries experienced declines in their Human Development Index in recent years (UNCTAD, 2023d). Carrying these greater debt burdens obstructs the mobilization of resources needed to achieve the goals of the 2030 Agenda.

"In the past decade, interest payments in many developing countries outpaced expenditures in critical sectors such as education, health, and public investment. Carrying these greater debt burdens obstructs the mobilization of resources needed to achieve the goals of the 2030 Agenda."

---

[6] UNCTAD calculations based on IMF Global Debt database. Note that IMF classifies 97 economies as emerging markets and developing economies. These include those that are neither advanced economies nor low-income countries.

Box II.2 Recent trends in official development assistance

For several low-income and lower-middle-income countries, diminished access to concessional official development finance has contributed to the increasing reliance on private external finance. This trend is particularly pronounced among recently promoted lower-middle-income countries that transitioned from low-income status shortly after GFC (e.g., Angola, Mongolia, Nigeria, Pakistan, and Viet Nam). These nations lost access to affordable concessional external finance from the Poverty Reduction and Growth Trust (PRGT) and the International Development Association (IDA). Thus, they represent the "missing middle of development finance" (United Nations, 2020).

Recent patterns in official development assistance (ODA) have also played a role. ODA takes the form of grants, loans to sovereign entities, debt relief and contributions to multilateral institutions (calculated on a grant-equivalent basis). In 2022, total net ODA from the Development Assistance Committee (DAC) member countries reached $211 billion, a rise from $186 billion in 2021, largely due to spending on refugees, much of it in the donor countries themselves. However, as a percentage of the gross national income (GNI) of DAC members, this equated to only 0.36 per cent, falling short of the target 0.7 per cent of GNI, which is only achieved by five donor countries. Furthermore, in 2021, DAC members disbursed $129 billion in ODA to developing countries, of which $84 billion (65 per cent) was directly allocated to these nations and $45 billion (35 per cent) was allocated to multiple regions (called "unspecified" flows). The difference of $57 billion in 2021 between the total net ODA aforementioned ($186 billion) and the amount disbursed to developing countries ($129 billion) is categorized as "unallocated" flows and relates to expenditures within donor countries, such as administrative costs and in-house refugee expenses.

Amid the context of ODA realigning away from central budget support towards in-donor expenditures and broader multilateral priorities, these "unspecified" and "unallocated" flows constituted, respectively, an average of 24 per cent and 30 per cent of net ODA from DAC members to developing countries between 2014 and 2021. It is anticipated that this proportion increased in 2022 due to the war in Ukraine.

Within developing countries, FMEs require particular attention. Collectively, this subgroup of economies within developing countries registered the fastest growth of external public debt over the last decade. It is therefore not a coincidence that even if FMEs altogether only represented, vis-à-vis the total of developing countries, 8 per cent of their GDP and 6 per cent of their total public debt in recent years, they accounted for 20 per cent of developing countries' total external public debt (figure II.12). In other words, FMEs, and especially their public sector, are now particularly exposed to the asymmetries and shortcomings of the international financial architecture, particularly with respect to the consequences of debt distress.

Part of this rapid increase of debt has relied on the global investors' idea that FMEs are the next generation of EMEs, with expectations of rapid and sustained economic growth linked to, and fuelled by, their increased integration into global financial markets. The growing significance of FMEs as an asset class over the past two decades has been influenced by three interconnected trends: the pursuit of higher returns by global investors, a divergence in the returns on bonds of different developing groups, and a compression of credit ratings of EMEs.

To begin with, non-resident portfolio inflows to developing countries were spurred by global push factors after the GFC. This pattern mirrored the historical capital flow cycles that followed the breakdown of the Bretton Woods system (Akyüz, 2017; TDR, 1998). Easy monetary and financial conditions in developed countries led investors to accept higher risks in their search for bigger returns (da Silva et al., 2021). Demand prompted the growth of alternative asset classes with the desired characteristics, including FME bonds.

While it is common to group flows to developing countries together, such practice masks a divergence in the return on bonds in different developing groups. Following the GFC, long-term returns on non-investment grade bonds from developing countries outpaced those of investment grade bonds consistently – except for a period during the onset of the pandemic shock of 2020 (figure II.13).

Moreover, investors' demand for non-investment grade instruments was affected by credit compression among EMEs, as most of these countries became investment grade. CRAs played a pivotal role in this dynamic due to their pro-cyclical behaviour. Market reactions are amplified by their ratings during both the boom and contraction phases of capital flow cycles (Griffith-Jones and Kraemer, 2021; Pretorius and Botha, 2017). As EMEs weathered the GFC in terms that beat market expectations, CRAs enhanced their assessments of these countries between 2006 and 2015. By 2015, 21 out of 31 EMEs had achieved investment-grade status, leading to a reduction in the potential supply of non-investment grade bonds among this group (figure II.14.A).

Figure II.12 Frontier markets contribute less than 10 per cent of developing countries' total output but carry 20 per cent of the external public debt

Shares with respect to all developing countries' aggregates, selected indicators

(Percentage)

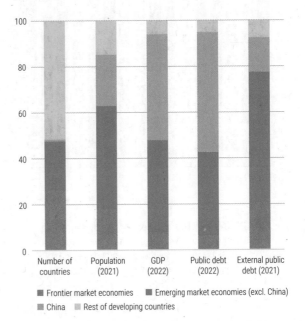

Source: UNCTAD calculations based on Refinitiv data.
Note: For each indicator, the year of reference is provided between parentheses.

Figure II.13 In the years after the global financial crisis, returns of non-investment grade bonds usually outstripped those of investment-grade bonds

Year-on-year total returns and their difference on public bond indices, selected grades

(Percentage)

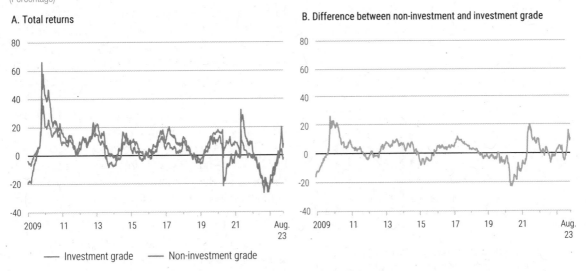

Source: UNCTAD calculations based on JP Morgan Emerging Market Bond Index (EMBI) Global Diversified Total Return Index.
Note: These indicators refer to year-on-year changes of dollar-denominated sovereign and quasi-sovereign indices and are provided on a weekly basis ending on 24 August 2023.

Figure II.14 Frontiers filling the vacuum in the non-investment grade segment

Distribution of credit ratings within selected country groups

(Percentage and absolute number of countries within bars)

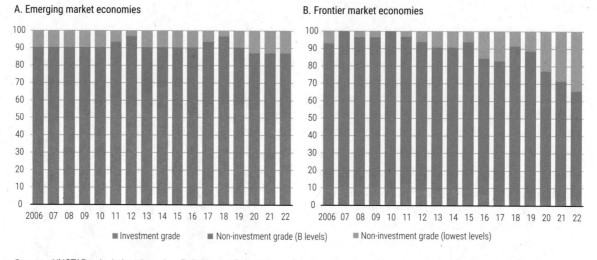

A. Emerging market economies

B. Frontier market economies

■ Investment grade   ■ Non-investment grade (B levels)   ■ Non-investment grade (lowest levels)

Source: UNCTAD calculations based on Refinitiv and Oxford Economics.

Notes: Average ratings between the three main credit rating agencies (CRAs): Fitch, Moody's and Standard & Poor's. "Non-investment (B levels)" refers to all the grades considered by CRAs as "speculative" and "highly speculative". "Non-investment (lower levels)" corresponds to the remaining grades within the non-investment heading, and thus carry even greater risks.

The decline in the number of EME sovereigns categorized as non-investment grade encouraged investors to seek higher yielding alternatives in the early 2010s. FMEs emerged to fill this void, with most of these countries being rated as non-investment grade (figure II.14.B). FMEs attracted investors in pursuit of higher returns, opening the doors to global financial markets for these countries. While only three FMEs had issued sovereign bonds denominated in hard currency between 2000 and 2009, this count surged to 27 countries in the ensuing decade. Annual bond issuance of FMEs reached a record value of $22 billion in 2018 and 2019, just before the onset of the COVID-19 pandemic (figure II.15).

Figure II.15 Frontiers' bond issuance was on the rise during the last decade until the COVID-19 shock

Gross issuances of hard-currency frontier markets' sovereign bonds

(Billions of dollars)

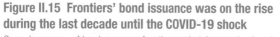
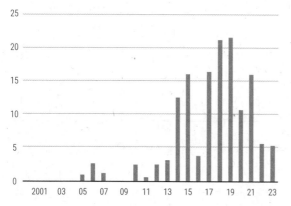

Source: UNCTAD calculations based on Refinitiv.

Notes: This figure only considers bonds issued by governments denominated in dollars, euro and yen with a minimum face value equivalent to $500 million. It includes rollover of previous bonds.

The surge in bond issuance by FMEs has been at the core of the massive accumulation of external public and publicly guaranteed (PPG) debt by these countries over the past decade. The stock of PPG bonds issued by FMEs rose sevenfold during the last decade, reaching $154 billion in 2021. As a result, since 2011, the portion of FMEs' PPG debt held by private creditors almost doubled from 19.6 to 35.9 per cent, with bondholders accounting for 8.8 per cent and 23.7 per cent, respectively (figure II.16). In total, FMEs' external PPG debt reached $651 billion in 2021, marking a threefold increase since 2010. For comparison, during the same period, external PPG debt of EMEs and remaining developing countries doubled (figure II.17).

The accumulation of external PPG debt is exerting significant pressures on the public finances of FMEs, as growing debt service obligations reduce available resources for crucial public expenditures. Debt service on PPG debt relative to government revenues surged from almost 6 to 16 per cent between 2010 and 2021. In contrast, for EMEs, this figure stood at 3 per cent, while it reached 7 per cent for other developing countries in 2021 (figure II.18.A). As of 2021, a minimum of 26 FMEs allocated 10 per cent or more of their revenues to debt service. Moreover, among the top 25 developing countries with the highest debt service to revenue ratio in 2021, 15 were FMEs (60 per cent of the total). The leading 4 countries on this list were all FMEs (figure II.18.B). As a result, the pressure of debt service on development expenditures has become substantial in FMEs. 26 out 37 FMEs were spending more on external PPG debt service relative to either education or health by 2021 (UNCTAD, 2023c).

External public debt in FMEs is also contributing to heightened external vulnerabilities. The ratio of external debt service to exports in FMEs rose from about 6 to 16 per cent between 2011 and 2021. In comparison, this metric stood at 15 per cent for EMEs and 10 per cent for other developing countries in 2021 (figure II.19.A).[7] To provide context, these aggregate figures are double or even triple the threshold established by the 1953 London Agreement on restructuring war debts for Germany. This agreement limited the portion of export revenues that could be allocated to external debt servicing to 5 per cent of the total, with the aim of ensuring the post-war recovery of the then Federal Republic of Germany would be sustainable (TDR, 2015). Furthermore, among the 25 countries with the highest proportion of export revenues allocated to total external debt servicing in 2021, over half (13 countries) were FMEs (figure II.19.B).

Cracks in the market façade of FMEs appeared in the aftermath of COVID-19. The buildup of debt vulnerabilities over the previous decade led to an increase in bond spreads of FMEs relative to that of EMEs (figure II.20). This shift indicates that markets are factoring in a heightened risk of default for this specific group of economies. In fact, most of the countries that have lost market access since 2019 fall into the category of FMEs (figure II.21). The number of FMEs trading with spreads surpassing the 1,000-basis points threshold – used to gauge market access – has notably increased from 1 to 13 between January 2019 and August 2023. In addition, it is mostly FMEs that have been downgraded in

---

[7] The high ratio in EMEs is a result of the higher share of the private non-guaranteed (PNG) debt in the long-term debt compared to FMEs (45.4 per cent and 32 per cent in 2021, respectively).

Figure II.16 The reliance on private creditors for external financing of frontier market economies has strengthened

Creditor composition of frontier market economies' external public and publicly guaranteed debt

(Percentage)

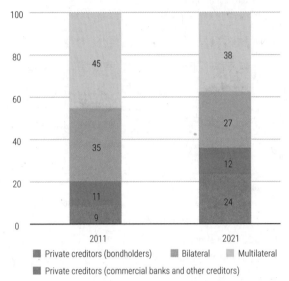

■ Private creditors (bondholders)　■ Bilateral　■ Multilateral
■ Private creditors (commercial banks and other creditors)

Source:　UNCTAD calculations based on World Bank International Debt Statistics.

Figure II.17 External public debt of frontier markets has grown faster post-financial crisis

Growth of public and publicly guaranteed external debt, selected groups of developing countries, 2010–2021

(Percentage)

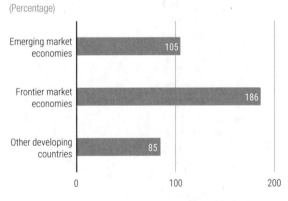

Source:　UNCTAD calculations based on IMF World Economic Outlook.

recent years by CRAs to a rating of CCC or lower, indicating substantial credit risks and likelihood of default (figure II.22).

With each subsequent shock since 2020, more FMEs have found themselves in a situation of debt distress, placing them at ground zero in the looming debt crisis (figure II.22). The developing countries that

Figure II.18 Frontier markets' public finances are under heavy pressure after a decade of debt accumulation

Public and publicly guaranteed external debt service relative to government revenues

(Percentage)

A. Selected country groups

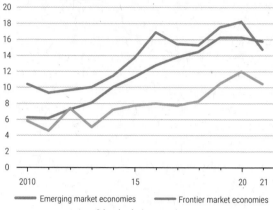

B. Top 25 within all developing countries in 2021

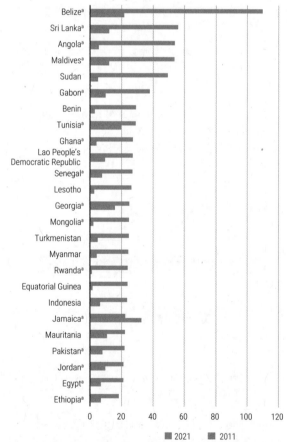

Source: UNCTAD calculations based on World Bank International Debt Statistics and IMF World Economic Outlook.

Note: Indonesia is the only emerging market economy in this group.

[a] Frontier market economies.

Figure II.19 Frontier markets' external debt service drains export revenues

Public and publicly guaranteed external debt service relative to export revenues

(Percentage)

A. Selected country groups

B. Top 25 within all developing countries in 2021

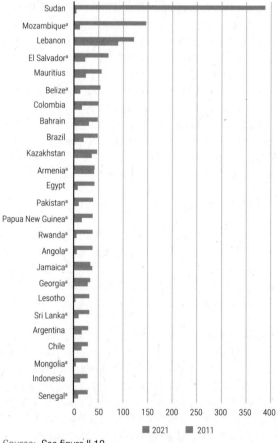

Source: See figure II.18.

Note: Argentina, Brazil, Chile, Colombia, Egypt, Indonesia, Kazakhstan and Lebanon belong to the group of emerging market economies (EMEs), while Bahrain, Lesotho, Mauritius and the Sudan do not belong to EMEs or the frontier market economies.

[a] Frontier market economies.

have been classified as in default by S&P Global Ratings as of July 2023 since the pandemic, are all FMEs (Ghana, Sri Lanka, Suriname and Zambia). In addition, Ethiopia applied for debt restructuring under the G20 Common Framework.[8]

The debt challenges faced by developing countries in general, and those of FMEs in particular, are set to increase as a large wave of bond repayments comes due in the coming years (figure II.23). FME bond repayments, including principal and coupon payments, will reach $13 billion in 2024 and continue to be high at least until the end of the decade. This raises concerns that more FMEs may default if their market access is not restored. Moreover, for EMEs and FMEs that have retained market access, new sovereign bond issuances will be costly given the higher interest rates in developed countries. Higher borrowing costs in a context of lower economic growth – and as discussed in chapter I, both are conditions that look set to last well into next year – will undermine debt sustainability. Without measures to effectively address this dynamic, most countries are expected to prioritize fiscal consolidation to stabilize debt levels (UNCTAD, 2023c). Regrettably, this dynamic will place the attainment of the 2030 Agenda further out of reach.

The trajectory of debt vulnerabilities in FMEs reveals the imbalance between the advantages and disadvantages of dismantling capital controls in developing countries and rapidly integrating into unregulated international private capital markets – a theme discussed in previous reports (TDR, 2015; 2019). While the benefits encompass access to external financing in countries constrained by balance of payments restrictions and limited domestic financial markets, as has been discussed above, the associated costs are exceedingly high.

Figure II.20 Frontier markets are at the forefront of compounding crises

Spreads with respect to the Treasuries of the United States, selected country groups

(Basis points)

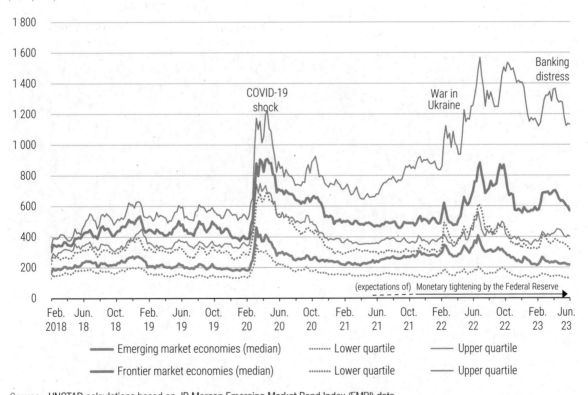

Source: UNCTAD calculations based on JP Morgan Emerging Market Bond Index (EMBI) data.

Note: Medians and quartiles are based on the availability of country-level data in JP Morgan EMBI–Global Diversified, a widely-followed dollar-denominated sovereign and quasi-sovereign index.

[8] Debt restructurings of Chad and Malawi (not considered as FME) have not been classified as in default by a rating agency.

Figure II.21 Growing number of frontier markets moving into debt distress

Emerging and frontier markets with bond spreads above 1,000 basis points over treasuries of the United States
(Number of countries)

■ Frontier market economies   ■ Emerging market economies

Source: See figure II.20.

Figure II.22 COVID-19 and other financial shocks increased debt vulnerability of frontier markets

Public debt situation of selected frontier market economies after COVID-19 and other subsequent major financial shocks

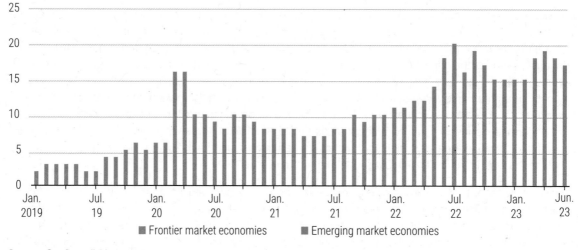

Pre-COVID-19	COVID-19 shock (March 2020)	Monetary tightening	
		War in Ukraine (February 2022)	Banking distress (March 2023)
Suriname	Angola	Belize	Belize
Zambia	Belize	El Salvador	Bolivia (Plurinational State of)
Angola	Cameroon	Ethiopia	El Salvador
Belize	Gabon	Ghana	Ethiopia
Bolivia (Plurinational State of)	Ghana	Pakistan	Ghana
Cameroon	Iraq	Sri Lanka	Maldives
Costa Rica	Mongolia	Suriname	Mozambique
El Salvador	Mozambique	Tajikistan	Pakistan
Ethiopia	Nigeria	Tunisia	Sri Lanka
Gabon	Sri Lanka	Zambia	Suriname
Ghana	Suriname	Maldives	Tajikistan
Iraq	Tajikistan	Mozambique	Tunisia
Kenya	Tunisia	Papua New Guinea	Zambia
Maldives	Zambia	Angola	Gabon
Mongolia	Costa Rica	Bolivia (Plurinational State of)	Kenya
Mozambique	El Salvador	Cameroon	Angola
Nigeria	Ethiopia	Costa Rica	Cameroon
Pakistan	Kenya	Gabon	Costa Rica
Papua New Guinea	Pakistan	Iraq	Iraq
Sri Lanka	Bolivia (Plurinational State of)	Kenya	Mongolia
Tajikistan	Maldives	Mongolia	Nigeria
Tunisia	Papua New Guinea	Nigeria	Papua New Guinea

■ Market access   ■ Almost at distress level   ■ Distress level

Source: UNCTAD calculations and typology based on JP Morgan Emerging Market Bond Index–Global Diversified indices.
Note: This figure only considers frontier market economies whose spreads reached 800 basis points or more since 2020. JP Morgan EMBI-Global Diversified tracks dollar-denominated sovereign and quasi-sovereign bonds. "Distress level" refers to spreads vis-à-vis the treasuries of the United States above 1,000 basis points (bp). "Almost at distress level" relates to spreads between 800–1 000 bp and "Market access" corresponds to spreads below 800 bp.

The analysis above has shown that the search for yield by global investors created global push conditions in which FMEs were flooded with capital inflows. However, the worsening of external financial conditions associated with compounding crises and downgrades by CRAs, has produced a rapid exit of those flows. This has triggered a further deterioration of financial conditions, cutting some FMEs off from accessing those markets altogether. Collectively, these factors have combined to place almost a third of FMEs on the precipice of debt distress, with five already falling over the edge. The international response to this problem has been insufficient. Urgent measures are imperative to prevent more FMEs from reaching the brink of financial distress, and worse still, tipping into default. Equally crucial is the reform of the international financial architecture, including the increase of reliable and affordable financial resources to fulfil the 2030 Agenda and the Paris Agreement, with effective and timely mechanisms of debt restructuring and relief. Otherwise, the siren calls of international financial markets will entice more low- and lower-middle-income developing countries on to the rocks of debt distress and default. Detailed discussions on these reforms can be found in chapters IV to VI of this Report.

"One third of frontier market economies are on the precipice of debt distress, with five already falling over the edge. The international response to this has been insufficient."

Figure II.23 Emerging and frontier markets face a wall of debt repayments from 2024 onwards

Bond repayment schedule from principals and coupons

(Billions of dollars)

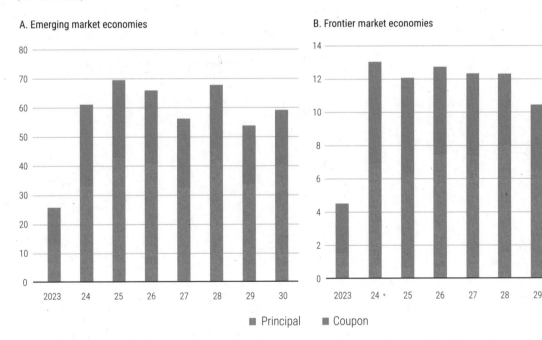

A. Emerging market economies

B. Frontier market economies

■ Principal   ■ Coupon

Source: UNCTAD calculations based on Refinitiv.

Note: This figure only considers bonds issued by governments denominated in dollars, euro and yen with a minimum face value equivalent to $500 million.

SPECIAL SECTION

Definition of the frontier market economies considered in chapter II

There is no formal definition of FMEs, although the term often refers to developing countries with small yet investable markets of recent origin, which are part of the next generation of EMEs (Schipke, 2015). For the sake of the analysis of this chapter, FMEs are identified with the 37 countries in the JP Morgan Next Generation Markets (NEXGEN) index, itself a subset of the larger JP Morgan Emerging Markets Bond index (EMBI). NEXGEN focuses on dollar-denominated government bonds from FMEs. This diverse group includes countries across all World Bank income classification levels, some of which are LDCs and small island developing States (SIDS) (table II.A.1). Of these, 14 FMEs were eligible for the International Monetary Fund (IMF) Poverty Reduction and Growth Trust (PRGT) and the World Bank International Development Association (IDA), with 10 participating in the heavily indebted poor countries (HIPC) initiative.

Table II.A.1 List of frontier market economies

Country	Region	Income group	SIDS	LDC	HIPC	PRGT and IDA eligible
Angola	Sub-Saharan Africa	LMIC		■		
Armenia	Western Asia	UMIC				
Azerbaijan	Western Asia	UMIC				
Barbados	Latin America and the Caribbean	HIC	■			
Belize	Latin America and the Caribbean	LMIC				
Bolivia (Plurinational State of)	Latin America and the Caribbean	LMIC				■
Cameroon	Sub-Saharan Africa	LMIC			■	■
Costa Rica	Latin America and the Caribbean	UMIC				
Côte d'Ivoire	Sub-Saharan Africa	LMIC			■	■
El Salvador	Latin America and the Caribbean	LMIC				
Ethiopia	Sub-Saharan Africa	LIC		■	■	■
Gabon	Sub-Saharan Africa	UMIC				
Georgia	Western Asia	UMIC				
Ghana	Sub-Saharan Africa	LMIC			■	■
Guatemala	Latin America and the Caribbean	UMIC				
Honduras	Latin America and the Caribbean	LMIC			■	■
Iraq	Western Asia	UMIC				
Jamaica	Latin America and the Caribbean	UMIC	■			
Jordan	Western Asia	UMIC				
Kenya	Sub-Saharan Africa	LMIC				■
Maldives	Southern Asia	UMIC	■			
Mongolia	Eastern Asia	LMIC				
Mozambique	Sub-Saharan Africa	LIC		■	■	■
Namibia	Sub-Saharan Africa	LMIC				
Nigeria	Sub-Saharan Africa	LMIC				
Pakistan	Southern Asia	LMIC				
Papua New Guinea	Oceania	LMIC				■
Paraguay	Latin America and the Caribbean	UMIC				
Rwanda	Sub-Saharan Africa	LIC		■	■	■
Senegal	Sub-Saharan Africa	LMIC		■	■	■
Sri Lanka	Southern Asia	LMIC				
Suriname	Latin America and the Caribbean	UMIC				
Tajikistan	Central and Southern Asia	LMIC				■
Tunisia	Northern Africa	LMIC				
Uzbekistan	Central Asia	LMIC				■
Viet Nam	South-Eastern Asia	LMIC				
Zambia	Sub-Saharan Africa	LMIC		■	■	■

Source: UNCTAD typology based on World Bank (July 2022) and UNCTADstat (2023) classifications.

Note: IDA: International Development Association; HIPC: heavily indebted poor country; LDC: least developed country; LIC: low-income country; LMIC: lower middle-income country; PRGT: poverty reduction and growth trust; SIDS: small island developing State; UMIC: upper middle-income country.

REFERENCES

Africanews (2022). Zimbabwe bans all lithium exports. 29 December.

Akyüz Y (2017). *Playing with Fire: Deepened Financial Integration and Changing Vulnerabilities of the Global South*. Oxford University Press. Oxford.

Amiti M, Redding SJ and Weinstein DE (2019). The impact of the 2018 tariffs on prices and welfare. *Journal of Economic Perspectives*. 33(4):187–210.

AP News (2023). EU lets Ukrainian grain ban expire even as some member countries impose their own. 15 September.

Baker D (2018). Is intellectual property the root of all evil? Patents, copyrights, and inequality. Working paper presented at "The Great Polarization: Economics, Institutions and Policies in the Age of Inequality" conference. University of Utah. Department of Economics. 27–29 September.

Benigno G, di Giovanni J, Groen JJJ and Noble AI (2023). A new barometer of global supply chain pressures. Federal Reserve Bank of New York. July release.

Bown CP (2023). US imports from China are both decoupling and reaching new highs. Here's how. PIIE blog. 31 March 2023. Available at: https://www.piie.com/research/piie-charts/us-imports-china-are-both-decoupling-and-reaching-new-highs-heres-how (accessed 27 July 2023).

Cavallo A, Gopinath G, Neiman B and Tang J (2021). Tariff pass-through at the border and at the store: Evidence from US trade policy. *American Economic Review: Insights*. 3(1):19–34.

da Silva VHCA, de Almeida LA and Singh D (2021). Determinants of and prospects for market access in frontier economies. Working Paper WP21/137. International Monetary Fund. Washington, DC.

Davies R, Banga R, Kozul-Wright R, Gallogly-Swan K and Capaldo J (2021). Reforming the international trading system for recovery, resilience, and inclusive development. Research Paper No. 65. UNCTAD.

Deconinck K (2021). Concentration and market power in the food chain. OECD Food, Agriculture and Fisheries Papers. No. 151. Organisation for Economic Co-operation and Development.

European Commission (2021). Carbon Border Adjustment Mechanism: Questions and Answers. Press release. 14 July.

Fajgelbaum PD, Goldberg P, Kennedy PJ, Khandelwal AK and Taglioni D (2023). Trade war and global reallocations. Working Paper No. 29562. National Bureau of Economic Research.

Fajgelbaum PD and Khandelwal AK (2022). The Economic Impacts of the US-China Trade War. *Annual Review of Economics*. 14:205–228.

FAO (2023). Food price monitoring and analysis (FPMA) Bulletin #6. Food and Agriculture Organization. Rome. 12 July.

FAO, IFAD, UNICEF, WFP and WHO (2020). *The State of Food Security and Nutrition in the World 2020. Transforming Food Systems for Affordable Healthy Diets*. Food and Agriculture Organization. Rome.

Fernandes AM, Freund C and Pierola MD (2016). Exporter behavior, country size and stage of development: Evidence from the exporter dynamics database. *Journal of Development Economics*. 119:121–137.

Fernandes AM, Freund C and Pierola MD (forthcoming). Preliminary release of the Exporter Dynamics Database. Advanced release kindly provided by the authors.

Financial Times (2023a). Maersk predicts long and deep contraction in global trade. 4 August.

Financial Times (2023b). How the US is pushing China out of the internet's plumbing. 13 June.

G90 (2023). G90 document for the special session of the Committee on Trade and Development (CTD-SS) on 10 agreement-specific special and differential treatment proposals. Submission by South Africa on behalf of the Organisation of African, Caribbean and Pacific States (OACPS), the African Group and the

LDC Group. Committee on Trade and Development – Special Session – Trade Negotiations Committee. Job/TN/CTD/2, Job/TNC/106. World Trade Organization. 28 February.

Garg K (2022). The Common but Differentiated Responsibilities – WTO Conundrum. Opinio Juris blog. 9 September. Available at: https://opiniojuris.org/2022/09/09/the-common-but-differentiated-responsibilities-wto-conundrum/ (accessed 27 July 2023).

Griffith-Jones S and Kraemer M (2021). Credit Rating Agencies and developing economies. DESA Working Paper No. 175. United Nations Department of Economics and Social Affairs.

Hansen H (2013). *Food Economics: Industry and Markets*. Routledge. London.

Hassan F, Rappoport V and Federico S (2020). Trade shocks and credit reallocation: Lessons from Italy. *VoxEU.* 25 June.

Hudson WM (2022). Revisiting Albert O. Hirschman on Trade and Development. *American Affairs*. 20 August.

IPES-Food (2022). *Another Perfect Storm?* International Panel of Experts on Sustainable Food Systems. Brussels.

IMF (2023). *Global Financial Stability Report*. International Monetary Fund. Washington, DC. April.

Levell P and Dorn D (2022). Changing views on trade's impact on inequality in wealthy countries. *VoxEU.* 14 February.

Luce E (2023) The new Washington consensus. *Financial Times*. 19 April.

Mirzabaev A, Olsson L, Kerr RB, Pradhan P, Ferre MGR and Lotze-Campen H (2023). Climate Change and Food Systems. In: von Braun J, Afsana K, Fresco LO and Hassan MHA, eds. *Science and Innovations for Food Systems Transformation.* Springer. Cham: 511–529.

Mohtadi S and Castells-Quintana D (2021). The distributional dimension of the resource curse: Commodity price shocks and income inequality. *Structural Change and Economic Dynamics.* 59(C):63–78.

Moody's Analytics (2020). Trade Diversion Since the U.S.-China Trade War. Available at: https://www.moodysanalytics.com/-/media/article/2020/Trade-Diversion.pdf (accessed 27 July 2023).

OECD (2022). The supply of critical raw materials endangered by Russia's war on Ukraine. Organisation for Economic Co-operation and Development. Paris. 4 August.

Pretorius M and Botha I (2017). The procyclicality of African sovereign credit ratings. In Tsounis N and Vlachvei A, eds. *Advances in Applied Economic Research*. Springer. Cham: 537–546.

Rabbi MF, Ben Hassen T, El Bilali H, Raheem D and Raposo A (2023). Food security challenges in Europe in the context of the prolonged Russian–Ukrainian conflict. *Sustainability*. 15(6):4745.

Rajan RG (2023). Unilateral action on climate change can have unintended consequences. *Financial Times*. 14 August.

Ray DK, West PC, Clark M, Gerber JS, Prishchepov AV and Chatterjee S (2019). Climate change has likely already affected global food production. *PLoS ONE.* 14(5):e0217148.

Reuters (2023). Namibia bans export of unprocessed critical minerals. 8 June.

Rodrik D (2022). A primer on trade and inequality. The IFS Deaton Review VI. Institute for Fiscal Studies. London.

Rodrik D (2023). What next for globalization? *Project Syndicate*. 9 March.

Saccone D (2021). Can the Covid19 pandemic affect the achievement of the "Zero Hunger" goal? Some preliminary reflections. *The European Journal of Health Economics.* 22(7):1025–1038.

Schipke A (2015). *Frontier and Developing Asia: The Next Generation of Emerging Markets*. International Monetary Fund. Washington, DC.

Siripurapu A and Berman N (2022). The Contentious U.S.-China Trade Relationship. Council on Foreign Relations. 2 December.

Sullivan J (2023). Remarks by national security advisor Jake Sullivan on renewing American economic leadership at the Brookings institution. The White House. Washington, DC. 27 April.

UNCTAD (2017). Using trade policy to drive value addition: Lessons from Indonesia's ban on nickel exports. Background document to the Commodities and Development Report 2017. UNCTAD/SUC/2017/8. Geneva.

UNCTAD (2019). Energizing South-South trade: The global system of trade preferences among developing countries. Policy Brief 74. Geneva.

UNCTAD (2021a). Export restrictions do not help fight COVID-19. 11 June.

UNCTAD (2021b). *A European Union Carbon Border Adjustment Mechanism: Implications for Developing Countries*. 14 July. UNCTAD/OSG/INF/2021/2. Geneva.

UNCTAD (2022a). *A Trade Hope: The Role of the Black Sea Grain Initiative in Bringing Ukrainian Grain to the World*. UNCTAD/OSG/INF/2022/6. Geneva. 20 October.

UNCTAD (2022b). The impact on trade and development of the war in Ukraine. 16 March.

UNCTAD (2023a). *South-South Cooperation and Economic Integration: The Vision and Roadmap*. Geneva.

UNCTAD (2023b). Recent developments, challenges and opportunities in commodity markets. TD/B/C.I/MEM.2/58. Geneva. 31 July.

UNCTAD (2023c). South-South Cooperation for Resilient Food Security. Geneva (forthcoming).

UNCTAD (2023d) *Trade and Development Report Update (April): Global Trends and Prospects*. UNCTAD/GDS/INF/2023/1. Geneva.

UNCTAD (2023e). SDG Pulse. First official estimates on illicit financial flows – UNCTAD SDG Pulse 2023.

UNCTAD (TDR, 1997). *Trade and Development Report 1997* (United Nations publication, Sales No. E.97.II.D.8. New York and Geneva).

UNCTAD (TDR, 1998). *Trade and Development Report 1998.* (United Nations publication, Sales No. E.98.II.D.10. New York and Geneva).

UNCTAD (TDR, 2015). *Trade and Development Report 2015: making the international financial architecture work for development* (United Nations publication, Sales No. E.15.II.D.4. New York and Geneva).

UNCTAD (TDR, 2018). *Trade and Development Report 2018: Power, Platforms and the Free Trade Delusion*. (United Nations Publication. Sales No. E.18.II.D.7. New York and Geneva).

UNCTAD (TDR, 2019). *Trade and Development Report 2019: Financing a Global Green New Deal* (United Nations publication, Sales No. E.19.II.D.15).

UNCTAD (TDR, 2022). *Trade and Development Report 2022: Development Prospects in a Fractured World: Global Disorder and Regional Responses.* (United Nations Publication. Sales No. E.22.II.D.44. Geneva).

United Nations (2020). External debt sustainability and development, Note by the Secretary-General to the General Assembly. A/75/281. Geneva. 30 July.

United Nations (2022). Global impact of the war in Ukraine: Billions of people face the greatest cost-of-living crisis in a generation. Brief No 2. UN Global Crisis Response Group on Food, Energy and Finance. 8 June.

United Nations (2023). A world of debt: A growing burden to global prosperity. UN Global Crisis Response Group on Food, Energy and Finance. 12 July.

WFP (2023). A global food crisis. World Food Programme. Rome. Available at: https://www.wfp.org/global-hunger-crisis (accessed 27 July 2023).

World Bank (2020). *World Development Report 2020: Trading for Development in the Age of Global Value Chains*. The World Bank Group. Washington, DC.

WTO (2023). *Trade Monitoring Updates: A Year of Turbulence on Food and Fertilizers Markets*. World Trade Organization. 28 February.

Chapter III

Food Commodities,
Corporate Profiteering
and Crises: Revisiting
the International
Regulatory Agenda

From excess to equity

The stark contrast between the surging profits of commodity trading giants and the widespread food insecurity of millions underscores a troubling reality: unregulated activity within the commodities sector contributes to speculative price increases and market instability, exacerbating the global food crisis.

This presents significant obstacles to effective policy measures. At the same time, an intricate web of cross-sector connections and high volume of intragroup corporate activity in the industry complicates efforts to establish transparency and accountability.

Profiteering from financial activities now drives profits in the global food trading sector. Yet commodity traders circumvent existing regulations: they are not regulated as financial institutions but are treated as manufacturing companies.

This report calls for a fundamental revision of this regulatory approach. It is imperative to develop tools to enhance transparency and accountability in this opaque yet systemically vital global industry. Policymakers and regulators need to foster a future where equity replaces excess, and the global paradigm shifts from profiteering to purposeful sharing for the betterment of all.

Specifically

- Profiteering prompts the need to reevaluate corporate group membership and the behaviour of major players in food trading.

- Regulators should recognize the financial aspects of food traders' activities as systemically important and extend relevant regulations. Measures proposed here at the corporate–finance nexus can enhance wider efforts to combat financial speculation and profiteering.

- A set of market-level, system-level and global governance reforms are needed to align the international financial architecture with recent developments in the opaque, underregulated yet strategically vital commodity trading industry.

A. INTRODUCTION

The cost-of-living crisis has become the hallmark of the post-COVID-19 recovery and continues to cascade through the global political economy. In advanced economies, the crisis is manifesting as high inflation and growing financial fragilities (chapter I). In the developing world, import dependencies, extractive financial flows, boom–bust commodity cycles, trade disruptions, the war in Ukraine and climate-vulnerable food systems are combining to destabilize finances, bringing countries closer to a debt crisis (chapter II; IPES, 2023).

In the interplay of crisis transmission mechanisms, a vicious cycle has emerged between higher energy and food production costs, reduced farm yields and higher food prices, more inflation pressures and subsequent financial tightening. Stricter financial conditions are eroding the buying power of currencies in developing countries and increasing the import costs of food and energy, reducing financial capacity and increasing the costs of servicing debt (GCRG, 2022). In a fragile global economy on the verge of a recession, volatility in commodity markets endangers access to most basic needs and rights, such as food and energy security for millions, potentially threatening social and political stability in many parts of the world.

But crises always present opportunities, at least for some. The last few years of commodity price volatility have coincided with a period of record profit growth by global energy and food traders. In the area of food trading, the four companies that conservatively account for about 70 per cent of the global food market share registered a dramatic rise in profits during 2021–2022. As figure III.1 shows, growth in profits of some of the largest food traders in 2021–2022 is at par with the profitability profiles of leading firms in the energy sector. Meanwhile, total profits of the nine big fertilizer companies over the past five years grew from an average of around $14 billion before the pandemic to $28 billion in 2021 and then to an astounding $49 billion in 2022 (IATP and GRAIN, 2023).

This chapter analyses some key dynamics of corporate profiteering through crisis, with a focus on the global food trading sector. The analysis presented below aims to identify and help address some of the destabilizing impacts of concentrated corporate control in the strategically vital, highly interconnected yet opaque and poorly regulated food commodity trading industry.

Figure III.1 Profits of main energy and food traders increased dramatically in 2021–2022

Profit (or loss) before tax, selected companies
(Millions of dollars)

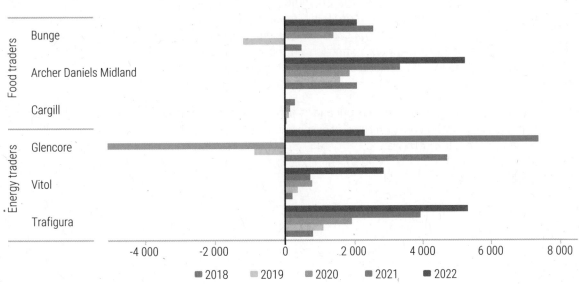

Source: UNCTAD calculations based on Orbis database.
Note: Based on corporate entities in the group with highest reported operating revenues.

Corporate profiteering in times of crisis is not a new challenge. At the very first United Nations conference, which took place 80 years ago in Hot Springs, Virginia, United States, 43 countries gathered to discuss the food and agricultural challenges faced by the post-war international order.[1] With many agricultural economies still suffering from the price collapses of the inter-war years and against a backdrop of famine conditions in parts of Europe and Asia, a central issue at the time was the problem of volatile prices, for both producers and consumers. But while there was broad agreement that the food question could not be left solely to market forces, there was less agreement about the best way to establish a more secure and stable global food system.

"In the context of cascading crises, there is a stark contrast between growing risks to the food security of millions and profiteering by corporations that control global food systems."

Today, in the context of systemic crises, the contrast between growing risks to food security of millions around the world and profiteering by the few corporations that control global food systems during times of volatility and shocks, is particularly stark. In the highly concentrated commodity trading industry, the super profits enjoyed by "agripolies" trickle down very slowly, if at all, to local farming communities.

In July 2023, Oxfam estimated that 18 food and beverage corporations made on average about $14 billion a year in windfall profits in 2021 and 2022, enough to cover the $6.4 billion funding gap needed to deliver life-saving food assistance in East Africa more than twice over (Oxfam, 2023). A recent study found that in Europe, up to 20 per cent of food inflation can be attributed to profiteering (Allianz, 2023). Some reports suggest that the ten leading "momentum-driven" hedge funds made an estimated $1.9 billion by trading on the food price spike at the start of the war in Ukraine (Ross and Gibbs, 2023).

However, according to two leading scholars, the issue is more enduring and rooted in structural factors. Growing cross-sectoral control over the food system by major agri-corporations raises the risk that extreme food-price swings will become the norm. Through decades of mergers and acquisitions, such firms have been able to expand their influence up and down the supply chain, while amassing huge amounts of market data. If a handful of companies continue to hold inordinate power over the world's food systems, any policy effort to mitigate the short-term effects of food price spikes will be futile in the long term (Clapp and Howard, 2023). Similar warnings are increasingly echoed by market analysts, civil society, regulators and international organizations concerned with the lack of regulatory oversight of commodity trading (FSB, 2023; Schmidt, 2022; Tarbert, 2023; Tett, 2023).

The analytical and policy challenges of regulating commodity trading cannot be overestimated. Opacity, lack of regulatory oversight – especially at the systemic level – cross-sector interconnections and intragroup corporate activity all pose major hurdles in efforts to scope the problem and identify risks and workable solutions. This can explain why, despite growing public attention on the issue of market concentration and profiteering, current policy debate on possible multilateral solutions to the food systems crisis has not addressed this question in depth.

This chapter is a step forward in this endeavour and its aim is two-fold. First, to examine the factors that enable corporate profiteering in food trading in times of crises and thus play a role in the current dysfunction of global food systems. Second, to put forward a set of regulatory measures that can help address the destabilizing impacts of concentrated corporate control in a strategically vital, highly interconnected yet opaque and poorly regulated industry.

---

[1] It is also worth noting that development issues were much more prominent in Hot Springs than they were a year later in Bretton Woods at the United Nations Monetary and Financial Conference (Daunton, 2023).

The analysis reveals that unregulated financial activity significantly contributes to the profits of global food traders. It also shows that corporate profits from financial operations appear to be strongly linked to periods of excessive speculation in commodities markets and to the growth of shadow banking – an unregulated financial sector that operates outside traditional banking institutions.

Specifically, during periods of heightened price volatility, certain major food trading companies gain amplified profits in the financial markets. Like a non-bank financial institution, food trading companies take positions and function as key participants in financial markets. This shadow banking function is not regulated in the current financial system. As a result, these companies are motivated to increase their already significant role in profiting from price differences in food markets. To help combat the problem of profiteering, arbitrage and unearned profits, a set of regulatory measures have been identified that can help address market dysfunction and risks of shadow financial trading.

The analysis does not necessarily establish that financial speculation is driving food prices up. Rather, it suggests a strong link between corporate profiteering through the use of financial instruments and the current period of market volatility. As figure III.2 shows, the past two years have been marked by high volatility in crop prices and in the financial markets for food, but correlation does not mean causation. Much more research needs to be carried out to establish the relationship between excessive speculation and price dynamics. Food prices are determined by an interplay of supply and demand conditions, including in retail sectors, food processing industries and conditions in labour markets (Scott et al., 2023). Therefore, while financial speculation, and excessive speculation specifically, may accentuate price swings, agriculture prices are highly affected by market conditions, geopolitical tensions, climate risks and trade measures.

In February 2022, threats to global food systems were amplified with the start of the war in Ukraine. Since 24 February 2022, 62 per cent of 667 export-related non-tariff measures recorded affected agricultural products or fertilizers. Of these, 267 are restrictive measures such as bans on the export of fertilizers and certain food products.[2]

Early in 2023, food prices came down from their 2021 peaks, yet the suspension of the Black Sea Initiative and the subsequent withdrawal of the Russian Federation from the deal has again sparked market volatility (figure III.2.B). In early August 2023, wheat remains more than twice as expensive as it was before the pandemic. In most developing economies, food price inflation is above 5 per cent, and as high as 30 per cent in Egypt and Rwanda (Clapp and Howard, 2023). And while it may seem straightforward that high agriculture prices benefit food producers, such assumptions ignore the major role played by the international agrobusiness firms that control many of the links in the global agrivalue chains and the dynamics of price formation in global food systems (Akyüz and Gursoy, 2020; Baines, 2017; Clapp and Howard, 2023; Staritz et al., 2018; UNCTAD, 2023).

With these qualifications, the findings presented in this chapter are indicative, and not definitive. More research is needed, and the challenge of incomplete data and non-transparency of the commodity trading industry is a major hurdle in this endeavour.

However, what is clear is that the fragmented and compromised set of regulatory norms governing the financial dimension of the global food trading industry has played a key role in enabling financial speculation, corporate arbitrage and profiteering in the global food industry since 2010. This problem was accentuated in the global context of compounding crises post-2020. Financial speculation in commodity markets, as well as the increasing role of financial assets under the control of large corporations that dominate the sector, point to the issue of unearned profits and the need to strategically regulate important modes of corporate control.

---

[2] UNCTAD calculations based on the Global Trade Alert database, available at https://www.globaltradealert.org/data_extraction, accessed on 20 August 2023.

Figure III.2 Food as an asset: Price and volatility high again

A. Price of selected crops

B. Volatility of selected commodity futures

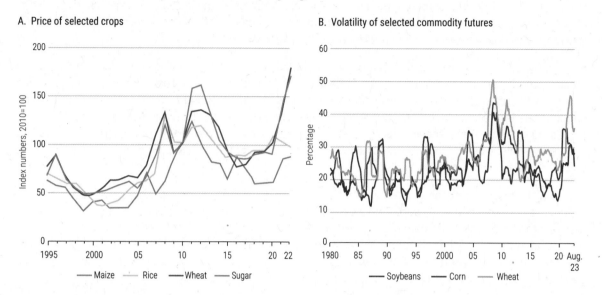

Source: Chicago Board of Trade (CBOT) commodity futures retrieved through Refinitiv database and World Bank data.

The chapter is structured as follows:

- Section B analyses the role of financial trades and speculation in food trading, finding a strong parallel between the period of high profits of major food traders and the wave of financial speculation in over-the-counter (OTC) markets.

- Section C investigates the conditions for corporate arbitrage in commodity trading created, in part, by the regulatory distinction between commercial and financial institutions. Findings show that this distinction is being eroded by the process of regulatory loopholing, corporate arbitrage and financialization of food trading.

- Analysing some of the concerns related to this process flagged by the Financial Stability Board in 2023, an indicator was developed (the asset dominance ratio, or ADR) to help locate and estimate the risks to financial stability in commodity trading.

- Section D concludes by charting policy solutions that aim to limit the systemic and distributional effects of unregulated financial activities in commodity food trading, at different regulatory levels.

B. FOOD AS AN ASSET: HEDGING, SPECULATION AND PROFITING FROM CRISES

Financial instruments and insurance products, known as commercial hedging tools, play a crucial role in risk management across all industries. Particularly vital in sectors such as agriculture, commodities, trade and investments, these tools contribute to market liquidity. They become even more significant due to their role in maintaining stable commodity prices, which in turn, rely on a stable commodity derivatives market. A notable aspect of this market are deferred settlements, a concept where transactions are settled at a later date. Derivatives are based on the principle of deferred settlements, and on the basis of being "a contract whose value depends on the price of underlying assets, but which does not require any investment of principal in those assets. As a contract between two counterparts to exchange payments based on underlying prices or yields, any transfer of ownership of the underlying asset and cash flows becomes unnecessary" (BIS, 1995:6–7).

Commodity futures markets bring together commercial operators who either produce, store or process commodities, and speculators, i.e., non-commercial operators who buy and sell futures contracts but have no specific interest in the use of the commodity; rather, they aim to make a profit exclusively from price fluctuations (Kornher et al., 2022; IPES, 2023).

A degree of speculation, and speculative liquidity, is essential for the stable operation of any financial market, as it helps price discovery and hedging. However, excessive speculation makes price swings larger than would have been the case based on supply and demand conditions alone. Under certain conditions, excessive speculation can become an independent driver of those price fluctuations. Excessive speculation, including in commodity markets, is intimately linked to the use of financial derivatives. These instruments mushroomed following the heightened uncertainty and unstable expectations that followed the end of the Bretton Woods system in 1973.

Speculation on food futures markets dates back to the mid-nineteenth century, when farm production expanded in the United States. At the time, small-scale farmers, being directly indebted to the banks which sold land, had to seek opportunities in markets much further afield. As international channels for trade in cereals had only just started to develop, control over the food chain became concentrated in the hands of a few powerful intermediaries, who are the ancestors of today's food multinationals (Vargas and Chantry, 2011). These markets came under federal oversight in the late 1930s, with stricter regulation introduced following the farming crisis and the Great Depression.

Over the past few decades, the structure of food speculation has become more complex. Two parallel forces have driven this shift: the maturing of speculation in financial markets on the one hand, including through the use of derivatives; and the liberalization of agriculture markets, on the other (Vargas and Chantry, 2011). This process has seen private equity funds, asset management companies, institutional investors, banks, and other financial institutions invest in "alternative assets" such as commodity futures, agricultural land and the crops it produces, which had hitherto been avoided by most investors as too high-risk (Murphy et al., 2012). Partly as a result of this process, the financial activities of non-commercial hedgers in commodity markets have become associated with excessive speculation and its impact on price levels, most dramatically seen during the commodity price crisis of 2008–2010 (Bicchetti and Maystre, 2013).

The current crisis accentuates two major effects of these developments. First, there is ample evidence that banks, asset managers, hedge funds and other financial institutions continue to profit from the most recent bout of commodity market volatility (Schmidt, 2022; Oliver Wyman, 2023; Ross and Gibbs, 2023). Second, by actively managing risk, commodity trading firms have assumed many financing, insurance and investment functions typically associated with the activity of banks. In this context, very large international trading firms, or ABCD-type companies[3] have come to occupy a privileged position in terms of setting prices, accessing funding, and participating directly in the financial markets. This not only enables speculative trades in organized market platforms, but a growing volume of transactions between individuals, or over-the-counter trades, over which most governments in the advanced countries have no authority or control (Suppan, 2010; Vargas and Chantry, 2011; Murphy et al., 2012).

Continuous lack of systemic regulatory oversight over the emergent segments of commodities trading reinforces this position. Market-based speculation, and operations in exchange-traded derivatives represent only a fraction of derivatives traded globally. Financial derivatives on agricultural commodities are mostly traded over the counter, which makes monitoring market trends and regulating risks in this sector a challenge (Schmidt, 2022).

In this instance, the geographical structure of global commodity derivatives trade is instructive (figure III.3). Many market-based instruments are traded in North America and Asia, reflecting major trading zones for key commodities, while Europe accommodates mainly OTC trading.

---

[3] Large firms of a size and stature akin to the four big commodity traders, Archer Daniels Midland, Bunge, Cargill and Louis Dreyfus Company, known as ABCD because of the coincidence of their initials.

Figure III.3 Most exchange-traded agriculture derivatives are traded in Asia and North America

Volume, by region

(Number of contracts, millions)

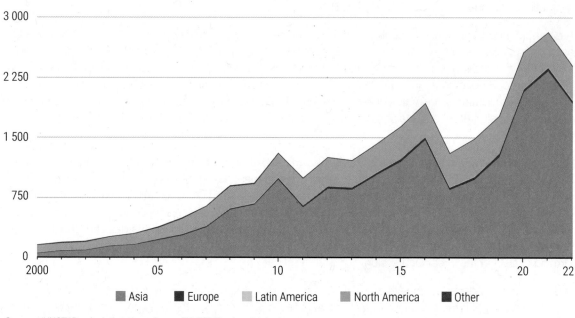

Source: UNCTAD calculations based upon FIA ETD Tracker database.
Note: Derivative contracts include futures and options.

Data from the Bank of International Settlements (BIS, 2023) shows that outstanding over-the-counter commodity derivatives relating to energy, food and non-precious metals experienced a sharp increase after 2020, with their gross market value increasing from less than $200 billion to $386 billion at the end of 2021 and peaking at $886 billion by mid-2022. This represents more than a fourfold increase compared to their 2015–2020 average. During the second half of 2022, this indicator declined by 45 per cent. Yet it still yielded a year-end value of $486 billion in 2022.

Notional principal values of these outstanding derivatives remained above $1.5 trillion at the end of 2022, its second highest since records began, after reaching an all-time-high of more than $2 trillion in mid-2022 (BIS, 2023). These trends reflect the uncertainty triggered by the war in Ukraine and other geopolitical tensions affecting commodities markets.

The central role of OTC operations in commodities trading points to one of the major challenges of regulating this notoriously inscrutable industry. The opacity of the global food trading sector has implications for the availability of data and therefore, definitive conclusions: only eight out of 15 main food trading companies examined in this chapter are publicly traded and required to publish consolidated accounts.[4] The lack of

---

[4] Given the diversified nature of the trades the largest agriculture corporations engage in, coupled with a high level of opacity inherent in current reporting, a pragmatic approach to sample selection was chosen. It was based initially upon current membership by "agricultural" firms in a leading trade body for the commodities sectors, the Commodities Market Council (CMC). As of March 2023, agricultural firms participating in the CMC are attributable to 9 distinct corporate groups. This membership is dominated by United States-centric firms. To help balance this bias out, 6 other major players from groups organized around several other major agriculture economies were identified. For all 15, the current structure of the corporate groups was mapped out, to identify which entities, from which jurisdictions, were producing consolidated and audited accounts on behalf of the corporate group as a whole. These steps were followed by assessment of available financial reporting by those entities. The data is gathered from the Orbis dataset provided by the commercial data publisher, Bureau Van Dijk. This is both because Orbis is the only consolidated source of information on the activities of public and private companies at a global level, but also because Orbis helps to standardize financial reporting to facilitate better comparisons for a global set of corporations. This also means that some firms, most notably Cargill and Noble Group, do not provide information at the standard required for the analysis undertaken here. While groups such as these do provide some figures publicly on their website, these represent unaudited and selective information which is unsuited to this analysis.

transparency within this sector means that generalizations about profit trends for individual companies, and a conclusive verdict on the exact impact of corporate profits on the overall price dynamics, are difficult to draw at this stage.

What does appear to be clear from analysing sector-wide profit trends is the relationship between companies' profits and price volatility. Figure III.4 presents the relationship between the (net) profits of the "ABCD" companies and food price volatility during the last decade.

Figure III.4 Profits of the "ABCD" food companies surge during periods of price volatility

Profits of selected large agricultural trading firms and food price volatility

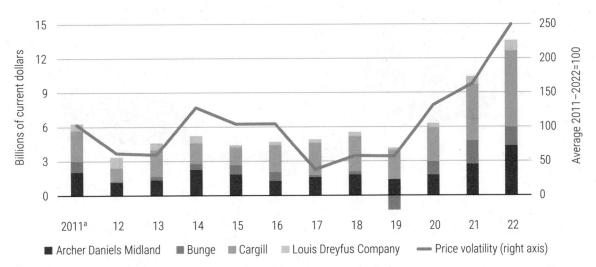

Source: UNCTAD calculations based on FAO *Real Food Price Index*, Blas and Farchy (2021: Appendix ii), Eikon Refinitiv, and Louis Dreyfus Commodities' Financial Results Reports (various issues).

Note: The underlying indicator for volatility corresponds to the yearly average of the monthly standard deviations of the FAO *Real Food Price Index* divided by the average of such figure for the 2011–2022 period. An hypothetical value of 200 would mean, for instance, that at a suppositional year, the average of the monthly standard deviations would have been twice as large as the average of the monthly standard deviations for the 2011–2022 period.

[a] Cargill's 2011 profits do not include the sale of its stake in the fertilizer group Mosaic that year.

As figure III.5 shows below, global food price volatility during the crisis of 2020–2022 is close to the levels of the commodity price crisis period of 2008–2010.

Two major issues are notable here. First, the profits of four major food traders rise during periods of market volatility and during crises, and this trend has been particularly pronounced during the pandemic. Second, in the context of compounding crises, the sources of the super-profits in the food trading industry warrant closer attention.

As noted in the seminal study by Oxfam (Murphy et al., 2012), prices in volatile commodity markets are as much about *anticipated* supply and demand as they are about existing conditions and potential risks. The level of risk and volatility in the trading of standardized and generic products pushes companies to look for strategies that will increase their stability and predictability. To achieve this, a range of financial techniques designated for commercial hedging can be used, such as futures and options. Commodity exchanges can also serve this purpose if traders, in addition to using publicly available information, trade using independent information derived from an intimate knowledge of specific events and their own plans to supply or demand commodities. However, in an inadequately regulated system, instruments officially designed (and regulated) as hedging tools are being used for speculating in food prices.

Figure III.5 Food price volatility increases during crises
Summary distribution of selected food price indexes, deflated by United States consumer price index
(Index numbers, 2010=100)

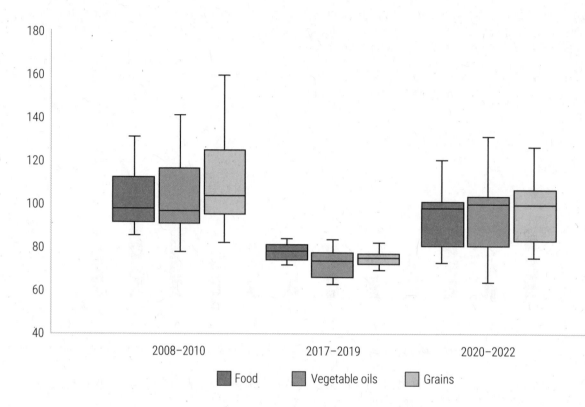

Source: UNCTAD calculations based on data of the United States Bureau of Labor.

Figure III.6 gives an indication of this phenomenon in the food commodities trading industry. It shows that profit indicators reflecting the dynamics of the core business of companies in the sector have followed a common trend since 2006. Yet in 2020, pre-tax profits, which can serve as an indicator of the profits (and losses) from purely financial operations (i.e., non-core business operations) became extreme, greatly exceeding profits/ losses from their core business operations. These are: operating revenues, gross profits and earnings before interest, taxes, depreciation and amortization (EBITDA).

This contrast in profit indicators leads to three key observations.

First, food trading companies have come to rely on the use of financial instruments and markets not simply to hedge their commercial positions, but to strategically ride the wave of market volatility (in other words, to speculate) using techniques of financial engineering. Second, market and price volatility appear to have a much more pronounced role in the sector's financial operations, in contrast to their core commercial activities. Third, financial instruments and techniques designed for hedging a range of commercial risks are being used by the sector for speculative purposes. This is enabled by the current regulatory architecture of commodity trading as a whole, which remains diluted and fragmented.

Figure III.6 Financial operations drive profit growth in the food trading sector

Median food traders' profits and revenues

(Index numbers, 2019=100)

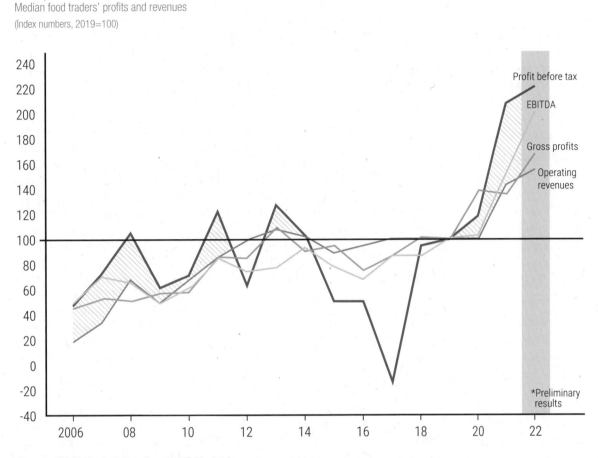

Source: UNCTAD calculations based on Orbis database.

Note: Based on available corporate data from Akira Holding, Andersons, Archer Daniels Midland, Bunge, Cargill, CGB Enterprises, CHS, CMOC Group, COFCO International, Glencore, GrainCorp, OFI Group, Noble Group, Scoular and Wilmar International.

Hedging activity, regardless of whether it is officially a hedge under the existing rules, or a hedge to bypass onerous regulations, should have a negligible impact on financial performance because, if done properly, that is the objective of the hedge. Most derivatives trading takes place in OTC markets, which are largely unregulated. Major commodity traders classify the bulk of their derivatives assets as normal speculative investments that contribute to the profit of the group as a financial gain (or loss). However, the unique nature of derivatives trading means it does not consistently deliver predictable results. Financial gains from derivatives activities are not equivalent to "financial income", but instead, are manifested as "fair value adjustments" based upon the difference of the original face value of the contract, and whether, over time, value differences generate gains or losses to be accounted for. Depending on how companies present their accounts, these "adjustments" can materialize in different places in the income statement present in annual reports. For some companies in the sample, the magnitude of these adjustments is consistent across time, except during periods of excessive derivatives speculation (discussed below). During such times, company accounts report unusually large adjustments, which boost overall profit levels and drive the observations detected in figure III.6. This attests to the disproportionate role that non-operating activities (speculation) play in the current era of super profits. This aligns with the timeframe during which excessive speculation in the OTC markets surged, as shown below.

Over time, large commodity trading companies have become major financiers. They act as creditors to governments and private entities, carry out proprietary trading (i.e., speculating on the future direction of prices, leveraging their large informational advantage), issuing financial instruments such as "secured amortizing notes" to third party investors such as pension funds, etc. (Blas and Farchy, 2021). Driven by the need to hedge their business transactions, and with the resources and opportunities to speculate, commodity traders today are key participants in derivatives trading. In 2017, the European Central Bank (ECB) found that 11 commodity dealers cover more than 25 per cent of the Euro area market in commodity derivatives, with more than 95 per cent of derivative contracts being non-centrally cleared OTC derivatives.[5]

"There is mounting evidence that speculative activity in food markets increases dramatically during crises."

There is mounting evidence that speculative activity in financialized food markets increases dramatically during crises, including the current period of 2020–2022/2023. Kornher et al. (2022) examine the drivers of excess price volatility of commodity futures markets and find that, following the period of extreme market volatility between 2007 and 2011, markets stabilized until the onset of the pandemic in 2020. Since the end of 2021, excessive price volatility surrounding commodity futures trades has grown significantly. The share of speculators (non-commercial traders) in hard wheat and maize corresponds to price spikes and has risen sharply since the end of 2020 (Kornher et al., 2022). In 2022, the share of long positions held by non-commercial traders was estimated at around 50 per cent, a figure similar to the period of high speculative pressure in 2007–2008 (Kornher et al., 2022).

"A group of 10 leading hedge funds made an estimated $1.9 billion trading on the food price spike at the start of the war in Ukraine...their activity contributed to speculative price rises and exacerbated the food crisis for millions around the world."

More recently, data compiled by French commercial bank, Société Générale, suggests that a group of 10 leading "momentum-driven" hedge funds made an estimated $1.9 billion trading on the food price spike at the start of the war in Ukraine in wheat, corn and soybean trades, after a period of years in which they had largely made losses on these food commodities in the same three-month period (Ross and Gibbs, 2023). Their activity contributed to speculative price rises and exacerbated the food crisis for millions around the world. Researchers have found that in the Paris Milling Wheat market – the benchmark for Europe – the proportion of buy-side wheat futures contracts held by financial speculators increased from 35 per cent of open interest in May 2018 to 67 per cent in April 2022 (Agarwal et al., 2022).

These findings are confirmed by the analysis of speculation in OTC derivatives presented in figure III.7. The available current data from the Bank of International Settlements indicates that financial speculation in commodities, including food, has risen dramatically during the two recent crises, 2008–2010 and 2020–2022.

The Bank of International Settlements offers two metrics which provide two ways of understanding the key dynamics in these markets. The first measure is "notional value of outstanding" OTC derivatives (blue line in figure III.7.A). It is a metric of value that aggregates the total "face value" of an underlying set of contracts. The second measure is the "gross market value of outstanding derivatives" (orange line in panel figure III.7.A). This differentiates the pool of contracts into those that are currently generating a profit, versus those that are generating a loss. The latter metric is particularly important for evaluating when speculation pursuits "overtake" break-even risk management hedge interests. Put simply, the blue curve in figure III.7.A shows the volume of bets taken in OTC commodities. Major increases in the orange curve indicate periods when there were more profit-making bets in the market.

---

[5] IMF (2023: 63) notes that "[m]ajor data gaps exist in the reporting of derivative exposures across [nonbank financial institutions] (NBFIs). Important details such as the direction of positions – long versus short – and information about counterparties are often missing in disclosures. For exchange-traded and centrally cleared over-the-counter derivatives, detailed data are available through central counterparties but are highly confidential and, therefore, require robust data-sharing arrangements with the relevant supervisors. Recent over-the-counter derivative-market reforms in the G20 have helped introduce central clearing requirements for interest rate and credit derivatives across a broad range of advanced and major emerging market economies. However, the reforms have generally not extended to foreign exchange and commodity derivatives." Moreover, BIS data still provides no disaggregation within the catch-all category that includes energy, food and other non-precious metals.

Taken together, the panels in figure III.7 present the evolution in the structure of speculative trades in OTC markets during the past two financial cycles. The data suggests that the OTC commodity markets have evolved through four phases. The first is the lead up to the global financial crisis, when the rapid growth of OTC markets coincided with a predominance of loss-making contracts (orange line in III.7.A), with a notable correction and growth in contracts that were profit-making immediately after the onset of the crisis in late 2007. This period of excessive profit making contracts gave way to a long period of stability with little volatility in the composition of profit versus loss-making contracts in the OTC markets from, roughly, 2010 until the end of 2020. Between 2021 and December 2022, the underlying composition of the OTC markets, compared to 2007–2009, has been marked by a disproportionately large number of profit-making contracts.

These metrics distinctly show when there are shifts towards excessive speculation in the OTC markets. They also show how this measure more effectively correlates with the timing of systemic shifts when profits are generated from financial activities, as reflected in corporate accounts. Together, the two measures indicate the timing of excessive speculation. The determining feature in when this happens appears to be external to the companies themselves. This reflects differences in how market investors estimate prices, compared to industry insiders' more precise knowledge of actual prices.

Moreover, as can be seen from figure III.7.A, while the speculative bout of 2007–2010 was driven by new entrants into the commodity markets supplying new liquidity (banks and other financial institutions), the current peak is mainly associated with the activity of the incumbent market players (see the much less dramatic rise of the blue curve in figure III.7.A reflecting the more limited injection of new liquidity).

Figure III.7 Hedging and speculation in OTC commodity markets

A. Change index of face value of all OTC traded contracts and the total value of positive versus negative contracts

B. Detecting hedging versus speculative periods in OTC markets

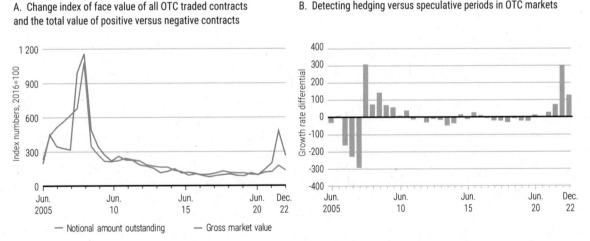

Source: UNCTAD calculations based upon BIS Global OTC Derivatives Market database (https://stats.bis.org/statx/srs/table/d5.2).

Note: Calculations based upon biannual gross market value and notional amount outstanding data for "Total instruments" and "Other commodities" covering the period June 2005 and December 2022. Panel B: Growth rate differential is measured as the difference in growth rates between the indices of gross market value and notional amount outstanding.

It is instructive in this instance that in the documentation presented by one of the ABCD giants, a listed company under strict obligation to disclose to the public the exact nature of its activities, it is made clear that:

> The majority of the Company's derivative instruments *have not been designated as hedging instruments*. The Company uses exchange-traded futures and exchange-traded and OTC options contracts to manage its net position of merchandisable agricultural product inventories and forward cash purchase and sales contracts to reduce price risk caused by market fluctuations in agricultural commodities and foreign currencies. The Company also uses exchange-traded futures and exchange-traded and OTC options contracts as components of merchandising strategies designed to *enhance margins* (Archer Daniels Midland, 2022:67, emphasis added).

"The blurred distinction between hedging operations by commercial traders and financial speculation poses a financial contagion risk and is a factor in price inflation."

The transformation of food trading companies into financial institutions is a problem long noted by analysts (Murphy et al., 2012; Gibbon, 2013). The blurred distinction between hedging operations by commercial traders and financial speculation poses not only a financial contagion risk but is also a factor in price inflation. This warrants a revision to the existing regulatory architecture of commodity trading. While the phenomenon of excessive speculation in commodities is linked to deregulation policies (de Schutter, 2010; Oxfam, 2011; Winders, 2011), there are growing concerns that financial activities within today's food trading industry give rise to unnoticed financial stability risks and strengthen corporate influence over strategically significant markets (FSB, 2023). Not only does this add to the challenges of detecting and curbing excessive market speculation in commodity and food trading; it also further complicates regulation of the shadow banking system and imperils financial stability. It also conceals risks and exposures in the poorly regulated yet highly interconnected and systemically important industry. These issues are addressed in the next section.

C. OF LOOPHOLES AND LOOPHOLING

"What might happen under legislation that would allow most OTC derivatives to remain in dark markets, thus preventing regulators from having timely access to all trading information, a prerequisite for effective regulation?", asked one contributor from the Institute for Agriculture and Trade Policy, to a 2010 UNCTAD symposium on commodity market regulatory pathways (Suppan, 2010).

More than a decade after the use of OTC derivatives in food markets raised concerns among regulators, some clear lessons can be drawn. They point to the incomplete, fragmented and diluted approach to regulating commodity trading. Increasingly, these concerns relate to heightened financial stability and opacity risks in the industry, where regulatory gaps have widened further since 2010. These gaps are being exploited by the corporate groups that dominate commodity trading. Moreover, commodity traders have not only circumvented existing regulations but also consistently avoided further attempts to regulate the financial dimension of their activities.

Regulatory competition, unique industry characteristics and efficiencies, as well as economies of scale, are typical arguments used by the industry to advocate the merits of the fragmented regulatory approach which has prevailed until today. Despite efforts to increase oversight, the food markets sector has resisted, arguing that it is indirectly supervised by banks.

"Commodity traders have circumvented existing regulations and consistently avoided attempts to regulate the financial dimension of their activities."

To a large extent, current gaps are the outcome of regulatory loopholing in the post-2010 financial architecture. These include caveats and exemptions to market-level regulations introduced in the wake of the global financial crisis; company-level techniques of financial and regulatory arbitrage; a persistent lack of a harmonized approach to regulating commodity traders generally, and of food companies more specifically.

There is also a more fundamental reason for the lack of appropriate regulatory treatment: the majority of food trading companies are not regulated as financial institutions but are treated as manufacturing companies. The ongoing crisis in the global food system underscores the need to rethink the regulation of food and commodity traders at a more coherent and systemic level.

"The majority of food trading companies are not regulated as financial institutions but are treated as manufacturing companies."

1. Dodd-Frank: an opportunity missed

Historically, the most important source of the public regulation and monitoring of futures exchanges has been the government of the United States, driven by farmer and consumer interests. Until the financial crisis of 2007–2009, futures exchanges in other jurisdictions, except for some developing countries, were typically subject only to light forms of self-regulation and little or no public monitoring. In the European Union, regulation of commodity derivative markets centred on the behaviour of *market participants* – in terms of capital requirements, organizational requirements and requirements to follow conduct-of-business rules, and even here with wide exemptions – rather than of *markets* (Gibbon, 2013).

Following the commodity price boom of the 2000s, financial market regulation concerns began to feature in the regulatory agenda of the United States and the European Union. Signed in 2010, the Dodd-Frank Act aimed to roll back the preceding liberalization of OTC and exchange-based trading. The Act prioritized measures and requirements for better (re)-capitalization of banks, and more discipline in the credit operations of commercial banks (Kornher et al., 2022). In the area of commodity trading, the main provisions in the Act were usefully summarized by Gibbon (2013):

(i) OTC swaps "taking a standard form", when traded by financial entities with portfolios with a notional value of more than $8 billion, will have to be cleared through centralized clearing houses and subject to reporting and margin requirements. The United States Securities and Exchange Commission (SEC) has announced a margin requirement equivalent to 15 per cent of the notional value of the acquired position. Crucially, "non-financial entities" hedging risk *will be exempted from the central clearing requirement* but will be subject to a requirement for central notification. Additional margin requirements were considered for non-cleared swaps.

(ii) Banks shall *spin off their commodity swap activities* to independent entities excluded from Federal Reserve Insurance arrangements and not engage in derivatives trading not directly related to the trading they do for customers (the so-called "Volcker rule").

(iii) Federal position limits shall be extended to all exchange-traded commodity contracts, and the aggregation of individual positions on a commodity for position limit purposes shall occur across all exchanges and trading venues, including non-United States exchanges and swap venues. The eligibility for hedgers' exemptions from position limits shall be narrowed to entities with positions exclusively in cash-settled contracts.

(iv) Spot month position limits shall normally be set at 25 per cent of the estimated deliverable supply.

(v) These rules shall also apply to activities on foreign exchanges and other trading.

(vi) Venues by "United States persons", foreign-registered subsidiaries of firms and foreign firms whose activities are likely to impact on the economy of the United States, except where foreign exchanges set rules that are deemed to be identical to domestic ones.

(vii) In early 2012, additional Presidential authority was granted for the Commodities Futures Trading Commission (CFTC) to increase margin requirements for oil futures and options contracts (Gibbon, 2013).

Not long after the initial adoption of the Act, its key principles started to be diluted, under the influence of industry interests, inter-agency competition, technical difficulties of implementation and opportunities of international arbitrage.

The coalition of companies using derivatives includes companies such as Bunge, John Deere and Cargill, which engage in both commercial hedging and financial speculation. The coalition has argued that OTC trades between financial institutions and non-financial institutions (such as the coalition members), should be exempt from requirements to clear those trades on public exchanges. At least three reasons are typically given to justify the exemption.

- First, non-financial firms pose no systemic financial risk and hence they should not be prevented from "customizing" their interest rate, currency rate, balance sheets and credit risk in bilateral deals with financial institutions;

- Second, the higher margin requirements of trading on exchanges will pose huge cash-flow problems for coalition members and imperil market liquidity;

- Third, if bilateral trades are pushed from the dark OTC market to exchanges or derivatives clearing platforms, trade risks will be concentrated in such quantity that these centralized clearing platforms will be unable to confirm and verify trades operationally (Suppan, 2010).

Some of the key effects resulting from regulatory loopholing in financial derivatives that ensued soon after the inception of the 2010–2011 regulatory norms are examined in box III.1. The overall outcome of diluting the set of financial reforms was the creation of an important regulatory loophole that is being used by financial institutions to speculate in commodity derivatives to this day.

Box III.1 It's all in the footnote: Dodd-Frank and financial regulatory arbitrage

With the adoption of Dodd-Frank, OTC trading for financial derivatives was supposed to be formalized and moved to central clearing platforms to boost market transparency. The measure was aimed primarily at swaps and security-based swaps (Kornher et al., 2022). Other important regulatory reforms included new position limits and restrictions on the use of swaps. However, although at the time the Commodity Futures Trading Commission (CFTC) issued comprehensive rules on position limits, the authorities failed to enforce them fully. Some funds, such as the commodity index and similar funds, were left unregulated. Regulation of swaps in particular became the centre of the regulatory loopholing that would soon ensue.

To understand its origins and the impact on the sector, a critical distinction needs to be drawn between "branches" and "affiliates" or "subsidiaries" in the structure of banking and corporate operations. The distinction is legally important and impacts the identification of the persons subject to legislation; it also defines how to potentially avoid (arbitrage) the application of legislation.

A branch is merely an office of a legal person; transactions concluded by personnel out of this office are transactions of the legal person owning the branch. An affiliate, or subsidiary, as opposed to a branch, is a separate legal person having its own legal personality, assets, and personnel. This separate legal person is an affiliate or subsidiary because its equity capital is owned by a parent company, which is itself also a separate and autonomous legal person. But legally speaking, as a matter of principle, it is an autonomous legal person. The activities conducted in the office can be exactly the same under both legal configurations. In the first case, they are attributed to the owner of the branch; in the second they are those of a separate legal person (the subsidiary), although 100 per cent of the share capital of the subsidiary may be owned by the "parent" company.

Under the International Swaps and Derivatives Association (ISDA) documentation applicable at the time, a legally separate subsidiary would in effect benefit from an unlimited parent guarantee. In the context of financial trading, for counterparties, this meant that the situation was almost "as if" they traded with the parent company, or a branch. The trade could be subject to local rules, but with a United States bank holding guarantee. This opened the possibility to enjoy the best of many different worlds: for instance, to trade under a more relaxed regime while benefiting from the parent's guarantee and the backing of the United States federal government in case of a bailout.

Dodd-Frank purportedly closed this possibility with Section 722(i). But the CFTC introduced a loophole in its own legislation making it possible to adapt the form of past practices and keep the substance. The July 2013 Guidance made "[United States] persons" in swaps trades subject to all Dodd-Frank's swap rules, regardless of the physical location of the swap execution.

However, footnote 563 of the Guidance stated: "The Commission agrees with commenters who stated that Transaction-Level Requirements should not apply if a non-[United States] swap dealer or non-[United States] major swap participant (MSP) relies on a written representation by a non-[United States] counterparty that its obligations under the swap are not guaranteed with recourse by a [United States] person."

Consequently, newly (officially) "de-guaranteed" foreign subsidiaries were no longer subject to Dodd-Frank. It has been reported and understood among swaps industry experts that a large portion of the United States swaps market shifted from the largest United States bank holding companies and their United States affiliates, to their newly de-guaranteed "foreign" affiliates, even though those swaps remained on the consolidated balance sheets of these United States institutions (Greenberger, 2018). Also, these huge United States bank holding company swaps dealers were often "arranging, negotiating, and executing" these purported "foreign" swaps in the United States, through United States personnel but then "assigning" those fully executed swaps to their newly "de-guaranteed" foreign subsidiaries, asserting that these swaps were not covered by Dodd-Frank even though completed in the United States.

By arranging, negotiating, and executing swaps in the United States, with United States personnel and then "assigning" them to their "foreign" newly "de-guaranteed" subsidiaries, these swaps dealers once again have the best of both worlds: swaps execution in the United States under the parent bank holding companies' direct control, but the ability to move the swaps abroad out from Dodd-Frank (Greenberger, 2018:126).

The 2013 Guidance and Policy Statement was superseded on 23 July 2020 by the CFTC which issued its Final Rules regarding the cross-border application of various requirements under the United States Commodity Exchange Act. Importantly, however, the definition of a "[United States] person" has been further narrowed. For example, a collective investment vehicle owned by [United States] persons was considered a "[United States] person" in the Guidance (although such a legal vehicle does not have legal personality). In the Final Rules, it is not a "[United States] person" anymore (CFTC, 2020).

Although a fully accurate estimate of the extent to which swaps have moved abroad from the United States is not available, it is estimated that up to 95 per cent of certain lines of swaps trading had moved outside the United States under the de-guaranteed loophole and thus were considered not to be subject to Dodd-Frank swaps regulations. An international race-to-the-bottom of swaps regulation ensued (Greenberger, 2018). Partly as a result of this regulatory loopholing, Greenberger estimated that, in the United States, the ratio of speculators versus hedgers, historically around 30 per cent speculators to 70 per cent commercial hedgers, has inversed: 70 per cent speculators to 30 per cent hedgers (Greenberger, 2013).

In the European Union, the European Commission broadly modelled its approach to OTC trading on Dodd-Frank. Yet its key regulatory issues, such as the regulation of OTC derivatives and the enforcement of aggregate positions limits for all market participants, have been controversial and divisive (Suppan, 2010). After the G20 meeting in Pittsburgh in 2009, position limits became a cornerstone of the regulatory approach.

Position limits imposed on market actors are supposed to ensure that derivatives markets work for the *commercial* producers, and not for purely *financial* operators with no intrinsic interest in the commodities themselves. Importantly, this means that industrial and financial market participants are to be treated differently. The classical method used is to set position limits and provide bona fide exemptions for commercial producers as in the Dodd-Frank Act. In the European Union, the Markets in Financial Instruments Directive (MiFID), notably MiFID I and II, apply to commodity derivatives, but include a number of key exemptions. Under MiFID II, a specific "ancillary activity exemption" is available where a firm's activities relating to commodity derivatives are "*ancillary*" to its main business.

2. Global food traders: Commercial hedgers or financial institutions?

At its core, the problem of regulatory gaps centres on the dichotomy between the regulatory treatment of commodity traders as manufacturing corporations on the one hand, and their increasingly more profitable (yet unregulated) activities in financial markets, on the other. The concept behind this distinction between commercial and financial market participants is that an industrial business should only look for security in prices; not betting for the sake of it. However, large grain processors with access to a wealth of information regarding food markets have a clear interest in using their hedging activities as a profit centre. In the process, they tend to change their business model and start operating like a financial actor, with the benefit of exemptions designed for purely commercial hedgers.

"Large grain processors with access to a wealth of information regarding food markets have a clear interest in using their hedging activities as a profit centre."

By using a series of subsidiaries located in appropriate jurisdictions, food monopolies have found a way to combine several advantages:

– A superior knowledge of the agricultural commodities markets (real-time supply and demand and prospective knowledge of their evolution);

– An ability to store agricultural commodities to harness price surges when they occur, ABCD have invested heavily in infrastructure for storage and built significant grain reserves; but with no obligation to disclose their grain stocks;

– Secrecy of their operations and the benefit from derogations to the rules applicable to pure financial actors. ABCD have all legally structured their operations using hundreds of subsidiaries incorporated to take advantage of the various menus of regulations (or lack thereof) offered by the different jurisdictions, including secrecy jurisdictions, around the world (table III.1).

Although some of the challenges of implementing regulatory reforms are due to the operational complexity and opacity of the global food trading industry (indicated in table III.1), many key arguments against closer regulatory attention are constructed by group politics.

Table III.1 Global food trading companies: Number of subsidiaries

Global ultimate owner	Number of subsidiaries
Glencore	877
Archer Daniels Midland	825
Cargill	780
COFCO International	734
Wilmar International	619
CHS	353
Bunge	352
OFI Group (includes Olam)	207
Akira Holding (includes Louis Dreyfus Corporation)	187
Andersons	150
CMOC Group	100
GrainCorp	60
Noble Group	56
CGB Enterprises	46
Scoular	20

Source: UNCTAD calculations based on Orbis database.

The core of regulatory arbitrage opportunities lies in the use of the concept of legal personality and subsidiaries. As the investigation shows below, in the case of major food giants, using hedging for purely speculative purposes appears to take place at the level of subsidiaries, often not being reported at a consolidated (GUO, Global Ultimate Owner) level.

Increasingly, however, in the context of 2020–2023 crises, there is growing recognition that such regulatory dichotomy poses a range of potentially systemic risks to financial stability (FSB, 2023), price stability and economic security (UNCTAD, 2022) and corporate governance, including through risks of illicit financial flows (OECD, 2023; Public Eye, 2023).

In 2012–2013, the Financial Stability Board (FSB) considered classifying large physical commodity trading houses (which are without exception major participants in derivatives markets) either as shadow banks or as "systemically important non-bank financial institutions" or both. This would have made them subject to greater regulation.[6] The industry pushed back, insisting that commodity trading is a highly complex, globally interconnected manufacturing sector managing a range of specialized risks on a large scale (Baines, 2017). In the event, the FSB concluded there was insufficient evidence to consider trading houses as shadow banks but left the door open for future revision of this stance (Gibbon, 2013).

In the absence of close regulatory oversight, the transformation of commodity trading houses into shadow financial institutions continued unabated. Following the implosion of the 2008–2010 commodity bubble, many of the world's largest banks have scaled down their commodity trading operations. Some institutions (e.g., Barclays, Deutsche Bank) have exited the business. These departures opened the space for less regulated entities such as commodity trading firms. As a result, "large trading companies have gained access to increasingly sophisticated instruments that offer them greater financial flexibility and enable them to avoid any controls by banks" (Public Eye, undated).

At the global level, large commercial groups ("ABCD"-type) with real commercial hedging needs have been developing additional financial strategies designed to enhance profit margins, further challenging the regulatory framework of the industry and posing potential threats to financial stability (FSB, 2023). Some of these risks came to the fore during the energy crisis in 2020 when commodity companies faced severe liquidity difficulties (Longley and Chin, 2022). Lévy-Garboua (2022) has called such traders "semi-financial" players, with one foot in finance (their liabilities, which make greater use of leverage than a company, albeit much less than a bank) and one foot in the real world (the raw materials they hold). Yet this real world is close to the financial markets, due to the extreme volatility of prices (Lévy-Garboua, 2022). Implications for financial stability arise from the fact that central banks are helpless when addressing such entities. They require intermediary institutions to take on the functions typically carried out by banks when dealing with commodity traders. From the perspective of central banks, only banks and, to a greater extent, central clearing platforms, are well-suited to this role.

---

[6] At the time, the initiative followed the disclosure of long-term lending to independent companies by Glencore worth $3 billion, and the trend for the largest trading houses to operate hedge funds or index funds or both, either alone or in partnership with investment banks (Gibbon, 2013).

Academics have long suggested that global food trading corporations have expanded the scope of control over the industry to become not simply oligopolies, but cross-sectoral value chain managers (Clapp, 2015). Crucially, this includes control over the financial assets. Yet methodologies or monitoring tools that would help capture the scale and impacts of this transformation at a systemic level were, up to now, lacking. The idea that the commodity trading industry will self-regulate means there is an absence of established regulatory guidelines in the industry, making it challenging to differentiate between commercial and financial institutions.

With this task becoming more urgent in light of recent volatility and crises, a new method is proposed below to advance this discussion.

3. How to differentiate between financial and commercial companies, using the "asset dominance" ratio

Analysis of the food trading sector's profitability presented in section B above established that non-operating activities were the main source of heightened profit growth in the food trading sector during 2020–2022. But what is the best way to gauge the level and impact of the financial activity undertaken by a global non-financial corporation?

The answer to this question presented below has its origins in corporate accounting methods.[7] In corporate accounting, financial instruments used in intrafirm financing are typically described on the balance sheet of entity filings. The method used here is based on examining the corporate filings of 13 of the major global food commodity traders and comparing the accounts of the corporate parent with the accounts of group subsidiaries. The result is measured by an indicator called the asset dominance ratio (ADR), which aims to capture financial (as opposed to "real") economic activity carried out inside a corporate structure. This is achieved by comparing information presented in the balance sheet with income statements in corporate filings. More specifically, ADR points to heightened use of intragroup transfers within private corporate groups. Intragroup transfers are financial transactions between legally independent entities within a corporate group.

As table III.1 shows, large companies such as food traders consist of a parent company and tens, in some cases, hundreds of subsidiaries. A great deal of intrafirm transfers take place among the parent and subsidiaries, and between subsidiaries themselves. There are two main types of such intragroup transfers: (a) transfer pricing, which involves trading activities between group members; and (b) intragroup financing, which involves using financial instruments to create debt or equity relationships between group members.

In corporate accounting, balance sheet items represent an approximation of all forms of financial investments by the reporting entity (e.g., a subsidiary or the corporate parent); while income statements document the amount of revenue harvested from those investments during the reporting period. Due to the known problem of tax avoidance through transfer pricing, corporate intrafirm trading is subject to considerable regulation. The regulation of intragroup financing, however, is less developed than transfer pricing, and is a concern for regulators. The study presented here is predicated on the assumption that tracking intragroup financing requires comparing balance sheets and income statements because financial instruments are accounted for on the balance sheet. This helps simplify the complexity of financial reporting within multinational corporations.

More precisely, ADR is computed as the mean average of all reported balance sheet items compared to the mean average of all income statement items presented by the corporate entities under examination. Note that:

- An ADR figure at or below 1 describes an industrial corporation in this sector;

- An ADR of more than 1 indicates that financial investment activity outweighs the earnings activities from core business and investments.

This metric focuses on the use of financial instruments in intragroup financing and gives weight to certain reporting patterns. Findings show that the use of intragroup financing is significant in generating excess profits.

[7] The method was developed on the basis of a research project on corporate arbitrage (CORPLINK, EU Grant agreement ID: 694943, DOI: 10.3030/694943).

It is commonly performed by select members of a corporate group whose primary role is corporate financing and treasury functions. The use of financial instruments is often reported in multiple places within accounting categories, and the magnitude of assets and liabilities involved is much larger than the values reported on the income statement.

For governance purposes, it is important to compare not only the subsidiaries within a group but also the consolidated parent company's reporting. Consolidated reporting, oriented towards shareholders, excludes intragroup transfers. Thus, analysing changes in excess values produced by subsidiaries excluded from consolidated reporting is crucial from the point of view of: (a) financial stability, (b) tax avoidance and fiscal revenues; (c) risks of illicit financial flows (IFF).

Figure III.8 illustrates the change in asset dominance ratio between the consolidated parent (GUO in most cases) and group subsidiaries for the 13 companies in the sample. It presents an analysis of the corporate activity, including at the level of subsidiaries, between two time periods:

- the period when hedging predominates in the OTC markets (2014–2018);

- the period of speculation on OTC markets and excessive corporate profits (2019–2022).

This analysis pinpoints shifts in the reports of these corporate groups, which indicate these entities are taking advantage of the profit opportunities that have arisen in recent years.

The distinction between data presented by the consolidated parent group (*y axis*) and data presented by the group's subsidiaries (*x axis*) is key. The diagonal in the graph depicts the points where subsidiary reports match the information presented in the consolidated public reporting. As positioned in figure III.8, being at or below 1 (e.g., GrainCorp in the sample) depicts an accounting profile of a typical industrial corporation. The diagonal differentiating the two halves of the graphic where there is a difference in the information presented by the financial reporting: one which is "hidden" (subsidiary level) and one which is "already public" (consolidated parent).

In figure III.8, the ADR is the ratio of the sum of all available balance sheet items to the sum of all available income statement items. The change in the ratio is illustrated by an arrow, where the starting point is the period of 2014–2018, and the endpoint of the arrow is the period of 2019–2022. Red arrows indicate corporations where asset dominance ratio has increased at the subsidiary level, while black arrows indicate the decrease of asset dominance ratio at the level of the parent.

"Profiteering reinforces the need to consider corporate group membership and the behaviour of major players in the food trading sector."

Three key conclusions can be drawn from these findings:

- First, the cases showing growth in asset dominance are observed primarily at the subsidiary level within the group, indicating increased use of intragroup transfers.

- Second, this suggests that the amount of excess profits being made could be underestimated when only looking at public profit and loss reporting.

- Third, profiteering is not limited to a specific sector but is specific to individual firms. There are concerns that excess profits may be linked to market concentration, benefiting only a few global players in the commodity trading community. This reinforces the need to consider group membership and the evolving behaviour of major international players in the sector.

It is pertinent that these three issues crystallized in the commodities sector at the peak of the energy crisis in 2020–2021, when market volatility threatened the financial stability of clearing houses and required the support of public liquidity injections. The financial crisis of utility companies highlighted the risks of liabilities on hidden balance sheets and underscored banks' exposure to commodity firms facing sharp market volatility (Petrou, 2022; Foroohar, 2020).

Figure III.8 Large food traders become unregulated financial institutions
Change in asset dominance ratio between the consolidated parent and group subsidiaries in the food trading industry
2014–2018 and 2019–2022

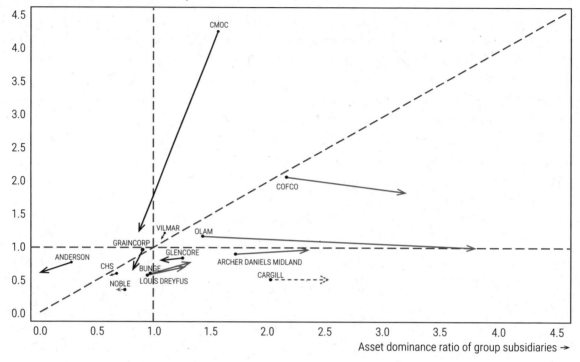

Source: UNCTAD calculations based on Orbis database.
  Note: Dataset on 13 corporate groups in the sample compiled in March 2023 from Orbis (BVD) data service. Corporate group definition: ownership >50 per cent by GUO entity (for Chinese SOEs, the GUO is the corporate entity owned by the Government of China). The asset dominance approach measures the ratio of the sum of *all* available balance sheet items to the sum of *all* available income statement items. The change between 2014–2018 and 2019–2022 is illustrated by an arrow. Red arrows indicate corporations where asset dominance ratio has increased at the level of subsidiaries, while black arrows indicate the decrease of asset dominance ratio at the level of the parent and the subsidiaries.

As monetary tightening continues in advanced economies, there are growing market fears that similar financial structures may arise and threaten the stability of individual companies, as well as the international financial system (FSB, 2023). Therefore, it is necessary to adopt rules to the effect that commodity derivatives play their useful social function while preventing excessive speculation in the financial markets for food and dysfunction of food systems globally (Thomas, 2023; OECD, 2023).

D. REGULATORY LESSONS

When asked who is monitoring the food system globally, beyond the prism of antitrust, a former senior economist at the United Nations Food and Agriculture Organization replied: *"Nobody"* (Thomas, 2023).

"The commodities sector is lightly supervised, much of it is opaque and regulation of key actors is close to non-existent."

The absence of harmonized global rules provides ample opportunities for regulatory arbitrage, which is exploited differently by different market participants. As noted above in section C, large United States banks use "de-guaranteed" subsidiaries to evade Dodd-Frank. Other actors use exemptions available thanks to their commercial activities in order to conduct what amounts to financial speculation. The United Kingdom Financial Services Authority (which oversees the world's second largest agricultural commodities market outside the United States) does not even distinguish between commercial and financial traders (de Schutter, 2010). As a result, the commodities sector is lightly supervised, much of it is opaque, and regulation of key actors is close to non-existent (Jones, 2022).

The current fragmented and outdated approach to regulating the global food industry has many causes. But with new types of risks and shocks confronting an already complex, opaque yet strategically important system, it is time to revisit the menu of available regulatory pathways. Such a challenge is vast. Below, measures are outlined relating to what are considered the root causes of the current regulatory gaps: the flawed distinction between commercial and financial operators, and an outdated set of systemic regulations that have not kept pace with financial, technical and legal innovation available to corporate groups. Possible solutions centre on three interrelated levels of policy reform that capture the connection between market practices and financial activities:

1. Market-level reform: close loopholes, facilitate transparency;

2. Systemic-level reform: recognize aspects of food traders' activities as financial institutions and extend relevant regulations;

3. Global governance-level reform: extend monitoring and regulations to the level of corporate subsidiaries in the sector to address the problem of unearned profits, enhance transparency and curb the risks of illicit financial flows.

Crucially, all three levels of necessary action require much more cooperation on data quality, disclosure and corporate transparency in the sector. The ongoing crises highlight that the historical approach, which distinguishes between commercial and financial operators in agricultural commodity derivatives, is ill-suited to the current economic and legal structures of global trade in certain agricultural products and their associated derivatives. While data transparency is necessary, it is insufficient for market participants to discover prices. What is required is a process in which all market participants contribute daily price information, and which is accessible to all participants and regulators on a daily basis.

Following the UNCTAD vision to reform the financial regulatory framework, scaling up could take place in a three-fold manner:

1. Market-level: close existing loopholes, facilitate market transparency and competition (Dodd-Frank, CFTC, MiFID, European Commission).

Consider applying several rules to all the exchanges around the world:

- Improve stock (public and private) information. Excessive speculation is made easier by a lack of transparency on stock levels. Information about one's inventory can be made a pre-condition to act on the derivatives market. The information can also be used to evaluate whether combined positions correspond to a hedging strategy or to excessive speculation.

- Build a highly disaggregated dataset with volume/weight of commodity, import price value, source and destination countries, all company names obtained via customs declarations linked to each unit of commodity movements, and time stamps for shipment and receipt.

Both proposals can build on the experience of the Agricultural Market Information System (AMIS), an inter-agency platform to enhance food market transparency. It was launched in 2011 by the G20 Ministers of Agriculture following the global food price hikes in 2007, 2008 and 2010. By bringing together the principal agricultural commodity trading countries, AMIS assesses global food supplies (focusing on wheat, maize, rice and soybeans) and thus helps alleviate market uncertainty.[8]

---

[8] AMIS is composed of G20 members plus Spain and seven additional major exporting and importing countries of agricultural commodities. Together, AMIS participants represent a large share of global production, consumption and trade volumes of the targeted crops, typically in the range of 80–90 per cent.

Clearly distinguish between commercial hedging and financial speculation, with the understanding that the historical segregation between commercial/financial does not apply to today's structure of the world agricultural commodities exchanges (de Schutter, 2010).

Current practices and unsupported assertions by market participants seeking minimal oversight of their trading activities cannot be the sole focus with respect to bona fide hedging recognitions. Legitimate hedging relating to physical commodities through derivatives markets must not be jeopardized by those seeking exposures for investment, speculative, or dealing reasons.

- Access to commodities derivatives markets could be restricted to traders and specialist brokers.

- The holdings of any single trader should be known to all. Strict position limits should be placed on individual holdings, such that they are not manipulative. UNCTAD (2011a) noted that determining appropriate levels of position limits is difficult, but as a first step, it might be useful to adopt position points at which traders would be required to provide additional information.

- The limits currently set in the United States and Europe are too high. For the same reason that the United States sets federal limits applying to all markets, this needs to be globally set. Position limits must address a proliferation of economically equivalent instruments trading in multiple trading venues. Position limits at the exchange level cannot suffice (Behnam, 2020).

- Improve market transparency in physical commodity markets, commodity futures exchanges and OTC markets. Require market participants to disclose their positions and trading activities (UNCTAD, 2011a, 2011b). There should be clearing to the maximum extent possible of OTC derivatives, so that there is real time reporting of all transactions made without information privileges for OTC traders. The small minority of OTC derivatives which cannot be cleared should nevertheless be reported within a short time lag.

- The unfair competitive advantage conferred by the OTC trade data reporting delay not only impedes price discovery but makes it harder for exporters and importers to manage price risks and investment, as UNCTAD has repeatedly noted. If developing countries continue to spend a high portion of hard currency reserves on food and energy imports, while the rate of return in commodity investments remains unpredictable, the "distortion of development" will intensify (Suppan, 2010; UNCTAD 2011a).

2. Systemic-level: Promote competition in commodity markets to curb the concentration of market power in the hands of a few large players.

Systemic reforms can include laws such as breaking up monopolies, promoting the entry of new market players, considering measures such as antitrust laws, adherence to modern international financing reporting standards (IFRS) in commodity trading, and supporting the participation of small farmers and producer organizations in commodity markets.

Regulation should support the development of physical markets to reduce the destabilizing impacts of unregulated financial instruments and promote price discovery based on physical supply and demand fundamentals. This could include measures such as supporting the development of commodity exchanges in developing countries and promoting the use of physical delivery contracts in commodity trading. Also, contingency plans need to be developed to deal with potential market disruptions.

More fundamentally, regulators should revisit the plans of 2010–2012 and recognize the financial aspects of food traders' activities as systemically important and extend relevant regulations. Like the previous set of measures, these date back to policy discussions in the wake of the 2007–2009 financial and commodity price crises. At the time, lack of evidence was cited as a reason not to pursue a closer regulatory focus.

Notwithstanding the existing rules, there is widespread agreement that as of late, the dynamics and price signals of supply and demand have been overwhelmed by financial speculators, making price discovery, and hedging, challenging, if not impossible (Tarbert, 2023). There are also warning signs from the financial risks in the underregulated energy market, where amidst the uncertainty of 2022, utility companies did not have enough working capital to meet big collateral calls. It became apparent that government regulators and private sector risk managers had failed to prepare for the crisis (Tett, 2022).

"Regulators should recognize the financial aspects of food traders' activities as systemically important and extend relevant regulations."

Measures to help mobilize fiscal resources, curb regulatory arbitrage and enhance corporate transparency also need to be expanded and updated. Conservative estimates suggest that today, multinational enterprises (MNEs) avoid tax payments of at least $240 billion per year, due to outdated international taxation rules. These rules allow multinationals to treat each national subsidiary as a separate "arm's-length" entity for tax purposes, and to move profits to low- or no-tax jurisdictions. The study presented above demonstrated some of the effects of this fragmentation for companies in the global food trading industry. Chapter VII of the 2022 *Trade and Development Report* analysed the problem of corporate arbitrage in the area of foreign direct investment (FDI).

There are mounting calls from academia and civil society to address the problem of corporate arbitrage at the regulatory level. For instance, tax and other forms of regulatory arbitrage can be prevented by recognizing that multinationals are global unitary businesses, and by abandoning the arm's-length principle. Multinationals' profits could then be divided among countries according to a formula based on the location of revenues, employees and so on (Ghosh, 2023).

3. Global economic governance: The evidence presented above underscores two dimensions of the regulatory impact of the financialization of food trading. At the level of companies themselves, their transformation into shadow banks poses systemic, regulatory and stability challenges. Additionally, there is a link that needs to be examined between the speculative activity of food traders in the financial markets, and price instability.

More and more evidence is emerging not only about profiteering in food and commodity trading, but of the role of unregulated financial activities and institutions inside commodity trading giants. An estimate of the scale of the phenomenon was provided above, but more research is needed. In addition to system-wide measures to strengthen regulation in food commodities and enhance food security – such as harmonized and clearer rules, enforceable controls to limit the destabilizing influence of high-frequency trading and position limits (Kornher, 2022) – regulators and policymakers should apply some of the financial stability measures developed for the banking system in 2011–2012 to large food trading giants.

This requires further work on the nature of systemic risk in the highly financialized industry. This can only effectively be done as part of the reform to the global financial ecosystem, an idea strongly endorsed by the first Financing for Development Conference organized by the United Nations in 2001. Since then, efforts at global reforms have been slow and often non-inclusive, while the unresolved problems of financial and resource asymmetries only continued to deepen (Ryding and Rangaprasad, 2022). In light of recent crises, such efforts should include regulation of corporate behaviour including at the subsidiary level, to address the problem of unearned profits, opacity and risks of illicit financial flows. This direction of work could capitalize on the plans for a United Nations Tax Convention (see Tax Justice Network, 2022) and be usefully supported by the work of the Independent Commission for the Reform of International Corporate Taxation established in November 2022 (ICRICT, 2023).

Some lessons from the recent attempts to increase transparency and regulate super profits in the energy sector are relevant here. Several countries have levied windfall taxes on the oil industry, following the dramatic rise in profits in the sector amidst the energy and inflation crisis of 2022. A similar strategy could be imagined with regards to the profits derived from speculation on the food commodities derivatives markets. At the same time, levying windfall taxes does not address the main issue for developmental purposes, which is to have commodities derivatives markets fulfilling their role: providing hedging solutions for producers and processors.

There are, moreover, numerous issues with the *retroactive* taxation of speculative profits. The first is that the profits have often been booked in tax havens whose cooperation is unlikely. Second, retroactive taxation creates constitutional issues in many jurisdictions. In some countries, it is unconstitutional, and, in many others, courts accept retroactive taxes only in limited circumstances, such as closing a blatantly abused loophole. A windfall tax would most likely be litigated in many forums with substantial chances of success. A windfall tax does not deliver on the opportunity created by illuminating that there are serious issues with the rules applying to the world food commodities derivatives markets. Although States may need to address their constituents' desire for the correction of what they perceive as an unfair outcome, the structural issue needs to be addressed via other means.

In this respect, a 15 per cent global minimum tax rate agreed to in 2021 by 136 countries, further to a plan by the OECD, is often seen as a major step towards countering tax avoidance and artificial arbitrage strategies by multinational groups of companies generally. Yet this is a compromise measure agreed after fraught international negotiations. Alternative measures, such as a median global tax rate of 21 per cent, as proposed by ICRICT, would serve to offset the potential revenue lost, making a significant difference to developing countries (Ghosh, 2023).

The tax is not and was not designed to address the specific issues raised by the strategies developed by global food traders. Their activity, as shown above, underscores the need for multilateral efforts to identify the true beneficial owners of all assets, financial and physical. As Ghosh argues, moving towards a global asset registry should be the ultimate aim, but this step shows that like-minded countries can cooperate without a global agreement. In July 2023, Latin American and Caribbean countries hosted the first regional ministerial meeting for a more inclusive, sustainable and equitable global tax order (Nicholls, 2023), aimed at addressing the development aspects currently not met by the architecture of global taxation. While this is only a start, it is a meaningful move towards a common approach to taxing multinationals and combating regulatory and jurisdictional arbitrage (Ghosh, 2023).

The role of monopolies in strategically important markets in times of crises and the complexity of global corporate and financial structures that enable speculation and profiteering, not only require close attention, but also smart policies (Lusiani, 2022). Regulation of these interconnected problems needs to be targeted to the specific issues at hand, at a multilateral level. The initiatives outlined in this chapter provide a systemic framework to the measures on food price and food security agreed by the G20 members in June 2023.

Crucially, in light of the lessons of past crises and the analysis presented above, reforms need to be conceived in an integrated way, targeting key priorities across the system. More specifically:

(a) The problem of excessive financial speculation in commodities markets needs to be addressed along with the problem of unregulated activities in this underregulated sector;

(b) The issue of corporate control over key markets cannot be resolved by anti-trust measures alone but requires a coherent framework of national competition and industrial policies;

(c) International cooperation and commitment are critical in the effort to enhance data quality and transparency in commodity trading and curb the risks of financial instability and illicit finance.

More generally, the case of a commodity price crisis and corporate profiteering in food trading indicate that an international tax architecture that works for the benefit of all countries needs to be an integral element of the International Financial Architecture, examined in detail in Part II of this Report.

REFERENCES

Agarwal K, Win T and Gibbs M (2022). Betting on hunger: Market speculation is contributing to global food insecurity. *The Wire.* 6 May.

Akyüz GA and Gursoy G (2020). Strategic management perspectives on supply chain. *Management Review Quarterly.* 70(2): 213–241.

Allianz (2023). European food inflation – hungry for profits? Allianz Research. 14 April.

Archer Daniels Midland (ADM). 2022. 10-K2022 FY Annual report. Filed: 14 February 2023. https://capedge. com/filing/7084/0000007084-23-000010/ADM-10K-2022FY.

Baines J (2017). Accumulating through food crisis? Farmers, commodity traders and the distributional politics of financialization. *Review of International Political Economy.* 24(3).

Barret P (2022). How food and energy are driving the global inflation surge. IMF blog. International Monetary Fund. 12 September.

Behnam R (2020). Statement of Dissent of Commissioner Rostin Behnam Regarding Position Limits for Derivatives. Commodity Futures Trading Commission. 15 October.

BIS (1995). *Issues of Measurement Related to Market Size and Macro-prudential Risks in Derivatives Markets.* Bank for International Settlements. Basel.

BIS (2023). OTC Derivatives Statistics. May. Bank for International Settlements. Basel.

Bicchetti D and Maystre N (2013). The synchronized and long-lasting structural change on commodity markets: evidence from high frequency data. *Algorithmic Finance.* 2(3–4):233–239.

Blas J and Farchy J (2021). *The World for Sale: Money, Power, and the Traders Who Barter the Earth's Resources.* London: Penguin.

Carbonnier G and Mehrotra R (2019). Abnormal Pricing in International Commodity Trade: Empirical Evidence from Switzerland. Discussion Paper No. R4D-IFF-WP01-2019. Swiss Programme for Research on Global Issues for Development.

Clapp J (2011). *Food.* Cambridge, United Kingdom: Polity Press.

Clapp J (2015). ABCD and beyond: From grain merchants to agricultural value chain managers. UWSpace. http://hdl.handle.net/10012/11493.

Clapp J and Howard P (2023). The Hunger Profiteers. Project Syndicate. 8 August.

Clapp J and Isakson R (2021). Speculative Harvests: Financialization, Food and Agriculture. Practical Action Publishing.

Daunton M (2023). The Economic Government of the World. London: Penguin.

de Schutter O (2010). Food Commodities Speculation and Food Price Crises. Regulation to reduce the risks of price volatility. United Nations Special Rapporteur on the Right to Food. Briefing Note No. 2. September. Available at https://www2.ohchr.org/english/issues/food/docs/briefing_note_02_september_2010_ en.pdf.

Financial Stability Board (FSB). 2023. The Financial Stability Aspects of Global Commodity Markets. Financial Stability Board. 20 February.

Foroohar R (2020). The next subprime crisis could be in food. Financial Times. 13 September.

GCRG (2022). Global Impact of the war in Ukraine: Billions of people face the greatest cost-of-living crisis in a generation. Global Crisis Response Group. Brief No. 2. June.

Ghosh J (2023). Finding the money to fix the world requires a rethink on tax. *The Economist.* 13 June.

Gibbon P (2013). Commodity Derivatives: Financialization and Regulatory Reform, Danish Institute for International Studies (DIIS). Working Paper No. 12.

Gkanoutas-Leventis A and Nesvetailova A (2015). Financialization of the Oil Market. *Energy Policy.* 86: 891–902.

Greenberger M (2013). Closing Wall Street's Commodity and Swaps Betting Parlors: Legal Remedies to Combat Needlessly Gambling Up the Price of Crude Oil Beyond What Market Fundamentals Dictate. *George Washington Law Review.* April 2013. 81(3).

Greenberger M (2018). Too Big to Fail – U.S. Banks' Regulatory Alchemy: Converting an Obscure Agency Footnote into an "At Will" Nullification of Dodd-Frank's Regulation of the Multi-Trillion Dollar Financial Swaps Market. INET Working Paper No. 74.

IATP and GRAIN (2023). A corporate cartel fertilizes food inflation. Institute for Agriculture and Tade Policy. 23 May.

ICRICT (2023). ICRICT's letter to United Nations Secretary-General António Guterres. Independent Commission for the Reform of International Corporate Taxation. 17 March.

IMF (2023). *Global Financial Stability Report.* April. International Monetary Fund. Washington, D.C.

International Panel of Experts on Sustainable Food Systems (2023). Breaking the Cycle of Unsustainable Food Systems, Hunger and Debt. Special Report. IPES. March.

Jones H (2022). LME nickel debacle shows need to scrutinize commodities, says IOSCO watchdog. *Reuters.* 26 April.

Kornher L, von Braun J and Algieri B (2022). Speculation risks in food commodity markets in the context of the 2022 price spikes. ZEF Policy Brief No. 40. Centre for Development Research. University of Bonn.

Lévy-Garboua V (2022). Shadow Commodity Trading. *Finance and Gestion.* 20 June.

Longley A and Chin Y (2022). Commodity Markets Contend With a Growing Liquidity Crisis. *Bloomberg.* 13 September.

Lusiani N (2022). Tax and Monopoly Focus: Reframing Tax Policy to Reset the Rules of the Monopoly Game. Tax and Monopoly Profits. Roosevelt Institute. 27 October.

Murphy S, Burch D and Clapp J (2012). Cereal Secrets. The world's largest grain traders and global agriculture. Oxfam Research Reports.

Nicholls A (2023). Latin America and Caribbean Tax Summit in Cartagena: A Caribbean Perspective. Caribbean Trade Law. 4 August. Available at https://caribbeantradelaw.com/2023/08/04/latin-america-and-caribbean-tax-summit-in-cartagena-a-caribbean-perspective/.

OECD (2023). Oil commodity trading and addressing the risk of illicit financial flows. Development Co-operation Directorate. OECD Publishing. Paris.

Oliver Wyman (2023). Commodity Trading's $100 bn year. Record trades, intense volatility, extraordinary endurance. March.

Oxfam (2011). Not a Game: Speculation vs Food Security. Policy Paper. 3 October. Available at: https://www.oxfam.org/en/research/not-game-speculation-vs-food-security.

Oxfam (2023). Big business' windfall profits rocket to "obscene" $1 trillion a year amid cost-of-living crisis. Oxfam. 6 July. Available at https://www.oxfam.org/en/press-releases/big-business-windfall-profits-rocket-obscene-1-trillion-year-amid-cost-living-crisis.

Petrou K (2022). Central bankers cannot afford to ignore the pain in commodities. *Financial Times.* 13 April.

Public Eye. Undated. *Trends and developments in the global agro-food sector.* Available at https://www.publiceye.ch/en/topics/soft-commodity-trading/trends-and-developments-in-the-global-agro-food-sector.

Public Eye (2023). War and crises – and commodity traders are making record profits. January. Available at: https://www.publiceye.ch/en/topics/soft-commodity-trading/war-and-crises-and-commodity-traders-are-making-record-profits.

Ross A and Gibbs M (2023). Top hedge funds made $1.9bn on grains ahead of the Ukraine war food price spike. *Unearthed.* 14 April. Available at: https://unearthed.greenpeace.org/2023/04/14/ukraine-wheat-food-price-crisis-speculation/.

Ryding T and Rangaprasad P (2022). 20 years after Monterrey, the UN Financing for Development process is as important as ever. Eurodad. 16 March. Available at: https://www.eurodad.org/20_years_after_monterrey.

Schmidt P (2022). Food price speculation in the aftermath of the Ukraine war, European Economic and Social Committee. Nat/873.

Scott F, Cowley C and Kreitman T (2023). Tight Labor Markets Have Been a Key Contributor to High Food Inflation. Economic Bulletin. April. Kansas City Federal Reserve. Available at: https://www.kansascityfed.org/research-staff/francisco-scott/.

Staritz C, Newman S, Troster B and Plank L (2018). Financialization and Global Commodity Chains: Distributional Implications for Cotton in Sub-Saharan Africa. *Development and Change.* 49(3).

Suppan S (2010). Commodity regulatory pathways not yet chosen. UNCTAD Public Symposium. 10–11 May. Geneva.

Tarbert H (2023). The CFTC needs to investigate the role and impact of speculation in commodity markets. Better Markets. 8 March.

Tax Justice Network (2022). UN tax convention proposed at General Assembly. TJN. 14 October. Available at: https://taxjustice.net/press/un-tax-convention-proposed-at-general-assembly/.

Tett G (2022). Brussels ignores derivatives at its peril amid energy crisis. *Financial Times*. 8 September. Available at: https://www.ft.com/content/b58480fb-b9de-4316-af21-b82167ef3e20.

Tett G (2023). Five reasons investors should expect the unexpected. *Financial Times*. 9 June.

Thomas H (2023). Murky world of global food trading is too important to ignore. *Financial Times*. 21 June.

UNCTAD (2011a). *Price Formation in Financialized Commodity Markets: The Role of Information* (United Nations publication. New York and Geneva).

UNCTAD (2011b). Policy actions to mitigate the impact of highly volatile prices and incomes on commodity-dependent countries, and to facilitate value addition and greater participation in commodity value chains by commodity-producing countries. UNCTAD, 2 February. Available at: https://unctad.org/system/files/official-document/cimem2d14_en.pdf.

UNCTAD (2022). A Double Burden: The effects of food price increases and currency depreciations on food import bills. 16 December.

UNCTAD (2023). *Trade and Development Report Update* (April 2023). Geneva.

Vargas M and Chantry O (2011). Ploughing through the meanders in food speculation. Mundubat.

Winders B (2011). The Food Crisis and the Deregulation of Agriculture. *The Brown Journal of World Affairs.* 18(1):83–95.

Chapter IV

Reforming the International
Financial Architecture:
The View from UNCTAD

A. INTRODUCTION

The international financial architecture (IFA) is a framework of institutions, policies, rules and practices that govern the global financial system. Its aim is to promote international cooperation with a view to ensuring global monetary and financial stability, enabling international trade and investment, supporting the mobilization of the stable and long-term financing required for economic development, combatting the climate crisis, and achieving the Sustainable Development Goals.

Recurring financial and debt crises, as well as the shortfall in required development and climate finance, reiterate that the existing framework of IFA is ill-equipped for today's world. Many of its shortcomings are of a systemic nature. Two specific issues have been apparent from an early stage. First, the structure of IFA and its institutions are not designed to deliver the kind of financial support that developing countries need to realize their growth and development ambitions (Kregel, 2018). Second, developing countries often have sizable and lasting current account deficits. As a result, they operate under a governance hierarchy that demands they make more stringent adjustments in the face of macroeconomic imbalances compared to advanced economies (Martin, 2023). This contributes to the accumulation of unsustainable external debt burdens.

The search for a new change of direction requires these systemic challenges to be comprehensively addressed. So far, the necessary global agreement and the political will to take reforms forward have been lacking. Instead, a wide range of piecemeal and ad hoc reforms have been pursued. A series of reform proposals (new institutions, new alliances between existing institutions, new policy instruments and new systemic thinking), often initiated by developing countries, are being proposed as an alternative to the current IFA.

"New proposals are widening the scope of institutional experimentation and may give rise to more participatory global financial governance."

These proposed revisions are often contested because they may appear incoherent both between themselves and with the current IFA. Yet, they are widening the scope for institutional experimentation and may eventually give rise to more participatory and sustainable global monetary and financial governance (Grabel, 2018).

For UNCTAD, the IFA should enable developing countries to integrate into the global economy in a process facilitated by successful structural transformation. Within this, the role of mechanisms and institutions within international finance is two-fold: on the one hand, to help alleviate trade deficits and unstable debt burdens; on the other hand, to enable financing for long-term, sustainable and transformative growth. The contribution of international trade and financial flows to growth and development is closely connected to a country's balance of payments position. It is also impacted by structural asymmetries in the international division of labour and international markets.

Importantly, the position of UNCTAD regarding IFA is informed by its broader vision of development and transformation. The UNCTAD approach to trade and development policy is multifaceted. First, it recognizes structural obstacles and constraints. In this context, UNCTAD also advocates for a more balanced and sensitive framework for international cooperation. This would address existing biases and help mobilize the requisite resources to raise investment levels in developing countries. Developing countries would be able to shift away from commodity dependence towards more diversified economies; initially, this could centre on a strong push for industrialization and be underpinned by a sustained acceleration in growth (Prebisch, 1964). This approach would inevitably involve a significant rise in the imports of capital goods, with developing countries needing to generate sufficient foreign exchange to cover the associated costs.

While chapters V and VI address in detail two other crucial areas – debt and climate finance – this chapter provides a survey of key recent proposals for IFA reform, examined through the lens of longstanding contributions by UNCTAD in this field. The ability to respond to today's challenges has been complicated by recent changes in the political and economic landscape, which is why this survey focuses on two key areas.

The first challenge relates to the promotion of economic and financial stability in a world that is becoming increasingly financially fragile and vulnerable to cross-border spillovers. The second challenge is the need to secure vast financial resources to support economic, social, and human development; to make progress towards the Sustainable Development Goals; and to develop frameworks for the type of cooperation that can address complex problems in the global commons (such as global pandemics, climate change, forced displacement, tax avoidance, and cyberrelated risks).

B. TOWARDS A DEVELOPMENT-CONSCIOUS INTERNATIONAL FINANCIAL ARCHITECTURE

A systemic approach

Access to foreign currencies is essential for two purposes. First, it enables financing of international trade transactions. In the absence of sufficient foreign exchange, economies are forced to cut down on imports during periods of sluggish export earnings growth or in response to external shocks. Developing countries in particular, are vulnerable to these circumstances. Second, foreign exchange is paramount for financing the imports of capital goods that are required for industrialization and economic advancement.

One source of foreign exchange is export revenues. It has long been recognized that export-oriented strategies not only increase allocative efficiency and larger market size, but also help overcome the balance of payments constraint (Thirlwall, 1979). The current global financial architecture evolved following the rejection at Bretton Woods of Keynes' plan for a symmetrical treatment of all trade imbalances. Keynes' plan for an International Clearing Union proposed preventing structural trade imbalances by penalizing trade surpluses, as well as deficits. Its rejection created structural impediments for developing countries and their ability to rely on export earnings for sustainable growth. It also led to two sets of structural problems.

First, with no moderating incentives introduced to surplus industrial exporters, the Bretton Woods arrangement placed the full burden of adjustments on deficit countries (except the one issuing the international reserve currency). Second, the pressure to preventively accumulate costly but idle international reserves further embedded a macroeconomic deflationary bias, hampering economic development more generally.

"There is a contrast between the growing trade and financial imbalances impacting heavily developing countries, and the efforts of advanced economies that seek to safeguard their own financing needs."

When UNCTAD was created in 1964, it coordinated the appeals of developing countries for a supplementary financing mechanism adapted to their liquidity needs and development aspirations. A central point of contestation has been the contrast between growing trade and related financial imbalances impacting heavily developing countries, and the efforts of advanced economies that seek to safeguard their own financing needs.

Earning foreign exchange through exports requires access to developed country markets and policy space at the national level to support the creation of competitive industries. As chapter II shows, both these conditions are increasingly difficult to meet in the current framework of international trade and finance.

Unequal gains from trade, market concentration and growing debt servicing burdens endanger many developing countries' social and financial sustainability. A balanced policy response at the multilateral level should include reforms to the governance ecosystem (chapter V), and revisions to existing trade agreements to create more ample policy space for countries to redesign their production, consumption and trading profiles to meet contemporary global challenges.

As the following two chapters show, many existing multilateral approaches to financial governance – including the principles of managing sovereign debt, financing the green transition and costs of the climate crisis, as well as crisis resolution mechanisms – urgently need to be recalibrated to address the new realities of the global political economy. A multitude of complex shocks have arisen since 2020 and have only been addressed in an ad hoc manner. As more stress is bound to arise and as crises become more complex, policy tools and coordination mechanisms must be adapted to address these shifts at a systemic level.

UNCTAD advocates for an integrated approach built on pragmatic sets of policy proposals to make economic governance more inclusive, international finance more stable and international markets more accessible and less volatile. In parallel, efforts have been directed to improving the response of the international community to economic shocks, with particular attention to the problem of growing debt.

UNCTAD understands the interdependence of finance, trade and development; the institution's insistence on structural transformation has put it ahead of the curve (table IV.1). Nevertheless, it is increasingly clear that a truly systemic approach means considering the relationship between trade and finance and incorporating the urgent challenges stemming from environmental shocks and sustainability, notably climate and biodiversity challenges, as well as geopolitical risks (IPCC, 2022; IPBES, 2019).

The work of the United Nations Global Crisis Response Group, set up in the aftermath of the start of the war in Ukraine, as well as the Black Sea Initiative, are recent examples of practical implementation of systemic thinking by UNCTAD. As this Report goes to press, it is becoming apparent that the scope of economic, social, environmental and humanitarian crises has expanded dramatically. To ensure that international governance can address these interrelated challenges and keep the demands of developing countries at its centre, the existing elements of the international financial architecture must be reformed. This must also be complemented by new institutional mechanisms and policies, as recently stressed by the United Nations Secretary-General (United Nations, 2023).

Enabling policy space for green industrial transformation

Successful structural transformations have generally relied on proactive government policies. At the same time, the instruments and strategies that brought about developmental successes in the 1970s and 1990s need to be adjusted to navigate today's priorities. These include the global green transformation and biotech revolution, the geonomics of global value chains, as well as the impact of the geopolitical-related economic restrictions by the major economies (Vidigal and Schill, 2021; Hrynkiv, 2022).

In its long-standing calls for strategies of a developmental State and more recently, a green developmental State (*Trade and Development Report 2021*), UNCTAD has stressed that structural transformation requires significant productive investment. It also requires imports of capital goods and equipment embedded with foreign technologies which will allow efficiency gains and promote productivity. This means that, in an economy where investment is growing both in absolute terms and as a share of GDP, such imports will also need to grow faster than GDP. The financing of these imports will seriously constrain structural transformation unless additional export revenue can be obtained.

The developmental State has been a strategic political choice of countries aiming to compete in the global economy, but this has largely been in the form of export targets and attracting FDI. In today's context of growing economic and non-economic uncertainties, policymakers need to be able to use a range of capital account management measures to insulate the domestic financial system from fluctuations in the global financial cycle and financial instability (Mayer, 2021). In particular, controls on short-term capital flows (bonds, equity, money market and derivatives) can help stabilize exchange rate developments while fending off speculative attacks on the domestic currency. These instruments can also have macroprudential functions in limiting capital surges and sudden stops, while more longer-term flows (FDI, real estate and credit) may remain less regulated, to benefit economic growth (Rademacher, 2023).

Table IV.1 The UNCTAD vision for reforming the international financial architecture

UNCTAD lens for financial governance challenges (and landmark policy proposals)	United Nations Secretary-General actions as formulated in the Common Agenda Policy Brief on Reforms to the International Financial Architecture
General	A1: Transform the governance of international financial institutions.
	A2: Create a representative apex body to systematically enhance coherence of the international system.
Liquidity	A10: Strengthen liquidity provision and widen the financial safety net.
1965: Universal SDR allocations with aid link;	
1971: Creation of the Group of 24.	A11: Address capital market volatility.
Investment	A5: Massively increase development lending and improve terms of lending.
1964: Multilateral interest equalization fund (Horowitz Proposal);	
1965: Universal SDR allocation with aid link;	A6: Change the business models of multilateral development banks and other public development banks to focus on the impact of Sustainable Development Goals; more effectively leverage private finance for Sustainable Development Goal impact.
1970: Official development assistance target of 0.7 per cent of gross domestic product;	
1971: Definition of least developed countries;	A7: Massively increase climate finance, while ensuring additionality.
2014: Support for Southern-led multilateral development banks (MDBs).	A8: More effectively use the system of development banks to increase lending and Sustainable Development Goal impact.
	A9: Ensure that the poorest can continue to benefit from the multilateral development bank system.
Debt	A3: Reduce debt risks and enhance sovereign debt markets to support Sustainable Development Goals.
1983: Creation of Debt Management and Financial Analysis System (DMFAS);	
2014–2015: United Nations General Assembly resolutions creating the Ad Hoc Committee on Sovereign Debt Restructuring, definition of basic principles.	A4: Enhance debt crisis resolution through a two-step process: A debt workout mechanism to support the common framework and, in the medium term, a sovereign debt authority.
Finance–corporate nexus	A12: Strengthen regulation and supervision of bank and non-bank financial institutions to better manage risks and reign-in excessive leverage.
1967: United Nations General Assembly resolution creating the Ad Hoc Group of Experts on International Cooperation in Tax Matters;	
2004: Upgrade into a Committee;	A13: Make businesses more sustainable and reduce greenwashing.
1975–1993: Creation of the Centre for Transnational Corporations.	A14: Strengthen global financial integrity standards.
	A15: Strengthen global tax norms to address digitalization and globalization through an inclusive process in ways that meet the needs and capacities of developing countries and other stakeholders.
	A16: Improve pillar two of the proposal by the OECD/Group of 20 inclusive framework on base erosion and profit shifting to reduce wasteful tax incentives, while better incentivizing taxation in source countries.
	A17: Create global tax transparency and information-sharing frameworks that benefit all countries.

Source: UNCTAD based on United Nations (2023), which contains more detailed lists of subactions.

Note: Blue shading indicates the action and/or subactions that deal with the transversal challenge of climate and environmental sustainability.

IV

Ultimately, the goals of today's developmentalism derive from the global agenda of decarbonizing economic activity and international efforts to tackle climate change. Therefore, linking nationally devised and implemented strategies is part of a much larger international climate action project. National strategies will need to reference their contribution to wider international endeavours on low-carbon development, such as the Paris Agreement (chapter VI).

> *"The goals of developmentalism derive from the global agenda of decarbonizing economic activity and international efforts to tackle climate change. Linking nationally devised strategies is part of a much larger international climate action project."*

In this context, conventional approaches to financial de-risking by the State need to be recalibrated for the age of climate crises (box IV.1). For instance, de-risking often implies a constraint on the very policy instruments that a green developmental State would apply. Regulatory de-risking can make it more difficult to maintain vertically integrated, State-owned energy utilities, to redirect subsidies from fossil fuel to renewable energy providers, such as via feed-in tariffs, or ensure guaranteed grid access for renewable energy sources. At the same time, financial de-risking tends to target green-oriented grants, tax relief, or debt-based instruments, thus creating a bias towards portfolio flows that can hamper macroeconomic and financial stability (Gabor, 2021). Chapter VI offers a detailed look at pathways for a sustainable transition away from fossil fuel dependence and public policy tools to accompany the divestment effort.

Transitioning to renewable energies and embracing the circular economy could boost industrialization in many developing economies. By decoupling economic activities and natural resources, activities related to the circular economy, or to producing renewable energy could generate business opportunities for small firms and rural areas. This would not only diversify economic production. It would also lessen the reliance on a narrow range of primary commodities, contributing to developing countries enjoying broader tax bases. Furthermore, decoupling could stimulate domestic resource mobilization as a source of development finance. These activities could help alleviate countries' balance of payments constraints. Relying on domestically produced energy and food could reduce the need to import virgin raw materials. This could free up limited foreign exchange to instead import capital goods that contribute to industrialization and economic advancement.

Box IV.1 The Horowitz Proposal for a multilateral interest equalization fund: Fit for the green transition?

Consideration of multilateral development finance within UNCTAD has centred on two themes. First, consistently strong support for the role of multilateral development finance in the overall provision of development finance. Second, proposals to reform institutional lending programmes and policies, in particular proposals that use the skill and prestige of those institutions to facilitate other flows, through the use of guarantees or by acting as intermediaries by borrowing and on-lending.

At UNCTAD I in 1964, discussions revolved around setting up mechanisms with the involvement of multilateral financial institutions. This would expand the use of private capital market finance. Among these ideas, Horowitz's proposal to create a multilateral interest equalization fund caught attention and was further explored by the members of the Committee on Invisibles and Financing related to Trade (CIFT) at UNCTAD II in 1968. This plan, generally known as the Horowitz Proposal[a] would have allowed an international institution to borrow funds in financial markets on commercial terms and relend these funds to developing countries at lower rates of interest and with longer maturities. The interest subsidies were to be covered by contributions from developed countries and from the World Bank.

While there was no concrete follow up to this proposal, in 1975 the World Bank did establish a scheme for interest subsidization through its "Third Window" Interest Subsidy Fund. The Conference, at its fifth session in 1979, recommended that early consideration be given to a proposal for establishing a long-term facility in the World Bank to finance purchases of capital goods by developing countries. In the early 1980s, due to the stagnation and subsequent collapse of developing country access to capital markets, attention turned once again to intermediation as a means of improving access and greater use of private direct investment.

To some extent, Horowitz's approach to private finance mobilization appears as a forerunner of contemporary de-risking, which dominates policy discussions on climate finance. Yet, even though the Horowitz Proposal would represent a significant improvement over the current situation, the logic of de-risking itself (and hence any mechanism inspired by it) increasingly appears as much too weak to address a challenge such as timely and adequate climate finance (Braun and Gabor, 2023).

Source: Based on UNCTAD (1984).

[a] The basic proposal was made to the first session of the Conference in 1964 by David Horowitz, at the time, Governor of the Bank of Israel and Head of Delegation of Israel to the Conference (E/CONF.46/C.3/2).

These aspirational international aspects of climate adaptation policies call for a new multilateralism. Such a paradigm would provide the global public good needed to deliver shared prosperity and a healthy planet. It would also ensure that no nation could pursue economic and environmental goals that were to the detriment of other nations. However, if these two conditions are absent, developing countries will need to rely on external financial inflows – private or public — for their foreign exchange and liquidity needs.

Developments in short-term liquidity provision

As soon as it was created, UNCTAD coordinated the appeals of developing countries for a supplementary financing mechanism adapted to their liquidity needs and development aspirations. While growing trade and related financial imbalances mostly impacted developing countries, efforts of the most advanced economies only addressed their own financing needs. This is reflected in efforts by the Group of 10 in 1962 to establish a General Arrangement to Borrow, which marginally increased the contributions of richer countries in their own currencies to IMF capital without changing the quotas or drawing rights of poorer countries (Toye, 2014). Later, the Group of 10 introduced a new source of liquidity, through the creation of SDRs, to supplement the role of the dollar.

Building on the expertise of the Bellagio Group[1] which had already convened in preparation of the first UNCTAD conference in Geneva, UNCTAD drafted a plan (UNCTAD, 1965) for augmenting the lending capacity of Bretton Woods institutions by extending the allocation of SDR on a universal basis. UNCTAD envisioned an "aid link" (Toye and Toye, 2004), i.e. a link between a universal SDR allocation by IMF and an automatic provision to the World Bank for development lending and investment (Orange-Leroy, 2023).

With the creation of special drawing rights in 1969 and with an initial general allocation of SDR $9 billion, IMF acknowledged the validity of the UNCTAD argument to support universal allocation, but the amount remained modest. It was further allocated in proportion with IMF quotas favouring developed countries. As IMF rejected the UNCTAD aid link concept, the development potential of special drawing rights was weakened.

Following the decision of the United States to suspend dollar gold-convertibility in 1971, pre-existing challenges of deteriorating terms of trade and volatile commodity prices were compounded by increased exchange rate

[1] The Bellagio Group was first convened in the 1960s by Professor Fritz Machlup to brainstorm the structure of the Bretton Woods System and what might follow. The group of about 30 economists (which included Charles Kindleberger, Robert Mundell and Robert Triffin) met over several months to construct a proposal for exchange rates and adjustment mechanisms for the international monetary system (see: https://bellagio.mit.edu/).

volatility, which required larger and more regular SDR allocations. However, such moves were resisted by the United States Treasury, strengthened in part by the rise of monetarist economics and like-minded officials in the Bretton Woods institutions. The result was a strengthening of stricter conditionalities for lending to developing countries, and active promotion of the role of private financial actors as the main providers of domestic and cross-border liquidity.

During the 1970s, the World Bank progressively moved from specific project lending to programme lending. Throughout the 1980s debt crises and until after the 1997 Asian financial crisis, IMF routinely only extended liquidity to deficit developing countries in exchange for domestic implementation of structural adjustment programmes. Such programmes embedded core measures supporting trade and finance liberalization and deregulation, thus penalizing developing countries that implemented industrial policies or capital controls recommended by UNCTAD.

However, as the narrative of the Washington Consensus crumbled with the 2008 financial crisis, many developed countries rediscovered the policy recommendations promoted by UNCTAD to avoid deflation. In addition to coordinated (though short-lived) countercyclical fiscal policies, two IMF allocations totalling $183 billion of special drawing rights soon followed, in 2009.

Similarly, special drawing rights played a positive role during the COVID-19 pandemic, as the largest ever allocation approved on 2 August 2021 tripled the total amount of SDR to $660 billion, sparing the world a full-blown cascade of liquidity crises and unnecessary economic deflation across vulnerable deficit countries. In parallel, IMF also backtracked from its earlier positions on external financial liberalization, supporting the persistent calls of UNCTAD for rehabilitating capital account management techniques, including capital controls, as a legitimate means for addressing exchange rate and financial volatility (IMF, 2013; 2022).

These policy reversals highlight the underleveraged potential of capital account management and SDR allocations for enabling deficit countries to manage and overcome short-term liquidity constraints. Since 2008, strengthened international calls for a GFSN have stressed how SDR allocation and unconditional multilateral lending more generally, along with regional financial arrangements and bilateral swap arrangements, can help vulnerable deficit countries to minimize the need for the costly and deflationary build-up of idle international reserves.

As called for by the United Nations Secretary-General (United Nations, 2023) there is an urgent need to update IMF quota formulas to reflect the changing global landscape and boost the representation of developing countries (see also the subactions A1, A2, A10 and A11 listed in table IV.1). There is also a need to de-link access to resources from quotas and conditionalities and determine their allocation based on need and vulnerabilities. Developing countries should be able to rely on the full capital account management toolbox and proactive intervention to reduce exposure to capital flows volatility. Crucially, SDR allocations should be automated and countercyclical. Although still contentious, allocating SDRs, coupled with the aid link envisioned by UNCTAD (1965) as a means to finance longer-term development and sustainability challenges, remains technically possible.

C. HOW TO DELIVER DEVELOPMENT FINANCE? HISTORICAL APPROACHES AND CONTEMPORARY TRENDS

In the area of development finance, the UNCTAD approach has historically focused on the need to recognize and respond to the special financing needs of developing countries and the policies that can enable growth, financial sustainability and long-term, climate-resilient development goals.

UNCTAD efforts to advocate for the special financing needs of developing countries resulted in the United Nations General Assembly adopting a resolution setting the ODA target for donor nations at 0.7 per cent of gross national income (United Nations General Assembly, 1970). Developed countries have acknowledged this target but, with a small number of exceptions, consistently failed to meet it over the past 50 years.

Much of the policy debate on the optimal balance of public and private funding has focused on overcoming the primary role assigned to private investors to invest in infrastructure and other development finance. This has opened up discussions of "de-risking" investment, a term that applies to securitized infrastructure bundles and to the investment environment. De-risking involves a greater scope for a variety of public guarantees, insurance programmes and other mechanisms that shift risk from the private to the public sector, often in ways that are non-transparent and compromise public accountability (Alexander and Rowden, 2018).

One widespread assumption about development finance is that leverage and crowding-in can deliver new and heretofore untapped pools of private investment, especially when it comes to financing social and economic infrastructure. However, as chapter VI shows, there is little empirical evidence to support arguments around the vast developmental potential of private financial flows and the use of public resources to leverage and crowd-in private investment. Empirical evidence suggests that domestic public finance has long played a central role in financing infrastructure. This is because infrastructure has a long maturity profile and is not a commercially attractive investment for private investors; it offers high risks and relatively low economic returns, especially in relation to opportunities in other areas (Griffiths and Romero, 2018).

Drawing on the seminal work of Albert Hirschman, UNCTAD has argued that if private finance has a role to play in supporting the development strategy, it is to be crowded-in as part of an integrated and thoughtful development pathway that involves significant public investment in infrastructure and that generates the backward and forward linkages necessary for structural transformation.

When the Group of 20 was created in the wake of the 2008 global financial crisis, promises were made about the reform of the international financial architecture, starting with IMF quotas. However, results were disappointing. In 2014, Brazil, China, India, the Russian Federation and South Africa established the BRICS New Development Bank and, in the same year, China gave the regional impulse for the Asian Infrastructure Development Bank. Both initiatives signalled that Bretton Woods institutions were failing to respond to the needs of developing countries and to adapt to evolving economic and geopolitical realities, not to mention the daunting environmental challenges.

In principle, sources of long-term financing include the use of hybrid capital, which allow MDBs to lend more without impacting their triple-A credit ratings, as these securities are treated as "equity" by credit rating agencies. However, being subordinated in the capital structure, MDBs pay significantly more for hybrid bonds than for conventional funding (Khadbai, 2023). Critics claim that financial conditions imposed by lenders can keep debt burdens heavy and cut into spending on development. According to recent reports, potential investors in hybrid bonds from the African Development Bank asked for a spread of 150–200 basis points over the Bank's usual cost of funding, aligning with the rates commercial banks and corporates usually pay for hybrid securities (ibid).

IV

It is against this record that the rise of Chinese development banks and the participation of China in international lending has reshaped the topography of development finance. Newly created institutions offered financing to countries that needed to mobilize capital for infrastructure projects and provided innovative financing models for developing countries to invest in their ports, roads and power grids. And while Chinese financial support tended to be relatively limited in the early stages, it has increased over the years.

Chinese development finance takes the forms of grants, interest-free loans and concessional loans. Data gathered in documents from the State Council Information Office of the People's Republic of China (2011, 2014 and 2021) suggests that the proportion of interest-free loans has diminished in favour of grants and concessional loans, with each type representing almost half of the total foreign aid by China. In terms of geography, two recipient regions stand out, with developing countries in Africa (44 per cent) and Asia (36 per cent) receiving the bulk of Chinese support in the 2013–2018 period. Data also suggests that Chinese development lending expanded in the first 15 years of the twenty-first century, peaking around 2016.

The impact of these capital injections and competition among lenders at the international, regional, subregional, and national institutions in the Global South and East on the trajectory of the green transition remains unclear. As infrastructure finance increasingly becomes a tool in global diplomacy, it may mean that environmental, social and transparency standards are lowered, while urgent financing needs of sustainable development and climate crises are overlooked (Alexander and Rowden, 2018). Chapter VI discusses the current state, challenges and opportunities for a climate-aligned system of financial governance in detail.

D. SOLVENCY, SOVEREIGN DEBT RELIEF AND RESTRUCTURING: EVOLVING CHALLENGES AND ONGOING ADVOCACY

As with the liquidity and investment challenges, UNCTAD has always recognized that there is an intimate connection between debt management, debt sustainability and the evolution of the external environment (*Trade and Development Report 1985*). In the three decades after 1945, although developing countries experienced recurrent liquidity and investment challenges, these rarely triggered sovereign debt crises. This meant that sovereign solvency was a less pressing issue when UNCTAD was created in 1964. Yet even in the early years, debt servicing was a pressing concern for developing economies.

Following the collapse of the fixed exchange rate regime in 1971–1973 and repeated oil shocks of the 1970s, developing countries were confronted with rising exchange rate and commodity price volatility, exacerbating their economic vulnerability and liquidity needs. Since 1978, UNCTAD proposals to address these issues informed the institution's position in the Paris Club (box IV.2).

In the early 1980s, the Federal Reserve of the United States embarked on aggressive interest rate hikes to stem domestic inflation. However, there was no consideration for international spillover effects, namely that numerous indebted developing countries were unable to refinance their debt at affordable rates. This transformed liquidity challenges into fully fledged and deeply damaging sovereign debt crises.

Lacking a systemic analytical framework for promoting a constructive multilateral vision, the Bretton Woods institutions treated emerging debt problems as a distinct problem specific to each debtor country. Accordingly, the remedies prescribed focused on debt rescheduling and domestic adjustment, irrespective of the costs in terms of forgone output, and thus, debt servicing capacity itself (UNCTAD, 2012a). Forced to accept the conditionalities of IMF structural adjustment programmes, developing countries agreed to adopt more flexible exchange rate regimes, to accept austerity measures, privatize public services and sell off public assets to domestic and foreign investors.

Box IV.2 UNCTAD and the Paris Club: 40 years of cooperation

Since 1978, representatives of the UNCTAD Secretary-General have participated in more than 260 Paris Club debt reorganizations for more than 60 countries. This is in accordance with resolutions 165 (S-IX) and 222 (XXI) of the UNCTAD Trade and Development Board. At these meetings, UNCTAD presents its view on the debtor country's economic prospects and expresses its perspective regarding terms of debt restructuring conducive to long-term sustainable development.

The participation of UNCTAD in Paris Club meetings has given the institution a unique opportunity to closely follow the evolving practices of Paris Club creditors – mostly from OECD member countries. The observer status of UNCTAD in Paris Club meetings and its work with debtor countries led the institution to realize that, for some developing countries, debt data recording issues can be a serious concern when devising their debt renegotiation strategy. This led to the creation of the DMFAS Programme which is currently in use in more than 80 institutions in 60 countries.

DMFAS advocated for a statutory process of sovereign debt restructuring modelled, in part, on chapter 11 of the United States bankruptcy code (*Trade and Development Report 1986*). Observing that the process of action and reaction by individual creditors and debtors is likely to be disorderly, UNCTAD proposed that a measure of debt or debt-service forgiveness must be part of the normal menu of financial techniques (*Trade and Development Report 1987*).

UNCTAD further advocated to establish an international debt facility (*Trade and Development Report 1988*), stressing that the failure to assign to any international financial agency the role of "honest broker" left the level of debt reduction to be shaped by the balance of negotiating strength rather than by objective needs (*Trade and Development Report 1990*).

The repeated nature of countries facing Paris Club debt rescheduling during the 1980s and 1990s highlighted the inadequacies of the then prevailing approach to restructuring developing country debt, and to LDCs in particular.

UNCTAD was one of the early proponents of the need for a new framework for dealing with the debt of the poorest countries. The institution supported the proposal for the HIPC Initiative launched in 1996 at the Group of Seven summit in Lyon, France. In the late 1990s, UNCTAD observed that the process for countries to benefit from the Initiative was lengthy and characterized by a complexity that burdened countries' already weak institutions. UNCTAD pushed for further enhancements to the Initiative, which led to the 1999 and 2001 reforms to eligibility thresholds and topping-up procedures.

The Paris Forum, which is jointly organized by the Paris Club and the Group of 20, held its first meeting in 2013. This is a very different gathering to a Paris Club debt rescheduling. Its main aim is to provide a discussion platform among creditors, debtors and international organizations regarding the main issues in the international financial environment and their impact on developing countries. UNCTAD began participating in these meetings in 2015 and has made regular contributions to discussions.

Source: UNCTAD.

IV

What ensued was a "lost decade" of deflation and disrupted development across many countries in the global South. Similar policy prescriptions led to comparable results in the 1990s and early 2000s in the wake of the emerging market financial crises of 1997–1998. In response, and to provide assistance to indebted developing countries, UNCTAD established DMFAS.

In the wake of the 1989 Brady Plan implemented by United States authorities, Bretton Woods institutions finally made a more concerted move to restructure unsustainable debts, along the lines proposed earlier by UNCTAD. This took the form of the HIPC Initiative adopted in 1996. Despite being plagued by slowness and a familiar set of policy conditionalities, the Initiative did allow a number of countries to re-enter international capital markets just as economic growth across the global South began to accelerate.

Following the Asian financial crisis, in 2002, IMF proposed a Sovereign Debt Restructuring Mechanism to compel all commercial creditors to agree on debt restructuring, although this was resisted by key members of the IMF Board. Instead, Group of Eight countries supported the Multilateral Debt Relief Initiative in 2005, a slight improvement on the HIPC Initiative.

With interest rates in advanced economies close to zero or negative during the decade following the 2008 global financial crisis, public as well as private debt soon soared in developing countries. This was especially acute in those that had opened up externally, i.e. to emerging and frontier markets, making them vulnerable to changes in the external environment.

Anticipating a repeat of the 1980s lost decade in the event of an unforeseen external shock, UNCTAD continued pushing for a more comprehensive approach to debt restructuring. In 2006 the institution embarked on an extensive consultative exercise with multiple stakeholders to design a set of principles for responsible lending and borrowing. The *Principles on Promoting Responsible Sovereign Lending and Borrowing* were launched in 2010 with a roadmap to push towards a sovereign debt workout mechanism (*Trade and Development Report 2015*). Based on resolution 69/247 approved in December 2014, the United Nations General Assembly established an Ad Hoc Committee on Sovereign Debt Restructuring Processes, which defined a set of basic principles on responsible sovereign lending and borrowing in 2015 (resolution 69/319). This built on the work of UNCTAD (2012b). The reluctance of creditor countries to engage with these discussions denied a consensus and institutional embodiment.

When the COVID-19 pandemic hit, sovereign debt challenges rapidly multiplied. In 2020, the Group of 20 and Paris Club countries acted quickly to implement the Debt Service Suspension Initiative (DSSI) and to develop a Common Framework for debt treatment. Once more, the preferred approach was to address the debt challenge based on a narrow initiative and to target countries on a case-by-case basis.

This piecemeal approach from the Common Framework continues to be dogged by slow procedures, offers too little relief too late and appears unfit to address forthcoming debt challenges. Indeed, a rising number of developing countries with high debt now also face growing climate vulnerabilities. This creates a vicious circle between rising investment requirements for a climate-resilient structural transformation and heavy reliance on increasingly costly debt-financing.

The collision of debt and climate challenges bears a very high risk of abrogating sustainability on both fronts. Breaking this vicious circle demands an ambitious multilateral policy agenda focused not only on scaling-up public-led and affordable development finance but also on reforming the approach of multilateral institutions to prevent and manage sovereign debt crises (UNCTAD, 2022). In this regard, the outcome of the 2023 Paris Summit for a New Global Financing Pact proved disappointing. Chapter V addresses the implications of some of these issues for the global ecosystem of debt governance.

E. CONCLUSION

The systemic challenges of the international financial architecture and balance of payments constraints tend to push developing countries towards accumulating external debt and/or financial liberalization, with the attendant exposure to the vagaries of the global financial cycle. Existing conditions of global financial governance reforms reinforce these problems. Holdings of borrowed reserves imply a negative resource transfer, while access to the global financial safety net is uneven and made more difficult for those most in need.

To address the systemic deficiencies of the international financial architecture, UNCTAD has advocated that:

(a)   Capital controls should be seen as part of a regular toolkit of pragmatic financial policy;

(b)   De-risking with a view to extensively using private capital for development finance is a misguided approach and has not delivered the anticipated results;

(c)   The way forward is to strengthen public sources of development finance, including official development assistance, SDRs (through more frequent ordinary issues, recycling of unused SDRs, and perhaps an SDR-aid link; also to underline the potential fiscal use of SDRs);

(d)   Multilateral Development Banks must be recapitalized, and their capital use reformed.

At the same time, reforms of monetary and financial policies and principles are not sufficient to deliver the structural support to mobilize the resources required in developing countries today. As chapters II and III of this Report show, market concentration, profiteering and increased asymmetries in the gains from trade are strongly linked to financialization of the global business and international corporate arbitrage.

In this light, redirecting the value-creating activities of multinational enterprises into the host economies of developing countries needs to be on policymakers' agendas. Taxing the activities of multinational enterprises is an important source of development finance. Until very recently, international initiatives around global taxation have been led by OECD, which blacklisted non-cooperative tax havens in 2009 and initiated the Base Erosion and Profit Shifting (BEPS) initiative in 2013. This programme developed a new global tax standard and minimum corporate tax rate of 15 per cent, starting in 2024.

While UNCTAD has supported efforts to curb illicit financial flows and tax avoidance, it has stressed the greater potential of unitary taxation to determine the geographical origin of value added, and its fair apportionment in an era of globalization and digitalization. Much like UNCTAD had recommended reviewing and amending existing trade and investment agreements that constrain the policy space of developing countries, the institution also called for a renegotiation of bilateral tax treaties to integrate rules reducing profit shifting, e.g. general and specific anti-avoidance rules, rules for controlled foreign corporations, for limiting interest deductions and for taxing capital gains arising from indirect transfers, etc. (*Trade and Development Reports 2014* and *2019*).

Such concerns should be addressed systematically within the international financial architecture, and it is notable that at present, no dedicated organization analyses the specific concerns of taxation/fiscal policy space in developing countries. In this respect, the United Nations Tax Cooperation Convention noted on by the United Nations General Assembly in November 2023 is a significant step towards systemic reform of the finance–corporate nexus led by developing countries. However, this is only the beginning of a long journey towards meaningful and effective change.

IV

REFERENCES

Alexander N and Rowden R (2018). Whither Democratization and Sustainability? A Critique of Key G20 Proposals to Further Expand the Role of Private Investment in Development. Heinrich Böll Stiftung North America. Washington, D.C.

Braun and Gabor (2023). Green macrofinancial regimes. Working paper. Open Society Foundation. 23 October.

China, State Council Information Office (2011). China's Foreign Aid. Available at http://www.china.org.cn/government/whitepaper/node_7116362.htm (accessed 7 November 2023)

China, State Council Information Office (2014). China's Foreign Aid. Available at https://english.www.gov.cn/archive/white_paper/2014/08/23/content_281474982986592.htm (accessed 7 November 2023)

China, State Council Information Office (2021). China's Foreign Aid. Available at http://english.scio.gov.cn/whitepapers/2021-01/10/content_77099782_4.htm (accessed 7 November 2023)

Grabel I (2018). *When Things Don't Fall Apart. Global Governance and Developmental Finance in an Age of Productive Incoherence*. Cambridge, MA. MIT Press.

Griffiths J and Romero MJ (2018). Three compelling reasons why the G20's plan for an infrastructure asset class is fundamentally flawed. European Network on Debt and Development. Brussels.

Hrynkiv O (2022. Export controls and securitization of economic policy: Comparative analysis of the practice of the United States, the European Union, China, and Russia. *Journal of World Trade*. 56(4)633–656.

IMF (2013). *The IMF's Institutional View on Capital Flows in Practice*. Washington, D.C.

IMF (2022). *Review of The Institutional View on The Liberalization and Management of Capital Flows*. Washington, D.C.

IPBES (2019). *Global Assessment Report on Biodiversity and Ecosystem Services of the Intergovernmental Science-Policy Platform on Biodiversity and Ecosystem Services*. IPBES secretariat. Bonn.

IPCC (2022). *Climate Change 2022: Mitigation of Climate Change. Contribution of Working Group III to the Sixth Assessment Report of the Intergovernmental Panel on Climate Change*. Cambridge University Press.

Keysser L and Lenzen M (2021). 1.5°C degrowth scenarios suggest the need for new mitigation pathways. *Nature Communications*. 12.

Khadbai B (2023). MDBs should be sensitive about the price of hybrid capital. Official Monetary and Financial Institutions Forum (OMFIF).

Kregel J (2018). The clearing union principle as the basis for regional financial arrangements in developing countries. In: UNCTAD, eds. *Debt Vulnerabilities in Developing Countries: A New Debt Trap? Volume II: Policy Options and Tools*. United Nations. New York and Geneva.

Martin J (2023). *The Meddlers. Sovereignty, Empire, and the Birth of Global Economic Governance*. Harvard University Press. Cambridge, MA.

Mayer J (2021). The "exorbitant privilege" and "exorbitant duty" of the United States in the international monetary system: Implications for developing countries. *Review of World Economics*. 157:927–964.

Millward-Hopkins J and Oswald Y (2023). Reducing global inequality to secure human wellbeing and climate safety: a modelling study. *The Lancet Planetary Health*. 7(2):e147–e154.

Orange-Leroy R (2023). UNCTAD experts as an intellectual basis for developing countries' involvement in the reform of the international monetary system (1965-1967). Paper presented at the Summer Institute of the Center for the History of Political Economy. Duke University. 19–22 June.

Picciotto S (2012). *Towards Unitary Taxation of Transnational Corporations*. Tax Justice Network.

Prebisch R (1950). *The Economic Development of Latin America and its Principal Problems.* Economic Commission for Latin America and the Caribbean and United Nations Department of Economic Affairs. New York.

Prebisch R (1964). *Towards a New Trade Policy for Development: Report by the Secretary-General of UNCTAD.* United Nations, New York.

Rademacher I (2023). Central bank independence, fiscal policy, and the varieties of capital control liberalisation, paper presented at the Council for European Studies conference in Reykjavik, June 2023.

Singer HW (1949). Economic development in underdeveloped countries. *Social Research: An International Quarterly.* 16(1):1–11.

Thirlwall A (1979). The balance of payments constraint as an explanation of international growth rate differences. *Banca Nazionale del Lavoro Quarterly Review.* 32(128):45–53.

Toye J (2014). *UNCTAD at 50: A Short History.* United Nations. Geneva.

Toye J and Toye R (2004). *The UN and Global Political Economy: Trade, Finance, and Development.* Indiana University Press. Bloomington.

UNCTAD (1965). *International Monetary Issues and the Developing Countries. Report of the Group of Experts.* TD/B/32. New York and Geneva.

UNCTAD (1985). *Trade and Development Report 1985.* (United Nations publication, Sales No. E.85.II.D.16, New York and Geneva).

UNCTAD (1986). *Trade and Development Report 1986.* (United Nations publication, Sales No. E.86.II.D.5, New York and Geneva).

UNCTAD (1987). *Trade and Development Report 1987.* (United Nations publication, Sales No. E.87.II.D.7, New York and Geneva).

UNCTAD (1988). *Trade and Development Report 1988.* (United Nations publication, Sales No. E.88.II.D.8, New York and Geneva).

UNCTAD (1990). *Trade and Development Report 1990.* (United Nations publication, Sales No. E.90.II.D.6, New York and Geneva).

UNCTAD (1996). *Trade and Development Report 1996.* (United Nations publication, Sales No. E.96.II.D.6, New York and Geneva).

UNCTAD (1997). *Trade and Development Report 1997.* (United Nations publication, Sales No. E.97.II.D.8, New York and Geneva).

UNCTAD (2005). *Beyond Conventional Wisdom in Development Policy: An Intellectual History of UNCTAD 1964–2004.* (United Nations publication, Sales No. E.04.II.D.39, New York and Geneva).

UNCTAD (2008). *Trade and Development Report 2008 – Commodity Prices, Capital Flows and the Financing of Investment.* (United Nations publication, Sales No. E.08.II.D.21, New York and Geneva).

UNCTAD (2012a). *Trade and Development Report, 1981–2011: Three Decades of Thinking.* Chapter IV. (United Nations publication, Sales No. E.12.2.D.5, New York and Geneva).

UNCTAD (2012b). *Principles on Promoting Responsible Sovereign Lending and Borrowing.* Geneva.

UNCTAD (2014). *Trade and Development Report 2014: Global Governance and Policy Space for Development.* (United Nations publication, Sales No. E.14.II.D.4, New York and Geneva).

UNCTAD (2015). *Trade and Development Report 2015: Making the International Financial Architecture Work for Development.* Chapter V. (United Nations publication, Sales No. E.15.II.D.4, New York and Geneva).

UNCTAD (2017). *Trade and Development Report 2017: Beyond Austerity – Towards a Global New Deal.* (United Nations publication, Sales No. E.17.II.D.5, New York and Geneva).

IV

UNCTAD (2019). *Trade and Development Report 2019: Financing a Global Green New Deal*. (United Nations publication, Sales No. E.19.II.D.15, New York and Geneva).

UNCTAD (2022). Tackling debt and climate challenges in tandem: A policy agenda. Policy Brief No. 104. Geneva

United Nations (2023). Our Common Agenda – Reforms to the International Financial Architecture. Policy Brief No. 6. New York.

United Nations General Assembly (1970). *Resolution adopted by the General Assembly on 19 September 1970*. (A/RES/2626)(XXV).

United Nations General Assembly (2014). *Resolution adopted by the General Assembly on 29 December 2014*. (A/RES/69/283).

United Nations General Assembly (2015). *Resolution adopted by the General Assembly on 10 September 2015*. (A/RES/69/319).

Vidigal G and Schill S (2021). International economic law and the securitization of policy objectives: Risks of a Schmittean exception. *Legal Issues of Economic Integration*. 48(2):109–118.

Wiedmann T, Lenzen M, Keysser LT and Steinberger JK (2020). Scientists' warning on affluence. *Nature Communications*. 11(1):3107.

Chapter V

Realigning the Global Debt
Architecture to Work
for Developing Countries

Towards a Development-Centred Debt Ecosystem

The aftermath of the global pandemic, marked by successive crises, has underscored the inequalities entrenched in the global financial system. This situation presents a compelling case for a paradigm shift in approaches to sovereign debt workouts. The traditional narrative attributing developing countries' indebtedness to their own mismanagement is losing ground, prompting a reassessment of how nations navigate the complexities of sovereign debt.

The current hierarchical structure of the international financial system is increasingly out of sync with development priorities and marked by resource asymmetries between borrowers and lenders. This, coupled with the vast financing gap for climate-related Sustainable Development Goals, forces many countries to take on more debt, exacerbating the challenges in mitigating climate events and amplifying the burden on developing nations.

Added to this, the continuous servicing of barely affordable debt drains resources from development. Despite more urgent needs provoked by the climate crisis, responses to sovereign debt challenges have been slow and insufficient, emphasizing the pressing need for systemic reform.

To change this dysfunctional debt architecture, a new, development-centred ecosystem is needed. This requires a comprehensive re-evaluation of factors that contribute to unsustainable sovereign debt such as climate change, demographics, health, global economic shifts, rising interest rates, geopolitical realignments, political instability, and the implications of sovereign debt on industrial policies in debtor States. New creative thinking needs to be developed along the entire sovereign debt life cycle. Such a renewed pathway can deliver a more equitable and resilient global financial landscape.

Specific pragmatic policy actions are:

- Increase concessional finance through capitalization of multilateral and regional banks, and issuance of special drawing rights.

- Enhance transparency in financing terms and conditions, using the digitalization of loan contracts to improve accuracy.

- Revise the UNCTAD *Principles for Responsible Sovereign Lending and Borrowing* to motivate and underpin the importance of guiding principles throughout the stages of sovereign debt acquisition.

- Improve debt sustainability analysis and tracking to incorporate consideration of the achievement of the Sustainable Development Goals and empower country negotiators with improved data on their potential for growth and fiscal consolidation.

- Enable countries to utilize innovative financial instruments such as sustainable development bonds and resilience bonds. Develop rules for automatic restructurings and guarantees.

- Enhance resilience during external crises, for example by implementing standstill rules on debtors' obligations in crises, and create a space to enable the avoidance of debt distress.

- Encourage borrowers to share information and experiences, drawing inspiration from private creditor coordination.

- Initiate work on a more robust debt workout mechanism and a global debt authority.

A. INTRODUCTION

The hierarchical and unequal structure of the international financial system has become increasingly disconnected from development priorities. This is reflected in the volatility of external private financing for developing countries, the higher cost of capital faced by these countries, the net negative international financial position of developing countries, the costs and risks associated with being unable to issue an international currency, unequal access to the global financial safety net and the growth of illicit financial outflows. But the clearest measure of the system's shortcomings is arguably its treatment of sovereign debt problems (Panizza, 2022).

If it is true that every crisis reveals an opportunity, the compounding crises since the global pandemic have brought to light inequalities in the global financial system that affect how countries acquire, manage and resolve sovereign debt,[1] especially external debt.

The narrative that unsustainable indebtedness of developing countries is solely a consequence of their own errors has never been less convincing. This awareness creates an opportunity to explore new approaches for bridging the persistent divide between statutory and contractual solutions.

Since the start of the millennium, developing country sovereign debts have piled up faster and become more difficult to manage. By the end of 2022, the stock of developing country sovereign debt had risen to $11.4 trillion, a 15.7 per cent increase since the end of 2019 and the start of the COVID-19 pandemic. The past three years have laid bare that an unforeseen shock can put many countries in a precarious position (chapter II, section D). Added to this, the continual servicing of barely affordable debt places countries under a considerable burden and drains resources from development. On average, at the end of 2022, the debt servicing burden as a share of export revenues for low-income countries was 22.6 per cent and 15.7 per cent for all middle-income and low-income countries.[2] This is clearly unsustainable (United Nations, 2023a).

"The continual servicing of barely affordable debt places countries under a considerable burden and drains resources from development."

The contemporary sovereign debt landscape is characterized by rapid expansion and increasing complexity. It involves a proliferation of public and private lenders, a richer menu of debt instruments and increasing presence of non-resident investors in domestic sovereign markets.

Since the 1990s, changes in the creditor composition of public and publicly guaranteed debt (PPG) have become more diverse, fragmented and complex. These trends were further reinforced after the global financial crisis and subsequent compounding shocks (figure V.1).

As figure V.1 shows, between 2010 and 2021, low-income countries saw a marked shift away from Paris Club bilateral creditors (down to 8 per cent of in 2021 from 13 per cent in 2010) to non-Paris Club official creditors and private creditors. Private creditors' holdings almost doubled to 13 per cent in 2021 (up from 7 per cent in 2010) with bondholders' share reaching 4 per cent (from 0 per cent participation in 2010).

As for lower-middle-income countries, the share of private creditors in PPG debt increased from 24 per cent in 2010 to 41 per cent in 2021, with the bondholders' share doubling from 16 per cent to 32 per cent. This group includes most frontier market economies that lost market access during recent external shocks (see also chapter II, section D). At the same time, the share of official creditors (multilateral and bilateral) decreased from 76 per cent to 59 per cent due to decreases in the shares of multilateral creditors (from 45 per cent to 39 per cent) and mainly, bilateral creditors (from 31 per cent to 20 per cent). For this country group, the decline in the share of non-Paris Club creditors (from 17 per cent to 10 per cent) was greater than in the case of Paris Club creditors (from 14 per cent to 10 per cent).

---

[1] When discussing sovereign debt, the terms "debt workout", "debt restructuring" and "debt resolution" are generally used interchangeably, and can involve suspending debt servicing, extending the maturity of the debt, reducing interest rates or cancelling the debt outright.

[2] Data for 2022 are UNCTAD estimations based on IMF, World Bank and national sources.

Figure V.1 An evolving debtscape: Growing reliance on private credit

Creditor composition of public and publicly guaranteed debt, groups of low-income and lower-middle-income countries, 2010 and 2021

(Percentage)

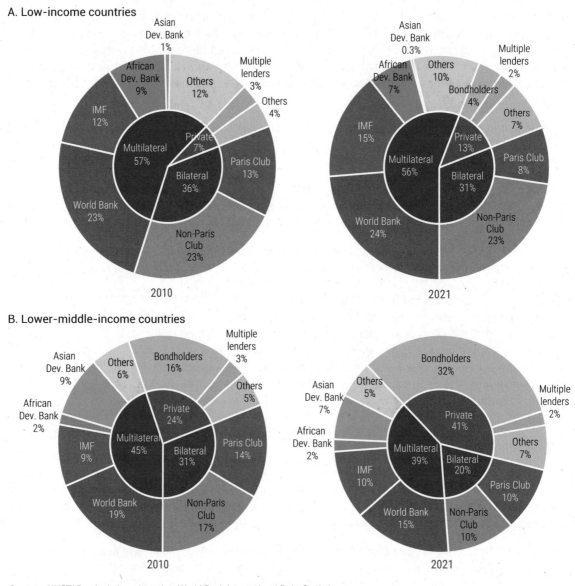

A. Low-income countries

B. Lower-middle-income countries

Source: UNCTAD calculations, based on World Bank International Debt Statistics.

This complexity has made the distinction between external and domestic sovereign debt more difficult to navigate. External sovereign debt is defined here as government (and publicly guaranteed) debt (loans and bonds) issued in international financial markets and denominated and settled in foreign currency.[3]

---

[3] The currency in which debt is denominated and settled affects external sovereign debt sustainability, creating a mismatch between the currency of the debt and the sovereign's tax revenues, which are in the domestic currency. Consequently, such sovereigns are vulnerable to currency depreciations, which are frequent in these countries due to their greater vulnerability to external financial shocks than developed countries (chapter II, section D). Depreciations increase the debt burden in domestic currency and shrink the country's fiscal space. The capacity of States to generate the necessary foreign currency depends on the country's balance of payment performance as influenced by external factors such as capital flow cycles, external demand and the vagaries of international pricing that influence the country's terms of trade (chapter II). The World Bank definition of total external debt shown in the *International Debt Report* publication and *International Debt Statistics* database is the sum of long-term external debt, short-term debt, and IMF credit, representing total debt owed to non-resident creditors and includes that repayable in both foreign and domestic currency.

Up until the 1980s, currency, jurisdiction, and residence criteria tended to coincide as most developing countries' external debt consisted of loans.[4] The lender was a non-resident (international bank) and the loan was issued in a foreign currency under foreign law. Since the early 1990s, the shift in debt instruments from syndicated bank loans to bonds means that bonds issued in domestic currency or under national law may be held by foreign investors. Conversely, residents may hold sovereign bonds issued abroad and denominated in a foreign currency (UNCTAD, 2015). The currency and jurisdiction criteria remain intertwined due to the structural features of the international monetary system; these require a developing country's debt issued in the international financial market to be denominated and settled in international currencies, mainly the dollar, which is at the top of the currency hierarchy (Fritz et al., 2018).

The treatment of sovereign debt challenges has a long history of delivering too little support too late to countries in debt distress. Due to the rise in volumes and complexity, debt restructuring is now even more difficult to coordinate, and the focus has become increasingly short-term. The only new mechanism to help manage debt restructuring in the current environment is the Group of 20 Common Framework for Debt Treatments beyond the Debt Service Suspension Initiative (Common Framework), which was introduced during the COVID-19 pandemic. Its procedures have proved to be laboured, its coverage incomplete and it is insufficiently innovative to be effectual (section B).

"To reform dysfunctional debt architecture, a new ecosystem is needed which places development at its centre."

To reform this dysfunctional debt architecture, a new ecosystem is needed which places development at its centre. A thorough re-evaluation of the factors leading to unsustainable sovereign debt is needed. This would address the contemporary complexities of climate change, demographics and health, along with changes in the global macroeconomic context, a rise in interest rates in developed countries, geo-economic shifts, issues around security and political stability and the implications of sovereign debt regimes on industrial policies in debtor States (Goldmann, 2023). To address these issues, creative thinking is needed regarding the entire life cycle of sovereign debt, including creditor and debtor due diligence; debt transparency; debt sustainability analyses and tracking and debt workout.

"New creative thinking is needed concerning the entire life cycle of sovereign debt, including transparency, debt sustainability tracking, debt resolution and restructuring."

This chapter sets out the sovereign debt life cycle, highlighting current inequalities, inflexibilities and problems as well as possible ways to address these shortcomings. In section B, the regulation of the key system failures is discussed. Section C unpicks the life cycle of sovereign debt and section D presents transformational proposals in four key areas: transparency, sustainability tracking, debt resolution and restructuring. Section E discusses the case for resilience in the debt life cycle and the chapter concludes with recommendations for transformation and the way forward.

B. REGULATING DEBT TO ADDRESS KEY SYSTEM FAILURES?

This section argues that the current situation regarding sovereign debt requires venturing into unexplored or underexplored directions. The opposition between statutory and contractual solutions seems insoluble for addressing contemporary dilemmas. Despite various innovations in sovereign debt over the past decades and

---

[4] The jurisdiction of debt issuance affects debt sustainability since it defines the rules under which disputes between debtors and creditors are negotiated and the process of debt workout. While external sovereign debt is governed by foreign laws and governments are treated as commercial actors in the international financial system, unlike corporations, sovereigns have no protections provided by bankruptcy laws or codes for efficient debt restructuring. Sovereigns are uniquely exposed to hostile creditor legal actions which can significantly delay the debt workout process (Guzman and Stiglitz, 2016; Buchheit et al., 2018; ESCAP, 2023).

even in the wake of COVID-19, changes have typically been incremental in nature, leaving the main pillars of the system unchanged (Bohoslavsky and Goldmann, 2016).

Since 1990, the regulation of sovereign debt has evolved through four distinct phases. This section outlines these different periods, providing a historical context for the current challenges and arguing for a paradigm shift in approaches to sovereign debt workouts (Gelpern, 2006).

The first of the four phases begins at the end of the Cold War. Around 1990, this period ushered in a new era in regulating debt and development. While the debt crisis that had its roots in the 1980s still persisted, the year 1991 marked the return of capital flows to Latin America (Calvo et al., 1992). The end of the East–West confrontation and impending liberalization of the worldwide economy replaced strategic considerations with market factors as the pertinent drivers of sovereign debt debate. To become independent from development aid and gain market access, highly indebted developing countries received more generous, though still insufficient, debt restructurings supported by governments and international organizations, particularly the Paris Club. This began with Brady bonds and culminated in the Heavily Indebted Poor Countries Initiative (HIPC) and Multilateral Debt Relief Initiative (MDRI). Middle-income countries achieved market access privileges and undertook institutional reforms under the guidance of international financial institutions. Still, adverse events such as the Asian financial crisis exposed the vulnerability of the system and prompted the IMF initiative to establish a statutory sovereign debt restructuring mechanism (Krueger, 2002).

A new phase began around 2000 with a shift to the markets. The IMF sovereign debt restructuring mechanism never materialized. Instead, for a variety of reasons, preference was given to market-based restructuring mechanisms, among them the recalibration of United States foreign policy under the Administration of the country's President at the time. Under the so-called contractual approach, debtor States negotiated a workout with their often-dispersed bondholders. Since the Argentine debt crisis beginning in 2001, Governments have sought to facilitate debt workouts through a series of collective action clauses (CACs), particularly majority voting clauses. This strategy has had some success, although its effectiveness has been limited by the long phase-in of new clauses. This is due to the long maturities of outstanding government bonds and the capacity of creditors to purchase a blocking minority when the price of a debt issue declines in times of crisis. Subsequent generations of collective action clauses sought to remedy these shortcomings. The experience with the Argentina and Greece sovereign debt workouts increased pressure to strengthen contractual frameworks and address collective action problems in sovereign debt workouts. Responding to this, in August 2014, the International Capital Markets Association developed a new model for CACs with aggregation features to make holdouts more difficult. The enhanced CACs include a "single limb" clause under which a single aggregated vote can be taken across all applicable bonds (Chung and Papaioannou, 2020).

The third phase took place in the aftermath of the global financial crisis of 2007–2008 up to recent years. During this time, opposition between the statutory and contractual approaches remained unresolved, despite unsatisfactory results. The global financial crisis triggered a need for debt workouts, including among developed countries. At the same time, creditor litigation became more aggressive and alarmingly successful. Meanwhile, calls for statutory solutions to ensure timely and effective debt restructuring attained only modest success, notably the United Nations General Assembly resolution 69/319 of 10 September 2015 and the 2015 UNCTAD *Roadmap on Sovereign Debt Workouts*. For the most part, the international community engaged in a practice of "muddling through", combining exchange offers with political pressure and an expansion of financial support instruments, particularly a proliferation of new funding instruments at IMF. Undergirding these efforts was the idea that austerity would re-establish creditor confidence, stabilize the fiscal position and trigger future growth. On the downside, debt workouts continued to cause considerable damage to the economic and social stability of the population in the borrowing country, particularly among less affluent and more vulnerable groups. Human rights challenges to austerity succeeded in only a small number of cases. Some of the more successful cases of debt restructuring, such as in Barbados and Greece, featured the retroactive insertion of collective action clauses into domestic debt (Anthony et al., 2020). Innovations in bond design such as bonds linked to GDP, issued for example by Argentina and Greece, were meant to allow smoother recoveries. However, in the case of Argentina, this resulted in litigation over the method of calculating GDP (*Financial Times*, 2023).

The COVID-19 pandemic and concurrent ecological and geopolitical crises have ushered in a fourth phase of sovereign debt regulation. When the COVID-19 pandemic required the healthcare system to be bolstered in order to overcome an economic crisis, traditional austerity measures of "growing by shrinking" – which have a track record of limited practical success (Blanchard and Leigh, 2013) – lost their theoretical appeal. It became evident that a lack of government investment in healthcare might do more harm than good. Climate change and the need for a transition to clean energy follow a similar pattern, requiring upfront investment to mitigate longer-term consequences.

At the same time, inflationary pressures associated with value chain distortions and energy issues in the wake of the war in Ukraine have created adverse conditions for borrowing countries, putting many at risk of downgrading (Fitch Ratings, 2023). IMF has signed credit agreements with approximately 100 Governments since 2020; 13 countries have since defaulted: Argentina, Belarus, Belize, Chad, Ecuador, Ghana, Lebanon, Malawi, the Russian Federation, Sri Lanka, Suriname, Ukraine and Zambia. In addition, exposure of borrowers to new non-Paris Club creditors calls into question an institutional structure centred on the Paris Club. In this context, the sovereign debt debate has shifted towards global public policy instruments as the elements below suggest:

- The rapid adoption by the Group of 20 of the Debt Service Suspension Initiative (DSSI) for countries eligible for the IMF Poverty Reduction and Growth Trust (PRGT) (May 2020–December 2021), provided a standstill on official bilateral debt payments for 48 of the 73 eligible countries. Of the 73 countries, 23 are low-income countries, 38 are lower-middle-income countries and 12 upper-middle-income countries according to World Bank (2022).

- The succession of the DSSI by the Group of 20 Common Framework for Debt Treatment beyond the DSSI. The Common Framework is criticized for not going far enough, in particular for an ineffective standstill rule requiring consensus, restricting the coverage of eligible countries, and the lack of obligatory private sector participation which allows non-participating creditors to benefit from regained financial strength (Munevar, 2021). So far, only four countries have sought relief under the latter.

- Development of new funding instruments such as the IMF Resilience and Sustainability Trust to allow for re-channelled special drawing rights; or the Next Generation E[uropean] U[nion] (NGEU), an investment and reform policy for the whole of the European Union, which provides opportunities to increase fiscal space and shoulder the rebuilding of the global economy in the wake of the pandemic.

- The rise of complementary new private lending instruments such as sustainability bonds and new restructuring methods, including "debt-for-nature" and "debt-for-climate" swaps.

- The initiatives under way to strengthen domestic law in the situation of harmful creditor action.

Towards resilience

While encouraging, these largely positive developments noted above remain insufficient to redress the deep structural asymmetries intrinsic to the prevailing international financial architecture. These asymmetries not only apply to the uneven access to long-term sustainable development finance, but also to the impact of exogenous shocks through exchange rate fluctuations, which have created a particularly toxic mix for least developed countries (LDCs) (UNCTAD, 2019a).

Some of the abovementioned developments show an increasing focus on resilience in sovereign debt regulation, particularly in relation to ecological and health risks, where "sovereign debt resilience" refers to the ability of a sovereign to avert debt distress in the face of external shocks; with resilience associated with the capacity of a system or a regime to adapt to exposure to stress and rebound to its original shape (Welsh, 2014).

The Secretary-General of the United Nations has called for a reconfiguration of the global financial architecture. This includes the need for sovereign debt restructuring to create the necessary conditions for public and private investments to deliver the Sustainable Development Goals and ensure resilience.

In this time of compounding crises, the existing inadequacies of the global financial architecture in addressing the sustainability of sovereign debt and long-run solvency have been laid bare. Long-run solvency is the condition that net liabilities – a stock, such as external debt – do not grow indefinitely in the long run, relative to a repayment capacity flow, such as export earnings (Domar, 1944). The reconfiguration of sovereign debt workouts needs to address the following resilience challenges, which have fiscal implications:

- **Ecological challenges.** Climate change and its related fiscal implications require the need for substantial private and public investments in new technologies and in infrastructure for adapting, mitigating and facilitating the transition to clean energy while minimizing biodiversity loss, within the context of the inequitable distribution of loss and damage associated with climate change.

- **Social challenges.** Sovereign debt restructuring needs to account for social issues in developing and developed countries, such as growing wealth inequalities in the wake of the shift towards a digital economy and consequent effects on tax revenue and fiscal resilience. Additionally, demographic changes exert an influence on fiscal capacity, and migration poses development risks to the countries of origin and imposes fiscal burdens on receiving countries.

- **Trade challenges.** The current development of the world trade system and its fragmented nature poses challenges due to industrial policies and subsidies that lead to market restrictions. These restrictions have adverse fiscal implications, especially for developing countries.

- **Debt challenges.** Borrowing countries are grappling with increasingly complex debt spaces. Contributing factors include scarcity of resources such as concessional finance and loss of control over value chains, giving rise to new forms of collateralized loans that carry risks for borrowing countries (Chellaney, 2017; Horn et al., 2021; Lippolis and Verhoeven, 2022). Additionally, debt transparency issues have emerged, particularly with the rise of syndicated loans (Gelpern et al., 2022).

- **Political challenges.** The slow – and piecemeal – relief to countries in distress will inevitably lead to political hurdles for Governments seeking debt relief, due to a loss of political capital. Associated security risks may affect countries' fiscal situations either directly or indirectly and compound the difficulty of debt restructuring efforts (e.g. United Kingdom Supreme Court, *The Law Debenture Trust vs Ukraine*, 2023).

Given the structural character of the current difficulties, a continued approach of "muddling through" with regard to sovereign debt is likely to cause significant widespread social and economic problems. A more proactive response is called for concerning every stage of the sovereign debt life cycle.

C. LIFE STAGES OF SOVEREIGN DEBT

The life cycle of sovereign debt is used here as a conceptual device to consider the way in which debt is incurred, how debt instruments are issued, how debt management is structured, how debt sustainability is tracked and the options for debt workout (figures V.2 and V.3).

Sovereign debt can be analysed through a framework comprising the five stages set out below. Challenges and failures can be identified at each stage, calling for improvements for a more robust system. As the stages in the life cycle of sovereign debt are highly interdependent, policy responses that lead to reconfiguration need to address each of them.

1. **Access to finance and markets.** This critical issue relates to the shortage of both concessional finance and affordable long-term capital. External financial shocks leading to capital outflows may mean countries

face extortionate spreads which imply loss of market access or unexpectedly high borrowing costs, which is further intensified by perceived high risks. These perceptions can be reinforced by benchmark-driven investment strategies and credit rating agencies' evaluations (chapter II).

2. **Debt issuance.** A lack of transparency hinders responsible lending and borrowing. Those that ultimately pay the price – citizens – are often kept in the dark. Contractual and cost terms are obscure, particularly if they contain potentially harmful clauses such as resource-backed collateral. While there have been innovations in related financial instruments (e.g. State-contingent clauses) and enhanced collective action clauses, there is still room for improvement. The UNCTAD *Principles for Responsible Sovereign Lending and Borrowing* (2012) are no longer at the forefront and, while other guidelines have emerged, a global consensus on principles for responsible lending and borrowing remains elusive.[5]

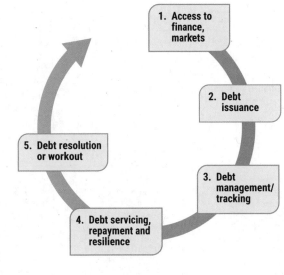

Figure V.2 Unpacking the sovereign debt black box
Life cycle of external sovereign debt expressed as stages

Source: UNCTAD.

3. **Debt management.** While countries have been increasingly empowered to manage their debt (including through the UNCTAD Debt Management Financial Analysis System, DMFAS), technical barriers remain. Countries need to be empowered to track their debt sustainability – including for subnational government and State-owned and parastatal enterprises – to be better able to assess their vulnerabilities and evaluate the debt sustainability analysis required by IMF.

4. **Debt servicing, repayment and resilience.** Ideally, debt servicing should go smoothly but the frequency of external shocks, including those that are climate-related, represents a barrage of externalities that can derail the process. Creating innovative financial instruments can be helpful for managing debt, but even the most effective of tools needs improving to ensure resilience. Limited access to the global financial safety net and the inability to address loss and damage hinders rather than improves resilience (chapter IV).

5. **Debt resolution or workout.** In the best scenario within the life cycle, debt is repaid or easily and affordably rolled over. This is referred to as resolution. If not, the country may have to seek a debt workout which could involve suspending the debt servicing agreement, extending the maturity, reducing interest rates and/or cancelling the debt outright (i.e. a haircut or a reduction in the value of the collateral). However, the institutions and mechanisms dealing with debt workouts have become increasingly disconnected from the realities and complexities of sovereign debt distress. The composition of institutions like the Paris Club are outdated and processes such as the Common Framework are inadequate. The ongoing absence of an automatic standstill mechanism during negotiations, incomplete creditor participation and delays in the process are among the underlying weaknesses.

"The institutions and mechanisms dealing with debt workouts have become increasingly disconnected from the realities and complexities of sovereign debt distress."

---

[5] Three years after the launch of the UNCTAD *Principles on Responsible Sovereign Borrowing and Lending*, Member States of the United Nations reiterated in the Addis Ababa Action Agenda that maintaining sustainable debt levels is the responsibility of borrowing countries but that lenders also have a responsibility to lend in a way that does not undermine a country's debt sustainability. Since then, other soft law approaches to responsible lending and borrowing have emerged, such as the Group of 20 Operational Guidelines for Sustainable Financing and the Voluntary Principles for Debt Transparency from the Institute of International Finance. None have gained widespread traction.

Figure V.3 Pitfalls along the path: The phases and failures of sovereign debt

Stage analysis of life cycle of sovereign debt

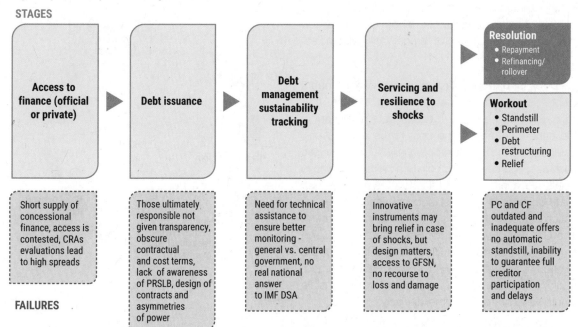

STAGES

Access to finance (official or private) → **Debt issuance** → **Debt management sustainability tracking** → **Servicing and resilience to shocks** → **Resolution**
- Repayment
- Refinancing/ rollover

Workout
- Standstill
- Perimeter
- Debt restructuring
- Relief

FAILURES

Short supply of concessional finance, access is contested, CRAs evaluations lead to high spreads	Those ultimately responsible not given transparency, obscure contractual and cost terms, lack of awareness of PRSLB, design of contracts and asymmetries of power	Need for technical assistance to ensure better monitoring - general vs. central government, no real national answer to IMF DSA	Innovative instruments may bring relief in case of shocks, but design matters, access to GFSN, no recourse to loss and damage	PC and CF outdated and inadequate offers no automatic standstill, inability to guarantee full creditor participation and delays

Source: UNCTAD.

Abbreviations: CF, Common Framework; CRAs, Credit Rating Agencies; DSA, Debt Sustainability Analysis; GFSN, Global Financial Safety Net; PC, Paris Club; PRSLB, Principles on Responsible Sovereign Lending and Borrowing.

D. TRANSFORMATIONAL PROPOSALS

This section sets out areas of potential transformation within the sovereign debt life cycle (figure V.4). While each of these proposals may have specific relevance to a particular stage, in all cases the stages and their outcomes are interdependent. The process also contains path dependencies; for example, weak transparency at the "access to finance" stage hinders the entire process.

1. Strengthening transparency across the sovereign debt cycle

Managing sovereign debt is a complex and intricate process that involves many stakeholders with an evolving interplay of incentives, interests and responsibilities. In this context, transparency is fundamental to every stage of the sovereign borrowing and lending cycle and extends beyond merely recording transactions. Transparency around sovereign debt transactions lies at the heart of the public covenant between Governments and their citizens. It ensures accountability, fosters trust and strengthens public institutions.

From the perspective of public financial management, debt transparency means providing a wide range of information about how public funds are used for development. This includes details of the financial and legal structure of a country's liabilities, the impact of financial needs and obligations on its development prospects as well as loan conditionalities and their relation to domestic policies. Collectively, these elements underpin sovereign debt transactions. Transparency is essential for ensuring legitimacy, accountability and sustainability of debt financing.

Debt transparency is not a static concept. The requirements to achieve transparency change relative to the specific institutional setting of the country and vary with the different stages of the sovereign debt life cycle. The following section provides general recommendations for enhancing transparency at each stage.

Figure V.4 Transformational goals along the sovereign debt life cycle
Aspirations to address the constraints stage by stage

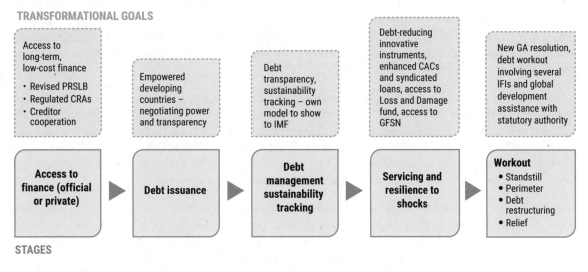

Source: UNCTAD.
Abbreviations: CACs, collective action clauses; CRAs, credit rating agencies; GA, General Assembly; GFSN, global financial safety net; IFIs, international financial institutions; PRSLB, Principles on Responsible Sovereign Lending and Borrowing.

a. Access to finance

The debt challenges of developing countries need to be considered in the context of the difficulties in fully implementing the Addis Ababa Action Agenda on Financing for Development (Inter-Agency Task Force on Financing for Development, 2023). Inequities in the international financial architecture create an explicit resource and information asymmetry between borrowers and lenders. The lack of viable alternatives for securing concessional development financing sets the stage for opaque and expensive sources of debt financing. The presence of confidentiality clauses limiting disclosure by sovereign borrowers and the use of collateralized loans or borrowing on commercial terms that are incompatible with long-term development requirements highlight these power asymmetries. These practices are the result of a system which increases the leverage of agents that can offer otherwise scarce financing, yet frequently at the expense of transparency and inter-creditor equity (Maslen and Aslan, 2022).

> *"Inequities in the international financial architecture create an explicit resource and information asymmetry between borrowers and lenders."*

A global economic system that allows countries to grow while borrowing, in order to develop trading capacities and transform structurally, whilst ensuring a fair international system of taxation would best help reduce the leverage of these agents. This requires greater progress towards a multilayered and resilient structure for development financing. Availability of overlapping and complementary sources of development financing and transparency can counteract questionable practices in sovereign debt markets.

While such improvements are necessary, they will be insufficient to fully achieve debt transparency. The impact of multilateral efforts to strengthen development financing must be mediated by efforts at the national level to ensure that resources are deployed towards the Sustainable Development Goals. Implementing integrated national financing frameworks at the country level can play a key role in developing comprehensive financing strategies that explicitly link sources and uses of financing in a transparent way for all relevant stakeholders (UNDP, 2023).

b. Debt issuance

Existing soft law approaches to promoting debt transparency, including the UNCTAD *Principles for Responsible and Sovereign Lending and Borrowing* and the Institute of International Finance Principles on Debt Transparency, fall in the realm of soft law and self-regulation. Despite some progress, significant gaps remain regarding timely disclosure of financial and legal terms of sovereign debt (United Nations, 2022b). Measures are needed to target the incentives that lead borrowers and lenders to turn to opaque financing mechanisms in ways that are counterproductive.

In the case of borrowers, national legal and regulatory frameworks play a crucial role in improving debt transparency and these efforts should be founded on the notion that transparency around public debt management is a public good (Gelpern, 2018). Legal frameworks for public debt management can help address key problems, including clear authorization mechanisms for the issuance of debt, parliamentary oversight, establishment of requirements for reporting transaction-level data regarding the financial and legal terms of debts and using standardized templates for disclosure (Maslen and Aslan, 2022).

In addition, legislation in lender countries and relevant jurisdictions should limit the recovery of opaque debts to discourage predatory lending practices. Robust debt disclosure requirements as part of public debt authorization frameworks ought to be a necessary condition for enforcing contracts in domestic and foreign courts (Group of 30, 2020). Effective regulation can help improve transparency and prevent harmful practices including collateralization and exploitative sovereign syndicated loans.

> *"Legislation in lender country jurisdictions should limit the recovery of opaque debts to discourage predatory lending practices."*

Financial innovations can be a challenge for effective debt management if not used correctly. Mechanisms such as climate-resilient debt clauses or debt-for-nature swaps can help improve resilience in the aftermath of a climate shock, or used to free up resources for conservation investments, if employed correctly. Full disclosure and transparency is required regarding the contractual terms of such mechanisms to ensure that borrowers and lenders can usefully integrate these tools into their financial assessments.

c. Debt management

Effective debt management is built on transparency and national capacity-building. It should be founded on debt management systems and the capacity to incorporate, analyse and report individual loan transactions. Improvements in debt management can be achieved through an international loans repository (ILR) as further addressed in box V.1. An ILR can improve debt management by digitizing loan transactions, ensuring consistent financial terms and providing reliable statistics.

There is also a need to bolster technical capacity at national levels to assess the financial and legal implications of the existing liability structure. Capacity-building ensures that countries can reduce their reliance on external assessments and enhance their sovereignty over financial operations. UNCTAD is leading in this area through its DMFAS programme. DMFAS has provided technical assistance to 116 institutions in 75 developing countries over 41 years (UNCTAD, 2012; 2022a). The DMFAS programme prioritizes developing and maintaining national capacity to ensure accurate information about public debt to support policy decisions and risk management.

Box V.1 Digitalizing loan transactions through an International Loans Repository

There is a broad consensus among the international financial community on the need to improve public debt transparency. Several initiatives and proposals are being discussed to tackle this, from addressing institutional, governance and capacity gaps in developing countries, confronting adverse incentives among borrowers and creditors to revising cross-country debt databases. The creation of an ILR is one such proposal (Rivetti, 2021).[a] An ILR can be described as a platform that reconciles external sovereign loans and records between borrowers and creditors, improving the accuracy of debt records and limiting operational risk. While enhancing public debt transparency will require a multi-pronged approach, such a repository would bring several benefits.

The problem: Loan data is shared manually

Contrary to debt securities, which are fully digitalized, information related to international loans and associated transactions rely on manually sharing borrower-creditor information. This arrangement leads to data inconsistencies among borrowers and creditors, such as misinterpretation of financial terms and conditions, missing information on transactions or errors in recording information. This then requires resource-intensive reconciliation and creates distrust in the quality and comprehensiveness of the data, which is an obstacle to debt workouts. Moreover, a lack of transparency creates opportunities for fraud and corruption.

Digitalizing international loan data and creating a public ILR could unlock problems related to debt transparency. An ILR could potentially provide a consistent set of all financial terms for each agreement, validate all loan and servicing transactions and present reliable and timely statistics.

Beneficiaries of an International Loans Repository

The ILR would serve borrowers and creditors as well as those using and compiling international debt statistics. Borrowers would be relieved of cumbersome and error-prone debt data recording processes and both creditors and borrowers would benefit from the information sharing it entails. Resource-intensive reporting obligations by borrowers would also be alleviated, facilitating access for all stakeholders in the borrowing country. Creditors would be assured that their debt records and the borrowers' debt records were produced according to international best practices, saving time on reconciliation exercises and possibly enhancing trust in the process. For those compiling international debt statistics, prompt updates to records would reduce costly and time-consuming cross-data checking exercises. Finally, all users of the data would have access to reliable, quasi real-time and verified debt data.

Benefits of an International Loans Repository: security, transparency, validation, automation

The key benefits of an ILR include: i) a secure platform for data exchanges relating to loan transactions, ii) validation of data between borrowers and creditors, iii) automation of borrowers' debt management and reporting systems, iv) enhanced transparency on loan financing conditions, v) promotion of near real-time dissemination of statistics, vi) standardized debt definitions for statistics and debt reporting (IMF, 2023) and vii) assisting borrowers and creditors to move to digital end-to-end processing of loan transactions (Rivetti, 2021).

Ultimately, the ILR may provide an incentive for standardizing and harmonizing international loan agreements. Debt managers in developing countries would benefit from complex financial terms embedded in loan and debt agreements being recorded accurately and automatically, and this data could be automatically fed into their existing debt management systems.

Implementing an international loans repository

The first stage of implementing the ILR would be to define technical specifications, aided by the existing technical working group on improving the World Bank's Debt Reporting System. This working group includes the Commonwealth Secretariat, IMF, UNCTAD and the World Bank. This would follow with a pilot ILR tested with volunteer multilateral development banks, bilateral creditors and interested borrowers.

Since the publication of an initial proposal to create the ILR in October 2021, criticisms of the ILR included the duplication of repositories, technological complexity, it being only a "partial solution", cost, data ownership and authorization for data dissemination.

Addressing concerns

- Duplication of repositories. The role of the ILR is not to duplicate existing databases but to improve data quality and reporting services. Data digitalization would ensure quality and enhance the reporting services offered by existing databases, and feed into existing debt management systems.

- Technological complexity. Borrowers' debt recording and management systems and creditors' loan monitoring systems are based on relational databases that rely on electronic data transmission. An ILR would build on existing systems, making the ILR technically feasible and cost-effective.

- Partial solution. While it is acknowledged that debt transparency requires a multifaceted approach, the ILR addresses a crucial aspect by transitioning from manual information sharing to digitalization.

- Costly. The upfront investment for creating the ILR is necessary yet manageable; and it is estimated that ongoing operational costs would be minimal compared to current practices. These costs need to be considered in relation to the costs currently incurred by borrowers, creditors and international institutions associated with collecting, compiling, reconciling and reporting data.

- Data ownership and authorization. Data handled by the ILR will remain encrypted and owned by data owners, with dissemination rights determined by them, aligning with existing authorization rules.

- Downsides of standardization. While standardized terms for financing instruments can be expected to facilitate debt restructuring, they may reduce policy space for tailor-made debt instruments addressing countries' specific needs. This means retaining some flexibility within the standardized reporting structures.

The creation of an ILR represents a possible step towards improving public debt transparency and streamlining international loan data management. By addressing key challenges and leveraging technological advancements, the ILR offers a valuable solution for borrowers, creditors and data compilers alike, ultimately promoting a more resilient international financial architecture.

---

[a] Rivetti D (2021), Debt Transparency in Developing Countries, Report No. 165760, World Bank, Washington, D.C.

d. Debt servicing

As debt is repaid, in the event of a shock, national authorities need a clear overview of how various debt instruments and obligations interact during times of crisis, to ensure resilience. This requires ongoing monitoring and modelling of debt dynamics and an understanding of the implications of financial innovations, based on disclosure and transparency.

National authorities also need alternative methodologies to assess their ability to service their debt in a complex world. The IMF–World Bank frameworks to assess debt sustainability are, at their core, risk management tools for creditors. As such, they are ill-suited to provide borrowers with a comprehensive overview of the linkages between debt sustainability and development financing requirements (UNCTAD, 2019b). To address this, UNCTAD has developed the Sustainable Development Finance Assessment (SDFA), which is further addressed in UNCTAD (2022b and 2022d).

The SDFA identifies the development finance needs of a country in order to meet the Sustainable Development Goals, together with pathways to make this compatible with external financial and public debt sustainability (section D.2 and UNCTAD, 2022c).

e. Maturity and debt restructuring

For countries that can repay their debts in a sustainable fashion, debt management offices ought to ensure adequate reporting of relevant payments. Records and assessments of transactions provide useful benchmarks for debt management relating to intermediaries, transactions and borrowing costs.

Countries in debt distress face additional difficulties, as a lack of debt transparency is closely linked to their financial challenges. Debt workouts provide a unique opportunity to improve transparency. The debt treatments from the Group of 20 Common Framework help achieve this by including a requirement for the full disclosure of contractual terms of debt, following a restructuring. Disclosure sets the foundations for improved debt management and equitable treatment of creditors. In the event of additional debt treatments, a mechanism for automatically disclosing debt workout agreements would reduce delays and minimize the risk of incomplete creditor participation and issues relating to comparability of treatment.
The United Nations General Assembly has invited relevant international institutions to consider creating a central data registry for debt workouts to compile precisely this type of information (United Nations, 2022c).

"The pursuit of transparency transcends mere data disclosure. It represents a commitment to building a global financial architecture that is fair and accountable to all."

In conclusion, transparency is a dynamic principle that evolves through each stage of the sovereign debt life cycle. The pursuit of transparency transcends mere data disclosure. It represents a commitment to building a global financial architecture that is fair and accountable to all. In addition to ongoing work by the DMFAS programme, the UNCTAD *Principles for Responsible Sovereign Lending and Borrowing* mark a milestone in multilateral efforts to improve debt transparency. The growing debt challenges faced by developing countries highlight the need to revisit these Principles and align them with broader development financing needs.

2. Debt management and debt sustainability analyses and tracking

Debt management offices in developing countries need to urgently strengthen their capacity to evaluate debt sustainability and undertake tracking. They should be able to simulate scenarios and use these as tools to guide economic policies. Policymakers must also enhance their capacity to collaborate effectively with IMF, conducting comprehensive debt sustainability analyses and strengthening their negotiation skills with the organization. Moreover, better integration of debt sustainability tracking – an upstream area of debt management which also includes governance and debt strategy – will benefit the borrower country as well as creditors.[6]

---

[6] See https://unctad.org/topic/debt-and-finance/dmfas.

In the current context of compounding crises, overlapping debt and climate challenges and mounting obstacles to achieving the Sustainable Development Goals and the Paris Agreement, the SDFA is designed to enable developing countries to track their sustainability progress against their development goals. It is one of several potential country-based tools that could be complementary to the work undertaken by the IMF before, and at the time of, debt distress. The SDFA evaluates a country's development finance needs to achieve climate-resilient, green structural transformation and the most fundamental Sustainable Development Goals while ensuring the sustainability of the external and public sector accounts. The SDFA considers all sources of external financing (foreign direct investment, foreign portfolio investment and external debt) as well as public sector finance (public debt and other public sector liabilities).

The SDFA shows that there are a range of policy options to attain or maintain external financial and public sector financial sustainability while also achieving the Sustainability Development Goals. The SDFA is founded on the assumption that long-run output growth is demand-led and the balance of payment performance is the dominant economic constraint to growth and development. This means that the external sector establishes an upper bound for long-term growth that is usually below full employment. Although, in theory, all countries face this external constraint (Thirlwall, 1979), it is more binding for developing countries due to their external position within the global economy (Prebisch, 1950 and 1959). This position has two interconnected dimensions. First, developing countries typically run trade deficits, reflecting the productive-technological dimension (Porcile, 2021). Second, developing countries do not issue an international reserve currency – a currency widely used in international transactions (predominantly the dollar), which reflects the monetary-financial dimension. The interplay of these two dimensions means that these countries cannot finance their structural balance of payment deficits in their domestic currency. The shortage of foreign currency associated with such deficits eventually leads to constraints on the long-term growth rate.

The SDFA puts the achievement of the Sustainable Development Goals at the centre of the analysis, allowing development ambitions to be explicitly considered within fiscal decision-making. This is contrasted with standard debt sustainability analyses (DSAs) which focus on the ability to repay. The SDFA goes beyond standard debt sustainability analyses to emphasize the broader dimension of external financial and public sector financial sustainability. It also extends Pasinetti's concept (1998) of an "area of sustainability" to external finance, external debt and public sector finance in developing countries.[7] The "area of sustainability" defines a range of values for sustainability indicators that are compatible with external financial and public sector financial sustainability.

The first version of the UNCTAD SDFA (Mark I) only considers the first four Sustainable Development Goals (Goals 1–4: no poverty, no hunger, good access to health services and access to quality education) which are expected to be fully (or largely) met by public sectors given their high, long-term social returns (Schmidt-Traub, 2015).

"The financing gap to achieve climate-related Sustainable Development Goals is enormous, requiring many countries to take on more debt."

The second version (Mark II) is under development and will expand on the first version. Notably, it will estimate the impact on external financial and public sector financial sustainability of meeting the 2030 Agenda and all the Sustainable Development Goals related to climate action (Goal 13 and climate aspects of other Goals). It is well known that developing countries are most affected by climate change and natural disasters that endanger their structural transformation (Intergovernmental Panel on Climate Change, 2023; Wu, 2023).

Moreover, these countries are in a more fragile position in terms of productive structure due to their greater dependence on brown sectors and insufficient financial and technological capacity to invest in green industries (UNCTAD, 2021). This means that the financing gap to achieve climate-related Goals through investments in climate adaptation and mitigation is enormous, requiring many countries to take on more debt. At the same

---

[7] Pasinetti (1998) was a reaction to the "Maastricht criteria" that set targets that the members of the European Union would have to meet to join the future monetary union. The targets were 60 per cent for the public debt-to-GDP ratio, 3 per cent for the fiscal deficit-to-GDP ratio and average inflation of no more than 1.5 percentage points above the rate of the three best-performing member States. He shows that, as the debt and deficit ratios change over time, the relation between them should be considered arbitrary and not fixed thresholds. Thus, different combinations of these two ratios ensure public debt sustainability.

time, the ability of developing countries to address mounting climate challenges is heavily impaired by existing unsustainable debt burdens (section D).

The UNCTAD SDFA Mark II will enable the assessment of a country's financial needs to undertake required investments and achieve a climate-resilient and green structural transformation. The SDFA dashboard allows testing of scenarios for sustainability tracking and assessing how different policy choices affect external public sector positions (Lockwood, 2022). The aim is to update the dashboard for the UNCTAD SDFA Mark II; this would help estimate the impact of climate-related shocks on the funding gap for achieving climate-focussed Goals. In this way, the SDFA will also improve the simultaneous technical evaluation of debt and climate challenges.

3. Debt workout and the global debt authority

Long, drawn-out and ineffective sovereign debt workout mechanisms can lock countries in a vicious cycle. This can cause loss of market access, capital flight, subdued economic activity, financial sector instability and a drying up of foreign direct investment. The consequences have been referred to as "incandescently painful" (Buchheit et al., 2018). The missteps of borrowers or creditors during restructuring can keep a country on the sidelines of the international finance playing field for some time. In particular, inadequate debt relief, overly optimistic projections of future growth, an inability to rally creditors and a lack of capacity to reduce fiscal deficits causes delays, holdouts and risk aversion.

For debt workouts to be transformed in such a way that they contribute to sovereign resilience, multiple innovations both of a private (contractual) and a public (statutory) nature are required. These need to be coordinated rather than played out against each other.

Improved sovereign debt workout requires substantive and institutional changes to the existing framework:

1. An automatic standstill for countries declaring distress, to concentrate the minds of creditors in the workout process. This would prevent holdouts and encourage debtor countries to enter the distress stage before it is too late. Early declaration of distress and early resolution could prevent countries being locked out of markets for a prolonged period. To ensure creditor equity, a standstill might be a useful device to ensure inclusion of private creditors, as would principles on comparability of treatment and rules need to prevent creditors from realizing collateral.

2. A mechanism is needed to determine the perimeter of legitimate debt. This relates to rules regarding unconstitutional debt resulting from corruption, opacity and secrecy, flawed authorization or reckless creditor practices.

3. At the country level, improved debt sustainability analysis needs to be available that reflects the need to achieve the Sustainable Development Goals and climate transition – including related investments and necessary industry policies – and that empowers country negotiators through improved data on their potential for growth and fiscal consolidation. This requires developing countries to have their own models, but it also requires greater transparency of the IMF debt sustainability analysis models and assumptions (and ideally, a willingness from IMF to modify them where necessary).

4. Recourse to regulation of capital flows as part of the ordinary toolkit of developing countries. This would allow monetary policy to be used to not only protect economies when threatened with outflows, but also when large inflows relative to the size of the economy during the expansionary phase of the global financial cycle threaten to create asset bubbles, financial fragility, currency overvaluation and superfluous imports (*Trade and Development Report, 2015*).

5. Improved innovative financial instruments such as debt-for-climate swaps and debt-for-nature swaps that provide mechanisms to enhance fiscal space in countries with sustainable debt – albeit at the margins. The aim is to generate fiscal breathing room through a debt workout to invest in mitigating the effects of climate change or preserving biodiversity. Results have been mixed, and rules that limit creditor control over the investment may be needed so that sovereignty and ownership is assured (Bolton et al., 2022).

6. An institutional framework that fosters resilience. Given the significant current ecological, social and geopolitical challenges, institutions charged with regulating sovereign debt need to bridge differences between constituencies and stakeholders. This speaks in favour of large, universal organizations, including the United Nations. Other actors such as the Group of 20 might play a crucial role, particularly in ensuring the support of a wide range of capital-exporting countries. While any major initiatives for restructuring debt would involve multiple institutions, an institutional "headquarters" with authority over sovereign debt workouts would be advantageous. Thinking about how and where such a technical and neutral Authority should be established needs to begin. It would require dealing with the failures of the system outlined above and obtaining the buy-in of creditors and borrowers alike, while being informed by multilateral institutional views, including of the United Nations (box V.2).

7. Establishment of a borrower's club. Since as early as 1956, official creditors have coordinated their efforts through institutions such as the Paris Club and various private creditor groups also exist (box V.3). Through a borrower's club, debtor countries could discuss technical issues and innovation, such as bond issuance experiences and novel debt instruments for sustainable development, and learn from each other's experiences. Debtor countries with recent experience could advise those facing debt distress on reducing their restructuring costs or building political relations between the debtor countries. This support could lead to a more stable and resilient global financial system, benefiting both borrowers and creditors.

Box V.2 UNCTAD and the evolution of a global debt authority as an institutional mechanism

In April 2020, as the reality of a global pandemic and related shutdown were beginning to be felt across the globe, UNCTAD called for an international developing country authority as part of a series of updates to its *Trade and Development Report* (UNCTAD, 2020). This was the latest in a long history of UNCTAD publications pointing out that since international financial stability and liquidity are global public goods, and the source of debt distress lies partially outside developing countries themselves, an impartial institutionalized mechanism to ensure fair sovereign debt workouts is needed.

In September 1980, the Trade and Development Board of UNCTAD endorsed a set of guiding principles relating to the international management of debt problems for interested developing countries. The guiding principles recognized that any such action should be:

- Expeditious and timely;

- Designed to enhance the development prospects of the debtor country, bearing in mind its socio economic priorities and the internationally agreed objectives for the growth of developing countries;

- Aimed at restoring the debtor's capacity to service its debts in the short- and long-term and should reinforce the developing country's own efforts to strengthen its underlying balance-of-payments situation; and

- Aimed at protecting the interests of debtors and creditors equitably in the context of international economic cooperation.

Lack of movement on this resolution resulted in the *Trade and Development Report 1986* noting that:

> "[The lack of a well-articulated, impartial framework for resolving international debt problems creates a considerable danger [...] that international debtors will suffer the worst of both possible worlds [...] being judged de facto bankrupt [...] largely without the benefits of receiving the financial relief and financial reorganization that would accompany a de jure bankruptcy."

Drawing on Chapter 11 of the United States Bankruptcy Reform Act of 1978, the *Trade and Development Report 1986* set out some of the procedures that could be used in an international bankruptcy framework, including: an automatic stay on creditor claims or judgements to provide the debtor with the space to formulate a reorganization plan; a cessation on interest payments on outstanding debts at the time of a bankruptcy petition; a negotiated plan between debtors and creditors and adopted by a specified percentage of creditors. Later, the *Trade and Development Report 1998* also considered various proposals to establish an international debt facility to advance the restructuring of commercial bank debt to developing countries.

Some of these ideas were revived in the UNCTAD *Roadmap and Guide for Sovereign Debt Workouts* (2015) which recommended the creation of a debt workout institute. The role of this institute would be to facilitate dialogues between the debtor country and all its creditors, as mediator and arbiter, provide technical and logistical support (including a public repository for the complete records of past workouts), to commission debt sustainability analyses and have the capacity to publicly determine the successful conclusion of a restructuring. It was suggested that a more coordinated, multilateral approach in establishing such a body would increase its legitimacy. These features would be fundamental to a global debt authority.

To date, proposals for creating such an institution have failed to gain traction. In part this has much to do with its nature, as its effective operation would amount to a global public good. But debtor countries, which may benefit from such a public good, have to balance defending their interest as individual borrowers and the collective interest in facilitating more efficient and equitable outcomes in the event of a sovereign default. Creditors would also have to be persuaded of the long-term benefits of such an institutional structure.

Establishing new rules and mechanisms for sovereign debt workouts is likely to be fraught with lack of consensus and institutional resistance. The way forward is not simply a legal one; the process is deeply political and will need support from a broad set of member States and actors, including courts and international institutions.

However, pushing towards establishing an authority to deal with global debt could lead to a substantive transformation of the sovereign debt workout regime. Such an Authority would promote and implement the substantive changes listed above. The road towards this aspirational entity could start with small beginnings.

Vision of the global debt authority

Initially, the global debt authority could begin as a coordinating and advisory institution. Instead of being established under a binding treaty with near-universal membership, the authority could be based on a non-binding charter adopted by a smaller group of interested countries. It would initially consist of a small group of permanent staff affiliated with an existing international organization and rely on ad hoc committees of experts.

The initial work of the global debt authority would be identifying tasks, coordinating existing efforts and making recommendations. The ad hoc committees of experts would identify existing issues related to sovereign debt and make recommendations for the authority to provide guidance on soft law, domestic legislation development and contractual approaches. Through the work of these ad hoc committees, the authority would establish its network with experts, international institutions, domestic lawmakers and civil society groups, among others. In terms of collecting sovereign debt workout data, staff of the global debt authority and ad hoc expert committees would develop and maintain databases of previous debt workout agreements, debt sustainability analyses and effective workout communication strategies. In this process, the global debt authority would build its relations with the officials involved in previous debt restructuring from debtor countries, creditor countries and international institutions. From this, the authority could begin its operations and build its network for further development. On this basis, the authority could develop the resources to play a significant role in sovereign debt workouts.

Legal basis of the global debt authority

While some consider it a gold standard to establish an international organization through a multilateral treaty and expand its influence by increasing member States, given the technical nature of the global debt authority and its need for neutrality, it may be both preferable and pragmatic to commence on a non-binding basis and gradually increase its influence through its work. The authority could be established as an autonomous entity, neither borrower or creditor, with the necessary technical personnel by a small group of interested and committed countries. This is rather common, as examples such as International Atomic Energy Agency (IAEA) have shown – which itself emerged from a charter negotiated by 12 countries (Fischer, 1997). Legitimacy and expansion of the global debt authority would arise as a consequence of substantive contribution and recognition, somewhat like the IAEA.

Setting up the global debt authority

The first step towards establishing the authority would be identifying a group of interested States as charter members. The charter member States can negotiate a more comprehensive founding document and more detailed governing structure. The authority would also welcome observer States. A preparatory commission of experts would advise on the drafting of the founding document and lay the groundwork for substantive workstreams and associated networks of actors and organizations. Logistical foundations for the authority would also need to be clarified, including its physical location, initial budget and hiring permanent staff.

To ensure adequate reviews of the global debt authority, regular plenary meetings could be organized with a broader group of stakeholders, with the aim of keeping them informed of activities and hearing their concerns and recommendations.

> ### Box V.3 Private creditor coordination – lessons for borrowers?
>
> Private creditors actively collaborate via established forums such as the Institute of International Finance (IIF), a global association of financial institutions; the London Club, an informal gathering of international commercial banks for workout processes with sovereign debtors; and the International Capital Markets Association (ICMA), an association focused on shaping international capital and securities markets. This type of coordination has become standard practice, with overlaps in private creditor institutional membership.
>
> Through ongoing dialogue, familiarity and cooperation, private creditors can influence the international debt architecture to their benefit and lobby for legislation that aligns with their own interests. Private creditors also have the capacity to draw out the restructuring process. Furthermore, there is a self-reinforcing dynamic at play: coordination enhances the influence of private creditors, cementing their interests, which in turn motivates further coordination.

The current global debt architecture is creditor-centric. Creditor coordination has influenced domestic legislation and promoted contractual tools. Relevant rules in key jurisdictions such as the United Kingdom and New York State, which govern most sovereign debt agreements, favour creditors. For example, in New York State, the existing rules do not impose any restrictions on holdout litigation. Proposals aimed at improving this situation continue to be rejected.[a] There is no legislation in New York State that compels private creditors to participate in international debt initiatives that would benefit sovereign debtors. The recent legislative proposal concerning this received unanimous opposition from private creditors.[b] Another example is the 9 per cent statutory pre-judgement interest rate in New York State law. This represents the annual interest rate applied to the outstanding debt from the time it falls into arrears until the court makes a judgement. It was set in 1981 when the annual inflation rate in the United States was 8.9 per cent and has remained unchanged even though inflation subsequently fell well below this rate for decades, before rising again in 2021.

Contractual clauses tend also to favour creditors. For example, bond contracts and loan agreements typically contain cross-default and acceleration clauses. Cross-default clauses allow all creditors to demand repayment if the borrower formally defaults on one of its debts. Acceleration clauses require the debtor to repay all outstanding bonds earlier than agreed if certain conditions are met (for example, in case of a default with another series of bonds). While such clauses are used to protect creditors' interests and ensure continuity of obligations, they also weaken the position of the sovereign debtor in negotiations and limit their flexibility in handling financial difficulties. For instance, debtor countries can be disincentivized to undertake voluntary rescheduling as this is considered a default under certain loan agreements.

The existing rules in the global debt architecture do not incentivize sustainable financing. Private creditors are not required to provide debt sustainability analyses to justify their lending and risk premiums. By comparison, IMF and the Paris Club have policies outlining that they should respect lending limits according to debt sustainability analyses, even though these rules are sometimes not respected. But there is no equivalent rule in the private sector. This leads to overlending and risk premiums that are disproportionately high. Moreover, despite the substantial risk premiums, in case of default, private creditors often manage to secure full recovery through holdout litigation, even when official creditors have granted debt relief. Private creditors enjoy high returns through unjustifiably high-risk premiums and full recovery at the cost of taxpayers in creditor States that grant debt relief. This gives private creditors incentives to drag out the debt restructuring process, exacerbating the situation for debtor States, as it hinders their ability to restore economic stability and regain market access. Historically, collective action clauses have facilitated some restructuring of private debt, but large creditors may acquire a blocking position. Moreover, they perpetuate dependence on the goodwill of private investors even if urgent public interests are at stake, including climate adjustment measures or essential health care.

How can debtor coordination improve the system?

In contrast to the creditor landscape, there is a substantial lack of coordination between sovereign debtors and room to counterbalance this asymmetry. In the borrowing stage, debtor coordination can promote fair rules and encourage a more balanced international debt architecture, with responsible borrowing and lending. In the restructuring stage, debtor coordination can empower debtor countries to have greater technical capacities, networks and access to information, leading to a more equal footing and less biased outcomes. This can help avoid protracted negotiations and restore debt sustainability and economic recovery.

While there are many benefits for debtor countries to coordinate, there are also disincentives. These include fears of downside risks or being penalized with credit rating downgrades. Furthermore, there is less likelihood of borrowers coordinating than creditors, given that sovereign States typically act alone to initiate debt workouts. While large regional crises can create a temporary common cause, this may unravel quickly – as in the case of the Cartagena Group.[c] While the Group was temporary, there were some gains from coordinating, including an increase in concessional finance, acceptance by creditors of growth-oriented IMF programmes, multi-year rescheduling agreements and increased lending by multilateral banks. Moreover, it is possible that the threat of joint default helped member countries obtain better deals.

[a] While the exceptional Champerty rule in New York State law prohibits third parties from funding a lawsuit in return for a financial interest in the outcome and specifically prohibits acquisition of debt for the purpose of bringing legal action, this is not applied in most sovereign debt disputes. This is because the prohibition only applies in instances where the aggregate purchase price is less than $500,000. See section 489 of the New York Judiciary Law; Elliott Associates, *LP v Banco de la Nacion*, 194 F.3d 363, 368 (2d Cir. 1999)

[b] Assembly Bill A2970 / Senate Bill S4747.

[c] In June 1984, foreign and finance ministers of 11 countries (Argentina, the Plurinational State of Bolivia, Brazil, Chile, Colombia, Ecuador, Mexico, Peru, the Dominican Republic, Uruguay and the Bolivarian Republic of Venezuela) met in Cartagena, Colombia, and formally established the Group by signing the Cartagena Consensus. By 1986 the Group no longer existed – diverging interests and economic performance of member States, political and ideological differences and the presence or absence of an IMF programme, all eroded their cohesion.

E. RESILIENCE IN THE DEBT LIFE CYCLE

Sovereign debt resilience refers to the ability of a sovereign to avert debt distress in the face of external shocks, through its capacity to adapt to a period of exposure to stress and ensure a rebound in growth and development.

Within the overarching global context of escalating global uncertainty and climate crises, and situated within the conceptual framework of the sovereign debt life cycle, the discussion below considers several crucial elements for a more resilient response to external shocks. These elements include access to national and international buffers, availability of grants and concessional finance and debt relief measures that allow space for recovery.

1. Buffers to support resilience

Data collected just before the COVID-19 crisis in 2020 showed that only one third of American families were ready to cope with a medium-sized shock, with 27 per cent indicating that they would be unable to raise $2,000 to meet an unexpected shock. Another third indicated they found it difficult to make ends meet in a typical month, even without a shock (Deevy and Streeter, 2021). This lack of anticipated household resilience is multidimensional and related to wealth, class and social status, savings and potential sources of liquidity.

Similarly, a sovereign's vulnerability to external shocks can be gauged by its GDP, level of development, foreign currency reserves and its access to global liquidity – for example through a global financial safety net. Typically, developed countries have greater resilience, and it is no surprise that economic recovery after the COVID-19 pandemic revealed considerable inequality gaps within and between countries (United Nations, 2022a).

Accumulation of foreign exchange reserves is a costly national exercise, especially in terms of achieving better returns or investment opportunities foregone. Increasingly, developing countries have relied on reserves as a form of self-insurance, with one measure being the level of reserves compared to short-term debt exposures. In 2022 for example, reserves as a share of short-term debt declined in every developing region, as countries acquired less short-term debt, or used reserves to defend their depreciating currencies (see, for example, General Assembly resolution 78/229).

In turn, the global financial safety net refers to international, regional and bilateral liquidity. Examples include emergency lending from IMF, regional financial arrangements and bilateral currency swap arrangements between central banks. In general, developing countries have diminished access to the global financial safety net relative to developed countries, and those countries without access to a regional financial arrangement are most disadvantaged (Mühlich et al., 2022).

In this context, the August 2021 issuance of special drawing rights to 190 Member States by IMF in response to the COVID-19 pandemic was widely hailed as necessary to boost global resilience. While the special drawing rights mostly accrued to developed countries, developing countries certainly benefited from their issuance (Cashman et al., 2022).

2. Anything but debt?

Additional debt may neither be sustainable nor desirable in the immediate aftermath of a crisis, but unless grants and concessional finance are on offer, this may be the only option. In a context where developing countries typically pay elevated rates to access debt markets anyway (United Nations, 2023b), taking on more debt in these circumstances can come with punitive rates. Borrowing to rebuild after a climate event – for example a hurricane – generally increases in the post-disaster period. At the same time, borrowing costs are also hiked to reflect higher perceived creditor risk (Buhr and Volz, 2018). As the COVID-19 pandemic clearly showed, taking on more debt may be unavoidable. However, a crisis is likely to be accompanied by a slump in government revenue, meaning that social and economic demands soar and compete with debt servicing costs. Resilient recovery in this context is undermined as scarce resources are diverted towards higher debt servicing costs. This increased debt-servicing burden as a proportion of government revenue prevents developing countries from being able to maintain sufficiently elevated levels of public spending on recovery, development objectives and structural transformation.

There is a strong argument for alternatives to debt. More work on alternative sources of finance needs to be done. Insurance, additional grant-based support and far greater access to low-cost, long-term concessional finance can all play a role. The aim is to ensure that lack of debt sustainability and prolonged economic distress does not become the "new normal".

While intergovernmental risk insurance schemes (such as the Caribbean Catastrophe Risk Insurance Facility) may contribute valuable emergency relief, they require a broad base of countries and institutions to support them.

For countries in or near debt distress, grants enable those whose national laws exempt grants from national primary expenditure growth caps to pursue necessary national development goals. This includes climate action to build their climate resilience (Achampong, 2023).

Regarding more concessional finance, the United Nations Secretary-General set out the *SDG Stimulus to Deliver Agenda 2030,* stating that more concessional finance by multilateral development banks is sorely needed, with calls to multilateral development banks to increase lending from around $100 billion a year to $500 billion per year by 2030 (United Nations, 2023b). Moreover, public development banks can provide finance at lower-than-market rates over and above that provided by the multilateral development banks. A recent counterfactual analysis suggests that the high interest rates which developing countries have faced in past decades has done much to undermine their debt sustainability and resilience (Panizza, 2022).

3. Measures that create respite

In the immediate aftermath of a crisis or shock, affected countries would greatly benefit from a general suspension of debt servicing (both principal and interest) from all creditors. In a similar approach to the Debt Service Suspension Initiative enacted by the Group of 20 as the pandemic hit, rules for this type of blanket standstill or moratorium for a specific period could be agreed by bilateral and multilateral creditors. Progress in this regard is welcomed: the United Kingdom is championing climate-resilient debt clauses (United Kingdom, 2023) and the World Bank announced a comprehensive toolkit to support countries after natural disasters. However, these measures should be considered more widely for international wars, pandemics and other crises.

Such a moratorium, especially if applied to all official and private creditors, could create a space for reassessing a country's debt situation. Ideally, this process would be administered by a neutral body, such as the global debt authority, in conjunction with creditors and the borrowing nation. The greater goal would be to provide an opportunity to reassess the sustainability of sovereign debt, and thus avert debt distress. This would enable countries to continue to build resilience in anticipation of a future shock.

F. RECOMMENDATIONS FOR TRANSFORMING SOVEREIGN DEBT AND A WAY FORWARD

1. Transforming sovereign debt requires increased mobilization of concessional finance, either through greater capitalization of multilateral and regional banks or new issuance of special drawing rights.

2. Greater access to financing should be guided by improved transparency of terms and conditions around how financing is used. Digitalizing loan contracts would significantly improve the automation and accuracy of this information. Rules regarding collateralized sovereign bonds would also protect developing countries.

3. Revising the UNCTAD *Principles for Responsible Sovereign Lending and Borrowing* could create momentum to underpin the importance of guiding principles throughout the stages of sovereign debt acquisition.

4. At the country level, improved debt sustainability analysis and tracking needs to be available, not only to reflect the achievement of the Sustainable Development Goals but also to empower country negotiators with improved data on their potential for growth and fiscal consolidation.

5. Access to a truly global financial safety net would greatly benefit developing countries. While all Member States ultimately have access to conditional financing from IMF, access to central bank swaps in a time of liquidity crunch would help avert crises.

6. To achieve the Sustainable Development Goals, countries need to be able to exploit the innovative financial instruments that best serve their needs. More work needs to be done to empower countries in this regard. Rules are needed regarding sustainable development bonds, resilience bonds and automatic restructurings and guarantees.

7. During a polycrisis, a country's ability to remain resilient while servicing debt is called into question. International and domestic rules for a standstill on debtors' obligations in case of climate, health and other external crises, such as climate-resilient debt clauses and the approach spearheaded by the World Bank, are initial steps that could benefit all sovereign borrowers.

8. In what is an increasingly complex environment, borrowers should draw inspiration from private creditors and cooperate to share information and experiences. Work should begin for a more robust debt workout mechanism and statutory global debt authority. In the process, discussions should take place around creditor treatment and equity and a balancing of borrower and lender rights.

REFERENCES

Achampong L (2023). In focus: Reforming climate finance. In: OECD, ed. *Development Co-operation Report 2023: Debating the Aid System*. OECD Publishing. Paris:71–81.

Anthony M, Impavido G and van Selm B (2020). Barbados' 2018–19 sovereign debt restructuring – A sea change? Working Paper No. WP/20/34. International Monetary Fund. Washington, D.C.

Blanchard O and Leigh D (2013). Growth forecast errors and fiscal multipliers. Working Paper No. WP/13/1. International Monetary Fund. Washington, D.C.

Bohoslavsky JP and Goldmann M (2016). An incremental approach to sovereign debt restructuring: Sovereign debt sustainability as a principle of public international law. *Yale Journal of International Law Online*. 42:13–43.

Bolton P, Buchheit LC, Panizza U, Weder di Mauro B and Gulati M (2022). Environmental protection and sovereign debt restructuring. *Capital Markets Law Journal*. 17(3):307–316.

Buchheit L, Chabert G, DeLong C and Zettelmeyer J (2018). *The Sovereign Debt Restructuring Process*. International Monetary Fund. Washington, D.C.

Buhr B and Volz U (2018). *Climate Change and the Cost of Capital in Developing Countries: Assessing the impact of climate risks on sovereign borrowing costs*. SOAS University of London. United Kingdom.

Calvo G, Reinhart C M and Liederman L (1992). Capital inflows to Latin America: The 1970s and the 1990s. IMF Working Paper 92/85. International Monetary Fund. Washington, D.C.

Cashman K, Arauz A and Merling L (2022). *Special Drawing Rights: The Right Tool to Use to Respond to the Pandemic and Other Challenges*. Centre for Economic and Policy Research. April.

Chellaney B (2017). China's debt-trap diplomacy. *Project Syndicate*. 23 January.

Chung K and Papaioannou MG (2020). Do enhanced collective action clauses affect sovereign borrowing costs? Working Paper No. 20/162. International Monetary Fund. Washington, D.C.

Domar ED (1944). The "burden of the debt" and the national income. *American Economic Review*. 34(4):798–827.

ESCAP (2023). *Economic and Social Survey of Asia and the Pacific 2023: Rethinking Public Debt for the Sustainable Development Goals*. (United Nations publication. Sales No. E.23.II.F.2. New York).

Financial Times (2023). Argentina faces €1.3bn bill after losing case over GDP-linked debt. 5 April.

Fischer D (1997). *History of the International Atomic Energy Agency: The First Forty Years*. International Atomic Energy Agency. Vienna.

Fitch Ratings (2023). Sovereign defaults are at record high. 29 March.

Fritz B, Prates D and de Paula LF (2018). Global currency hierarchy and national policy space: A framework for peripheral economies. *European Journal of Economics and Economic Policies: Intervention*. 15(2):208–218.

Gelpern A (2016). Sovereign debt. Now what? *Yale Journal of International Law Online*. 42:45.

Gelpern A (2018). About government debt… who knows? *Capital Markets Law Journal*. 13(3):321–355.

Gelpern A, Horn S, Morris S, Parks B and Trebesch C (2022). How China lends: A rare look into 100 debt contracts with foreign governments. *Economic Policy*. eiac054.

Goldmann M (2023). Industrial policy and sovereign debt. SSRN.

Group of 30 (2020). Sovereign debt and financing for recovery after the COVID-19 shock. Preliminary report and conclusions of the Working Group. Washington, D.C.

Guzman M and Stiglitz JE (2016). Creating a framework for sovereign debt restructuring that works. In: *Too Little, Too Late: The Quest for Resolving Sovereign Debt Crises*. Columbia University Press. New York:3–32.

Horn S, Reinhart CM and Trebesch C (2021). China's overseas lending. *Journal of International Economics*. 133:103539.

IMF (2023). *Making Public Debt Public – Ongoing Initiatives and Reform Options*. International Monetary Fund. Washington, D.C.

Inter-Agency Task Force on Financing for Development (2023). *Financing for Sustainable Development Report 2023*. (United Nations publication. Sales No. E.23.I.6. New York).

Intergovernmental Panel on Climate Change (2023). Climate Change 2023: Synthesis Report. Contribution of Working Groups I, II and III to the Sixth Assessment Report of the Intergovernmental Panel on Climate Change. IPCC. Geneva.

Krueger A (2002). *A New Approach to Sovereign Debt Restructuring*. International Monetary Fund. Washington, D.C.

Lippolis N and Verhoeven H (2022). Politics by default: China and the global governance of African debt. *Survival*. 64(3):153–178.

Lockwood K (2022). User manual: UNCTAD sustainable development finance assessment framework policy dashboard. In: UNCTAD, ed. *COVID-19 Response and Recovery: Mobilizing financial resources for development* (United Nations publication. Geneva).

Maslen S and Aslan C (2022). *Enhancing Debt Transparency by Strengthening Public Debt Transaction Disclosure Practices*. EFI Insight. World Bank. Washington, D.C.

Munevar D (2021). *Sleep now in the fire: Sovereign bonds and the Covid-19 debt crisis*. Eurodad.

Mühlich L, Zucker-Marques M, Fritz B and Kring W (2022). No-one left behind? COVID-19 and the shortcomings of the global financial safety net for low- and middle-income countries. Paper for UNCTAD DA Project: Mobilizing finance for development in the era of COVID-19. Paper 05/22.

Panizza U (2022). Long-term debt sustainability in emerging market economies: A counterfactual analysis. Background for the 2022 Financing for Sustainable Development Report. Working Paper No. HEIDWP07-2022. Graduate Institute of International and Development Studies.

Pasinetti L (1998). The myth (or folly) of the 3% deficit/GDP Maastricht "parameter". *Cambridge Journal of Economics*. 22(1):103–116.

Porcile G (2021). Latin-American structuralism and neo-structuralism. In: Alcorta L, Foster-McGregor N, Verspagen B and Szirmai A, eds. *New Perspectives on Structural Change: Causes and Consequences of Structural Change in the Global Economy*. Oxford, Oxford University Press: 50–71.

Prebisch R (1950). *The Economic Development of Latin America and its Principal Problems*. Economic Commission for Latin America and the Caribbean. United Nations Department of Economic Affairs. New York.

Prebisch R (1959). Commercial policy in the underdeveloped countries. *American Economic Review, Papers and Proceedings*. 49(2):251–273.

Schmidt-Traub G (2015). *Investment Needs to Achieve the Sustainable development Goals: Understanding the Billions and Trillions*. United Nations Sustainable Development Solutions Network.

Thirlwall AP (1979). The balance of payments constraint as an explanation of international growth rate differences. *Banca Nazionale del Lavoro Quarterly Review*. 32(128):45–53.

UNCTAD (2012). *Principles on Promoting Responsible Sovereign Lending and Borrowing* (United Nations publication. Geneva).

UNCTAD (2015). *Trade and Development Report 2015*: *Making the International Financial Architecture Work for Development* (United Nations publication. Sales No. E.15.II.D.4. New York and Geneva).

UNCTAD (2019a). *The Least Developed Countries Report 2019: The Present and Future of External Development Finance – Old Dependence, New Challenges* (United Nations publication. Sales No. E.20.II.D.2. New York and Geneva).

UNCTAD (2019b). *Trade and Development Report 2019: Financing a Global Green New Deal* (United Nations publication. Sales No. E.19.II.D.15. Geneva).

UNCTAD (2020). *Trade and Development Report Update: From the Great Lockdown to the Great Meltdown: Developing Country Debt in the Time of COVID-19* (United Nations publication. Geneva).

UNCTAD (2021). *Climate Change, Green Recovery and Trade* (United Nations publication).

UNCTAD (2022a). *Debt Management and Financial Analysis System Programme Annual Report 2022* (United Nations publication. Geneva).

UNCTAD (2022b). *Sustainable Development Finance Assessment Framework* (United Nations publication. Geneva).

UNCTAD (2022c). Staying afloat: A policy agenda for climate and debt challenges. COP27 High-Level Event Series. Background Note.

UNCTAD (2022d). UNCTAD Sustainable Development Finance Assessment (SDFA) Framework: Linking debt sustainability to the achievement of the 2030 Agenda. DA COVID-19 Project Paper 16/22.

UNCTAD (2023). Delivering development finance to achieve the 2030 Agenda for sustainable development: Making development finance contribute to environmentally sound industrialization. Note by the UNCTAD secretariat for the 7th Intergovernmental Group of Experts on Financing for Development. 23 August.

United Kingdom (2023). Climate Resilient Debt Clauses – Legal template for the Climate Resilient Debt Clauses developed by UK Export Finance. 22 June. Available at: https://assets.publishing.service.gov.uk/government/uploads/system/uploads/attachment_data/file/1164721/Climate_Resilient_Debt_Clauses.pdf (accessed 22 November 2023).

United Kingdom Supreme Court (2023). *The Law Debenture Trust vs Ukraine*. Case ID. 2018/0192 Judgement. 15 March.

United Nations Development Programme (2023). Integrated national financing frameworks and sovereign thematic bonds. Policy Brief. UNDP. New York.

United Nations Environment Programme (2022). *Adaption Gap Report 2022*: *Too Little, Too Slow – Climate adaptation failure puts world at risk*. (Nairobi).

United Nations, Department of Economic and Social Affairs (2022a). *World Economic Situation and Prospects 2022* (United Nations publication. Sales No. E.22.II.C.1, New York).

United Nations, General Assembly (2022b). External debt sustainability and development. Note by the Secretary-General. A/77/206. New York. 21 July.

United Nations, General Assembly (2022c). Resolution adopted by the General Assembly on 14 December 2022. External debt sustainability and development. A/RES/77/153. New York. 20 December.

United Nations, General Assembly (2023a). External debt sustainability and development. Note by the Secretary-General. A/78/229. New York. 25 July.

United Nations (2023b). United Nations Secretary-General's SDG Stimulus to Deliver Agenda 2030. New York.

V20 (2022). *Climate Vulnerable Economic Loss Report*. The Vulnerable 20 Group. Geneva.

Vivid Economics (2021). *Greenness of Stimulus Index. An assessment of COVID-19 stimulus by G20 countries and other major economies in relation to climate action and biodiversity goals.* Available at: https://www.vivideconomics.com/casestudy/greenness-for-stimulus-index/ (accessed 22 November 2023).

Welsh M (2014). Resilience and responsibility: Governing uncertainty in a complex world. *The Geographical Journal.* 180(1):15–26.

World Bank (2022). Brief: Debt Service Suspension Initiative. 10 March. Washington, D.C.

World Bank (2023). Factsheet: World Bank Group Announces Comprehensive Toolkit to Support Countries After Natural Disasters. 22 June.

Wu R (2023). Natural disasters, climate change, and structural transformation: A new perspective from international trade. World Economy. 46(5):1333–1377.

Chapter VI

The Need for Financial Reform for Climate-Aligned Development

Reconciling ecological and developmental priorities

Despite decades of pledges, the international financial system has delivered only a fraction of the financing needed to meet global climate and development targets. To achieve the Sustainable Development Goals and inclusive growth for all, financial resources need to be scaled up in the framework of a climate-aligned development agenda. To accomplish this, two main challenges should be overcome.

First, the roles and modes of engagement for both the public and the private sectors need to be reassessed, in terms of how the sectors participate in and contribute to enabling economic transformation. Second, continued biases in financing, both public and private, often lead to climate goals being undermined, directly and indirectly. This includes the trillions of dollars still supporting fossil fuels.

Within its call for a Global Green New Deal, UNCTAD proposes a range of policy actions to redress the current impasse.

Recommendations

- Pay the public funds pledged for official development assistance and climate finance, ensuring these funds are readily accessible to those who need them.

- Support the public banks and funds doing the heavy lifting by increasing their capitalization and prioritizing long-term investment.

- Develop new models of deployment, and more equitable and effective means of harnessing private finance and commercial banks.

- Cut finance to activities that accelerate the climate crisis and redirect funds to activities consistent with climate pledges. This includes turning off the finance taps for new fossil fuel exploration and for fossil fuel subsidies, while establishing alternative long-term support for low-income and poor households.

A. INTRODUCTION

After more than two decades of global discussions – from the first United Nations International Conference on Financing for Development in Monterrey (2002), to the Copenhagen Accord (2009), the United Nations Conference on Sustainable Development (2012), the Paris Climate Agreement and the Addis Ababa Action Agenda (both 2015), along with numerous Group of 20 gatherings – the international financial system has only delivered a fraction of the financing needed to meet the agreed climate and development targets to guarantee a prosperous and sustainable future for all. Even when finance has been mobilized for longer-term investments in public goods and services, it has rarely flowed to the countries most in need. In some areas it has even been at odds with agreed goals, for example the trillions of dollars supporting increased fossil fuel production. The widening gap in annual investment needed by developing countries to achieve the Sustainable Development Goals currently stands at $4 trillion per year, almost double what it was in 2015 when the Sustainable Development Goals were adopted (UNCTAD, 2023a).

This chapter proposes a series of policy reforms and realignments. It presents a particular focus on addressing persistent asymmetries in the international financial system which, if resolved, could help developing countries mobilize the required resources. The main premise is that climate finance should be an additional and complementary component to development needs. The current negotiations regarding the climate agenda offer an opportunity to harmonize the two.

B. THE UNDERLYING CAUSES OF FINANCING GAPS IN A CLIMATE-ALIGNED DEVELOPMENT AGENDA

1. Private finance and the "missing trillions"

While private capital plays a role in meeting the development goals and the energy transition, the record so far has been disappointing. This is unfortunate as, according to various estimates, the annual investment needed for climate goals and the Sustainable Development Goals is less than 1 per cent of the current value of total global financial assets (around $4 trillion per year). Through a combination of financial innovation, technocratic acumen and decisive political leadership, it should be possible to redirect a portion of those assets into tangible investments to meet climate and development goals.

Private capital flows globally are immense in scale but tend towards short-term gains. Moreover, private sector levels of investment in gross fixed capital formation have been stagnant at suboptimal levels or in decline in most countries for decades. In 1980, private sector investment in developing countries was over 20 per cent of GDP, but has now fallen to roughly 18 per cent, a figure that would be lower still if China was excluded from the calculation. And, as discussed in chapter I, the drop has been most pronounced in advanced economies.

"The annual investment needed to meet climate goals and the Sustainable Development Goals is less than 1 per cent of the current value of total global financial assets."

The structural pressures and policy decisions that lie behind these trends have not received sufficient attention from those making a case for greater reliance on private finance to deliver development and climate goals (UNCTAD, 2019; Gabor and Braun, 2023). For instance, the 2016 *Roadmap to US$100 Billion* for the Paris Agreement expressed confidence in reaching the goal of mobilizing $100 billion per year by 2020 for climate action in developing countries. In its base projections, a companion document anticipated that public sources would provide about two thirds of the $100 billion target while private sources would provide the remaining one third (OECD, 2016).

The public part of the vision was almost achieved. Climate finance for low-income and middle-income economies from the world's main multilateral development banks ($38 billion), public direct mobilization ($8 billion) and public cofinance ($18 billion) amounted to more than $64 billion in 2020. Yet, a closer examination reveals that the figures for the private sector fell short of expectations, as the total private mobilization that year stood at less than $10 billion (African Development Bank et al., 2021: table 23). The calculation of this last figure, however, was carried out using generous interpretations. Under more stringent definitions based on only direct and not indirect cofinance, the amount received was just $3.5 billion. Hence, of a total of $74 billion of funds for low-income and middle-income countries, 87 per cent came from public banks and public cofinanciers. Such a small amount of private cofinancing was never envisaged.

Yet, the consensus narrative and expectations for financing climate and the Sustainable Development Goals have not fundamentally changed in recent years. In line with recommendations of the Group of 20 Eminent Persons Report on Global Financial Governance (Group of 20, 2018), developed countries continued to call for increased public finance to be used as a tool to draw out the elusive private finance outlined in the 2021 Climate Finance Delivery Plan (COP26, 2021). As cited in a UNFCCC Report (2022:101), "All developed countries need to step up efforts to meet the goal, implying the need to scale up public finance". At the same time, the optimism of 2016 is repeated: "The scale of private finance mobilization is not where it was projected to be in the 2016 Roadmap, demonstrating that further efforts are needed to improve the effectiveness of mobilizing private finance from public interventions" (ibid).

Some investment needs or activities will always be unappealing for the commercial or private sector. According to one extensive assessment of the blended finance landscape, "Each $1 of multilateral development bank and DFI [development finance institutions] invested mobilizes on average $0.75 of private finance for developing countries, but this falls to $0.37 for LICs [low-income countries]. Expectations that this kind of blended finance can bridge the Sustainable Development Goals financing gap are unrealistic: 'billions to billions' is more plausible than 'billions to trillions'" (Attridge and Engren, 2019:11). The OECD estimates that development finance institutions have mobilized only $81 billion towards the Sustainable Development Goals through blended finance since 2000 (OECD, 2023), and the mobilization of private climate finance has underperformed against developed countries' expectations by up to 60 per cent (UNFCCC, 2022).

Similarly, the high hopes for green bonds as a powerful source of climate finance have turned out to be unrealistic. UNCTAD (2023a) estimated that green bonds issued in 2022 experienced an annual decline of 3 per cent, down to $500 billion; a tiny addition to the $100 trillion stock of existing regular bonds worldwide (Newell et al., 2023).

Moreover, while markets for green bonds and environmental, social and governance (ESG) investments more generally are growing, the question of additionality is unresolved. Studies show that the risk and return profile of ESG investments is roughly congruent with their conventional counterparts (Jain et al., 2019; Pietsch and Salakhova, 2022), suggesting the majority of ESG investments would have been implemented with or without the ESG label. While there is evidence of a slight cost advantage of green bonds over conventional bonds, it is unclear whether this reflects investors' willingness to pay a "greenium" for such instruments, or a potentially temporary imbalance of supply and demand. However, stronger evidence for a "greenium" on government-issued and investment-grade bonds that follow strict reporting standards suggests that credibility matters (UNCTAD, 2023a).

None of this is intended to diminish the need for scaling up private investment in achieving climate and development goals, but it clearly matters how this is approached, managed and complemented.

2. The forward march of fossil fuel finance continues

One area where finance does continue to be forthcoming on a significant scale is fossil fuels. In 2015 in Paris, all nations committed to substantially reducing global greenhouse gas emissions to limit the global temperature increase in this century. Agreed-upon targets were 2 degrees Celsius while pursuing efforts to limit the increase even further to 1.5 degrees. The Paris Agreement did not mention fossil fuels, even though they account for 80 per cent of the world's energy supply and have directly caused over 90 per cent of global CO_2 emissions, or 75 per cent of global greenhouse gas emissions in recent years (Hausfather and Friedlingstein, 2022).

In the challenging context of transitioning away from fossil fuels, it is a major concern that funds continue to flow into fresh exploration and new projects, particularly in developed countries, which already benefit from high levels of energy access. A recent study (UNEP et al., 2023) finds that Governments still planned to produce more than double the amount of fossil fuels by 2030 than are compatible with the 1.5-degree target. Against this backdrop, simply subsidizing the production of non-fossil fuel energy infrastructure and supply to tweak relative prices will not be enough to turn off the fossil fuel CO_2 emissions tap.

Today there is a growing policy consensus that any credible strategy relies on a substantial and rapid reduction of fossil fuel finance, extraction, trade and consumption – for which regulation will be key, as voluntary actions can only go so far. At the twenty-sixth session of the Conference of the Parties in Glasgow in 2021 (COP26), more than 40 countries pledged to "phase down coal" (UNFCCC, 2021), backtracking from earlier wording proposing a coal "phase out". A smaller group led by Costa Rica and Denmark established the Beyond Oil and Gas Alliance (BOGA). The Powering Past Coal Alliance provided another pledge, and the private sector also promised to act.

In recent years, most airlines and even oil majors have pledged to become carbon neutral, although academic research stresses existing technological limitations and the need for scaling down such environmentally harmful sectors by about 85 per cent (Nick and Thalmann, 2022; *Bloomberg*, 2023).

At COP26, private financial actors launched the Global Financial Alliance for Net Zero (GFANZ) to better coordinate the $130 trillion of assets under the management of its members across all sectors of the financial system (banking, insurance, asset management, etc.) to accelerate the transition to a net-zero global economy. As the coal, oil and gas sector is highly capital-intensive and fossil fuel businesses rely on external credit and investment, the creation of GFANZ appeared a welcome step, and research commissioned by GFANZ (Lubis et al., 2022) reveals a need to swiftly cut fossil fuel finance. Specifically, the average annual level for the period from 2020–2030 must be halved in order to achieve net-zero ambitions.

Yet, research suggests that finance for fossil fuels is still on the rise, with fossil fuel investments forecasted to exceed $1 trillion in 2023 (figure VI.1). Other estimates of fossil fuel finance that track financial transactions between banks and fossil fuel companies also show that credit extended under the form of loans and underwriting services to fossil fuel companies has not declined.[1]

"Finance for fossil fuels is still on the rise, with fossil fuel investments forecasted to exceed $1 trillion in 2023."

Fossil fuel finance is strongly led by advanced economies. While banks with headquarters in developed countries are responsible for 61 per cent of fossil fuel credit extension, with the United States alone accounting for 22 per cent, credit from China amounts to 30 per cent. All other developing country banks only originated 9 per cent of global fossil fuel credit.

VI

---

[1] Since 2016, private and public banks have provided more than $5.8 trillion worth of credit for new fossil fuel development projects to companies identified on the Global Coal Exit List (GCEL) and on the Global Oil and Gas Exit List (GOGEL) compiled by the environmental and human rights organization, Urgewald. However, as bilateral credit transaction between banks and fossil fuel companies (only syndicated loans are reported) as well as transactions between MDBs and fossil fuel companies are not included in the data gathered by Urgewald and Reclaim Finance (2023), the estimates presented in figure VI.1 might be seen as conservative. Importantly too, unlike the estimates of the International Energy Agency (IEA) on fossil fuel investment based on corporate accounts and surveys about planned corporate capital expenditure (IEA, 2022, 2023a, 2023b), estimates of the support that banks provide to fossil fuel companies through loans and underwriting services do not include the profits reinvested by fossil fuel companies, which tend to increase in periods of high energy prices.

Figure VI.1 Fossil fuel finance unabated even after the Paris Agreement

Capital expenditure by fossil fuel companies and credit support provided to fossil fuel companies, by country (group) of financial institutions headquarters

(Trillions of dollars)

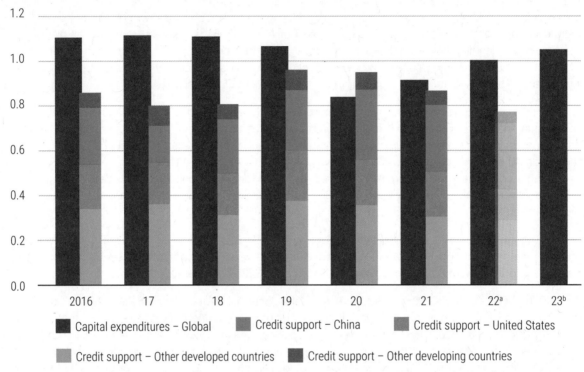

Source: UNCTAD calculations based on Reclaim Finance (2023); a 2022 update of Urgewald (2021); and IEA (2023a and b).

Note: Urgewald data on credit support (including loans and underwriting services) extended by public and private banks to GCEL companies runs until August 2022, and Reclaim Finance data on credit support to GOGEL companies runs until mid-September 2022. This data was gathered in Bloomberg, Refinitiv and IJGlobal. More methodological details in Warmerdam (2022), https://www.coalexit. org/methodology and https://gogel.org/about-data. IEA global figures refer to capital expenditure on fossil fuel without CCUS and are based on corporate accounts, surveys and estimates.

[a] As credit support data for the year 2022 only extends over 8 months (and not 12), the credit support figures for 2022 have been multiplied by a factor 1.5.

[b] The capital expenditure figure for 2023 is a projection.

Although the magnitude of credit activities by Chinese banks in support of fossil fuel companies, especially in the coal sector, exceeds any other individual country, the relative contribution of other countries to support existing and new fossil fuel projects is much more significant when viewed on per capita terms. As shown in figure VI.2, in terms of average annual fossil fuel credit activities per capita, those of developed economies such as Bermuda ($2671), Switzerland ($1857), Canada ($1463), Luxembourg ($964), Japan ($812), the United Kingdom ($730), France ($598) and the United States ($579) are significantly higher, compared to those of China ($183). A handful of high-income developing countries, such as Singapore ($930), Bahrain ($429), Kuwait ($387) and the United Arab Emirates ($305), are also high contributors according to this metric.

A comparable gap is evident between the climate goals and pledges of Governments and corporations and actual financing trends, as seen in the petrochemical industry. Petrochemicals constitute a lucrative end-stage of the fossil fuel value chain and the start of a vast global value chain in plastics. Both plastics and petrochemicals are increasingly seen as problematic for global pollution and health. UNCTAD research into loans and bond issuances in the petrochemicals sector shows a significant rise in new transactions each year after the Paris Agreement, rising from $15 billion in 2016 to over $50 billion in 2019. Current total active bonds and loans are valued at more than $250 billion, on top of existing equity holdings (Barrowclough and Finkill, 2021).

Figure VI.2 Mature financial centres most involved in keeping fossil fuel finance alive and kicking

Average annual credit support provided to fossil fuel companies in per capita terms, by economy (group) of financial institutions headquarters, 2016–2022

(Dollars per person)

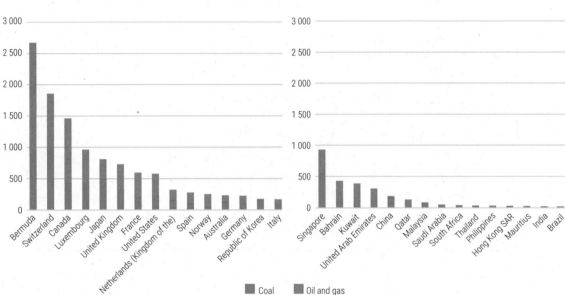

A. Top 15 developed economies

B. Top 15 developing economies

■ Coal   ■ Oil and gas

Source: UNCTAD calculations based on data from Reclaim Finance (2023) and on a 2022 update of Urgewald (2021).
Note: See note for figure VI.1.

While the public sector has generally decreased financial support in line with climate pledges, private finance has driven it much higher. Plastic production has increased sharply: it is seen as an attractive source of profits as other uses of fossil fuels decline. This indicates some of the complexities of the processes of transformation that lie ahead. Moreover, even as finance for the petrochemicals sector has continued unabated, only a small portion is going into "greening" the sector. Out of more than 2,000 active bonds issued by the petrochemical industry with a value of $218 billion, only 20 were designated "green". Their value was just $5 billion (UNCTAD, 2023b).

> *"Out of more than 2,000 active bonds issued by the petrochemical industry with a value of $218 billion, just 20 were designated 'green'."*

3. The role of public banks and funds in financing the shift to climate-aligned development

The fact that private finance flows into some activities in developing countries and not others is no new concern. It is one reason behind increased support of official developmental assistance, the creation of dedicated global funds and, more recently, for philanthropic sources of project finance. It is also the starting point for a serious reappraisal of public banks, including for development (Stiglitz, 2019; Griffith-Jones, 2022).

As the record of many countries shows, projects that are intrinsically unappealing to commercial banks and private interests, even where capital markets are relatively developed, include those with high upfront capital costs, low and unpredictable revenue flows and a long and uncertain lead time between taking the financing risk and capturing revenues. This is especially the case when the investment concerns something new and potentially risky, as depicted in the area to the left-hand side of figure VI.3, where risks are high and revenues uncertain.

Figure VI.3 The catalytic role of public banks and funds to finance the transition to green projects
Risks, revenues and reforms needed for patient capital to finance the shift to renewable energy

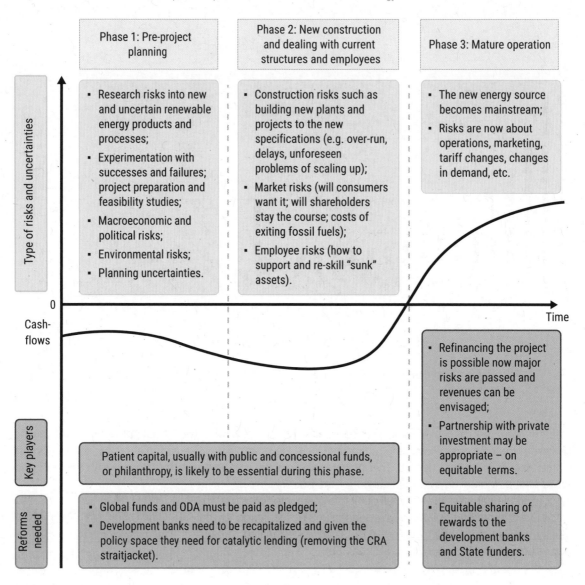

Source: UNCTAD.

Most countries found that it is best to create separate banks to provide long-term capital at near-commercial rates and "policy banks" to provide credit to special areas, such as agriculture or small-scale sectors, where interest rates must be subsidized and grace periods have to be longer. A similar division of labour can be found with international development banks, whether multilateral or regional, which tend to have distinct eligibility criteria for countries seeking access to concessional or grant-based financing windows.

The reason public banks can potentially play this catalytic and patient role is that they tend to be mandated to follow different operating principles compared to commercial banks. In addition, public banks cultivate technical and managerial skills and the ability to coordinate with government ministries as well as private interests (Griffith-Jones and Ocampo, 2018; *Trade and Development Report 2019*; among a growing body of literature on this). Their support can be tailored to specific projects and may last for a long time, requiring these banks to develop appropriate exit strategies for their lending to minimize the threat of capture and abuse of funds. In recent decades, many new banks have been established for this purpose, including several important banks led by developing countries (Barrowclough et al., 2021).

Revitalizing public banking institutions at all levels will be fundamental to financing a just transition to a zero-carbon world (*Trade and Development Report 2019*), just as such institutions were crucial for the reconstruction of war-torn Europe (and beyond) at the end of Second World War. This was the task of the International Bank for Reconstruction and Development, better known today as the World Bank, as well as the Marshall Plan, which took on the initial reconstruction effort. Other multilateral development banks were subsequently established at the regional level, such as the Asian Development Bank, the European Investment Bank and others (*Trade and Development Report 2022*).

"Revitalizing public banking institutions at all levels will be fundamental to financing a just transition to a zero-carbon world."

There are now 45 multilateral development banks with just over $2 trillion in assets in total, the largest being the World Bank and its regional counterparts. Alongside Western-led multilateral institutions, hundreds of national and regional development finance institutions have since emerged across the developing world. Today, there are over 450 of these institutions with total assets of $11.6 trillion which may finance upwards of $2 trillion on an annual basis, representing roughly 12 per cent of total world investment (Xu et al., 2021).

While public banks take on direct responsibility for financing public goods and can substitute for reluctant and impatient private finance in critical sectors, it is also recognized that the latter is usually more forthcoming once the riskiest periods are past, and revenue streams become more predictable, meaning that there is a good chance of making a profit (figure VI.3). Whether and how, and the extent to which this crowding-in takes place, can be a challenge for policymakers. It may be that some larger undertakings are always better done by public finance and remain in public ownership (*Trade and Development Report 2015*). For others, new modalities of risk- and profit-sharing will likely be needed to ensure the balance between public and private is fair and effective, as noted in the bottom row of figure VI.3.

Parts of the climate-aligned development agenda may remain unappealing to private investors because they embody elements of a public good, where earnings could be difficult. Examples of this include investments in climate change adaptation, as opposed to mitigation activities where future revenues may be possible (*Trade and Development Report 2021*), and efforts to control air and ocean pollution (Sustainable Development Goals 3, 11 and 14; Vivas et al., 2021).

These public good characteristics create different and longer-lasting problems for attracting finance from the market and rely heavily on regulations as well as other public sources of finance, such as official development assistance. In some instances, blended finance or the use of public–private partnerships can be used, although as noted in past *Trade and Development Reports* and in a wide range of literature (Matsumoto et al., 2021; Gabor, 2019), with due caution. This will likely only be an option in cases where some revenues and profits are envisaged or where philanthropy is active, such as in the "debt-for-nature" instruments discussed in previous Reports. Policymakers are advised to seek partnerships with an equitable balance of risks and returns.

A related challenge includes examples where historically costly investments have passed into the positive revenue zone and are now seen as problematic for other reasons, as in the case with today's high-carbon activities. Why would firms willingly leave this zone of profitability – with often very high profits – and pursue high-cost/uncertain-revenue investments? The clear answer is that the costs of being exposed to carbon-based activities lies in the future. If shareholders are not already fleeing newly "subprime" assets or pushing for change (Giraud et al., 2019; Caldecott, 2017), firms and investors will not voluntarily divest from profitable activities (Christophers, 2022). In addition, publicly listed firms, pension funds and other institutions may find themselves constrained by institutional rules or obligations, preventing them from taking such actions. What is needed are regulations requiring them to do so; compulsory disclosure of the extent to which firms and funds are exposed; and shareholder willingness to forego profits and make a major shift.

At the same time, it is not the case that public sources of finance have been sufficiently forthcoming – even when these come with pledges and public commitments made by their Governments. Public banks and funds are, in many developing countries, sorely underfinanced for the task.

VI

A key part of the financing challenge facing all countries, and particularly developing nations as they strive to build sustainable growth paths, is how to divest from existing sectors. This is due to the significant social, economic and financial costs that come from halting even unproductive or harmful investments, including those involving ecologically destructive practices. While the "no change" option will also bring costs, these are not equally shared nor are they immediate, for many people. Climate inequalities and injustices mean that it is the bottom 50 per cent of the world who is suffering climate impacts now; the richest decile is (currently) only marginally impacted (box VI.1).

Voluntary divestment and a significant shift in direction are unlikely to happen if there are substantial costs associated with winding down and transforming current industry practices and products. These are highly profitable for some and, as with the case of fossil fuels, today's economies are largely dependent on them, including through existing structures and patterns of production and trade. Stopping the exploration of new fossil fuel sites and reducing existing sites requires winding down and transforming numerous activities. This would impact a huge number of workers who could either face job losses or need to be retrained to access new job opportunities in the green economy (as shown in figure VI.3). Changing course also impacts the value of holdings for pension funds, sovereign wealth funds and other public and private institutions, potentially spreading shocks through the financial system (*Trade and Development Report 2019*). There is a great deal that needs to be in place for this path to be selected.

C. STEPS FORWARD

A more sustainable model is needed. Such a model would successfully mobilize private finance and break the climate investment trap by building a track record of investments through public-led intervention. This, in turn, can crowd-in complementary private investment, including through reinvested profit. Investment decisions by public actors should move beyond a project-level focus to support more holistic roadmaps that can develop low-emissions markets, exceed the critical "renewables deployment threshold" and initiate a virtuous cycle that lowers risk and the cost of capital. International efforts should target the evolution of low-emissions sectors through public investment in infrastructure; strengthening of supply chains; expanding project preparation support and knowledge-sharing; and developing networks of relationships between domestic private actors.

Strengthening policy and regulatory environments will also help to boost total finance flows. Finance flows into wind and solar energy, for example, have been preferentially channelled into countries with strong climate ambitions and renewable policies. Egypt, Jordan and Viet Nam all saw sharp increases in investment following the introduction of renewable energy targets and strengthened renewables policies (Rickman et al., 2023). International efforts can support the expansion of policy and fiscal space to deploy industrial policy tools such as subsidies, tax breaks, guarantees and information tools where developing countries are unable to mount expensive green initiatives on their own.

Developing countries will need to mobilize additional domestic resources to undertake their required investment push. Serious attempts to map the scale and composition of the financing challenge for developing countries often relies on mobilizing increased domestic resources to fill the gap. However, there is little indication of how this would happen, given the current macrofinancial constraints facing most developing countries (Bhattachariya et al., 2020). As suggested above, making better use of the over 500 national, regional and subregional development finance institutions will be critical and will also require significant increases in international support.

1. Scaling up additional public finance

a. Multilateral funding

As discussed earlier, development banks have the mandate to follow social and economic imperatives beyond maximizing short-term profits. They have the capacity to create credit and leverage beyond the funds they receive. They also have access to concessional finance that can be used to lend to other banks and private investors.

However, these development banks are often sorely underfinanced for the heavy lifting required. World Bank lending has fallen steadily over the last four decades relative to the size of the global economy (figure VI.4). This is a problem for climate and development finance because multilateral development banks are still the most important source of long-term finance for some regions and countries (*Trade and Development Report 2022*). In 2020 they provided a record $230 billion. Slightly more than half of their lending is typically concessional with respect to the interest rate charged to borrowers, maturity and other characteristics, compared to commercial lenders and grant-based lending (OECD, 2022).

For these and other reasons, the Secretary-General of the United Nations recommends boosting lending by multilateral development banks to 1 per cent of global gross domestic product, from $500 billion to $1 trillion a year (United Nations, 2023), increasing their ability to extend new sources of finance in the form of both concessional lending and grants.

This can be accomplished by increasing the base capital of development finance institutions, expanding their lending headroom and mobilizing capital from the commercial sector. Since the global financial crisis, some of these institutions have made significant increases to the amount of DFI capital in the world economy, but a stepwise increase from these levels is still needed. Leading contributions have come from China, which has increased the assets of the China Development Bank by $1.5 trillion since the crisis, with roughly one fifth of its balance sheet now in overseas financing to sovereign Governments outside China. What is more, China has helped establish two new multilateral development banks: the Asian Infrastructure Investment Bank and the New Development Bank. Many national and subregional development banks in emerging market and developing countries also replenished development finance institutions or created new ones as they accumulated reserves due to the commodity boom in the aftermath of the crisis.

Figure VI.4 · The downward slide in global development finance
World Bank lending as a share of world gross product
(Percentage)

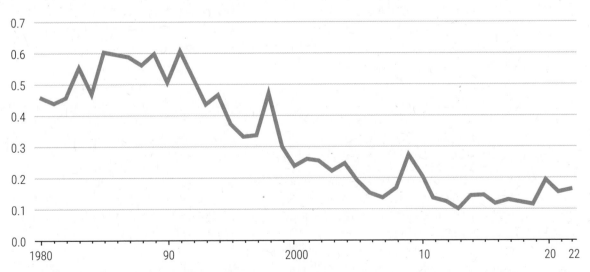

Source: Gallagher et al. (2023), derived from IMF data on lending by the International Bank for Reconstruction and Development and International Development Association.

In addition to further capital increases, some development finance institutions have significant lending headroom to provide more financing while continuing to maintain strong credit ratings. Recent studies, including by rating agencies themselves, have estimated that multilateral development banks could increase their lending headroom by $598 billion to $1.9 trillion under various scenarios. Without a capital increase, if multilateral development banks optimized their balance sheets at an AAA rating, the increase ranges from $598 billion to $1 trillion. With a capital increase of 25 per cent by major multilateral development banks, lending could expand by $1.2 trillion to $1.7 trillion. If some multilateral development banks were to optimize at an AA+ rating, expansion could reach close to $2 trillion dollars. Optimizing at AA+ would, however, have

"Climate finance is perpetuating inequalities that see the poorest regions of the world, such as sub-Saharan Africa, receive only a tiny fraction of climate mitigation investment."

a negative impact on profitability, although according to some, the net benefits are still likely to be positive (Humphrey, 2018; Gallagher, 2020). In addition to expanding their lending headroom, some development finance institutions are considering securitizing their loan portfolios, although there are few examples of securitization. Estimates of the benefits and costs of such an approach are mixed at best (Humphrey, 2018; Gabor, 2019).

Expanding should also be accompanied by extending. Climate finance, as with traditional development finance, is perpetuating inequalities that see the poorest regions of the world, such as sub-Saharan Africa, receive only a tiny fraction of climate mitigation investment. This is even though they account for about one sixth of the global population. Inequalities are made worse because the vast majority of finance comes from the global North (box VI.1).

The modalities through which multilateral development banks lend to national banks can also impact the synergy between climate and development finance and influence the borrowing capacity of developing countries. The provision of loans in local currencies, as opposed to dollar loans, is one change that can make a big difference for developing country borrowers who face exchange rate risks when exposed to debt in a foreign currency. This is especially notable for fossil fuels, which are priced in dollars. At the same time, if foreign investors take up locally issued bonds, this does not stop the country being exposed to exchange rate shocks if they decide to exit sharply.

Box VI.1 Targeting climate and fossil fuel finance inequalities

In common with unequal access to development finance in general, the countries and communities that are most in need of climate finance receive the least. In addition to their unmet needs for adaptation finance, there is a perverse mitigation effect. As most carbon emissions have been created by advanced economies, targeting these countries to reduce emissions would have the most impact (Chancel et al., 2023). However, halting global warming cannot be achieved unless developing countries also progressively change their carbon use.

Apart from the question of fairness, the fact is that those with the greatest capacity to provide finance are the top 10 per cent of the world's population. This decile causes 48 per cent of global carbon emissions, experiences the least losses, and accounts for almost 80 per cent of the world's wealth. Compare this to the 50 per cent of the world's population that has only 2 per cent of the global total wealth, is causing only 12 per cent of emissions, while registering 75 per cent of losses and damages (Chancel et al., 2023).

Moreover, current investment trends in the fossil fuel sector are only adding to these inequalities. Most finance in the sector is raised from banks in developed countries, and spent by companies with headquarters in developed regions, even if these funds are also used for fossil fuel extraction in developing countries. There is a development tension here. If the investments are used for electrification in developing countries, this could be seen as a way to reduce the energy gap and support economic diversification. On the other hand, certain fuels, whether used directly or indirectly to produce manufactured goods, are bound for advanced country markets. While this creates jobs and export revenue, it also exposes these countries to the downsides of hosting coal, oil and petrochemical activities. This includes being hit by trade policies and other regulations targeting carbon emitters.

Banks with headquarters in advanced economies originated 61 per cent of the total $5.8 trillion in loans and underwriting services from 2016 to 2022 (see footnote 1), compared to 30 per cent for China and less than 9 per cent for other developing countries (figure VI.B1.1). On the recipient end, most of the global fossil fuel finance is received by firms whose headquarters are domiciled in advanced economies, with bank loans and underwriting services totalling almost $3 trillion. By contrast, Chinese fossil fuel companies almost exclusively relied on domestic banks to fund expenses amounting to $1.7 trillion. Fossil fuel companies headquartered in other developing countries, however, received most credit support from banks headquartered in developed countries: $555 billion out of a total of just over $1 trillion.

Figure VI.B1.1 Developed country banks originate the bulk of credit support to fossil fuel companies, except in China

Cumulative credit support provided to fossil fuel companies, by country (group) of bank and fossil fuel company headquarters, 2016–2022

(Billions of dollars)

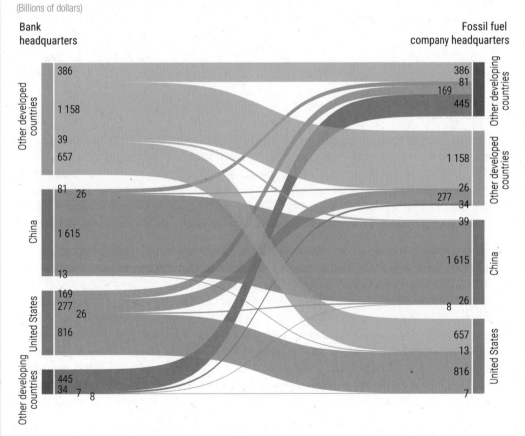

Source: UNCTAD calculations based on data from Reclaim Finance (2023) and on a 2022 update of Urgewald (2021).
Note: See note for figure VI.1.

A similar trend is observed at the petrochemicals end of the fossil fuel value chain, which is the source of fertilizers and plastic (and constitutes 70 per cent of petrochemical finance). Lund University and UNCTAD research investigating sectoral bond and bank transactions found most bond issuances and lending came from advanced economies, with Europe and North America providing the majority of finance designated for activities taking place in developing countries (Barrowclough and Finkill, 2021; UNCTAD, 2023b). During the years immediately following the Paris Agreement, more than one third of total sector bonds and financial transactions flowed from European sources, while a very small fraction, just 3.6 per cent of it, was spent in developing countries.

After the shock of COVID-19, in the year and a half from 2020, some new trends emerged. Notably the Asia–Pacific region became a source of finance as well as a host, as total investment increased sharply; but the general trend, whereby developed countries and regions dominate, continues. European and North American financiers provided $61 billion of petrochemicals credit, with the Asia–Pacific region providing $19.5 billion. Financiers in the Middle East and North Africa region provided $2.3 billion, with Latin America providing $0.7 billion.

This highlights the tendency of modern-day industry and manufacturing to "export emissions" (Kanemoto et al., 2012; Liddle, 2018), a scenario where high-income countries lower their territorial emissions by boosting production capacity in emerging economies. Most of the end-use products are then imported back into the high-income regions while the associated burden of carbon emissions is exported to the countries of production (Scott and Barrett, 2015; Jiborn et al., 2018).

b. Development assistance

Official development assistance is particularly important in filling financing gaps facing developing countries. Of all the sources available, it is the most likely to be provided as grants or at concessional rates and with long-term maturities. This is critical in those areas where private finance is unlikely to flow. Adaptation financing is one such area, given that financing climate adaptation is not likely to generate income-earning opportunities. Augmented official development assistance support will be critical to undertaking the required investments, particularly in developing countries already vulnerable to heightened climate shocks (UNCTAD, 2021).

An immediate challenge is the failure of richer countries to deliver the climate-finance sums they promised at the Copenhagen Summit in 2009. Rather than the $100 billion per annum pledged, the latest figures for 2022 reported by Development Assistance Committee (DAC) donor countries were just $83.3 billion (OECD, 2022). According to the Oxfam Climate Shadow Finance Report (Oxfam, 2023), the accounting methods used overstate even this amount. As in previous years, the Oxfam estimates are to the tune of $21–24 billion. Beyond the figures, the way in which funds are distributed is crucial. It is a concern that only one quarter was provided as grants and the remainder was given as loans, thereby adding to the debt burden of already suffering countries. Moreover, the loans were seldom concessional, with few offered at rates below the market (Oxfam, 2023). The final problem, according to Oxfam, is that one third of the climate fund payments were drawn from existing official development assistance budgets, so they were not truly "additional" funds.

In 2022, official development assistance did increase significantly (up 143 per cent) to $204 billion, reflecting increased spending on humanitarian activities, including support to refugees. Even with this increase, the total funds paid are only 0.36 per cent of DAC donors' combined gross national income, which is much less than the 0.7 per cent pledged by these donor countries decades ago. Just 5 of the 32 DAC member countries spend at or above their pledged target.[2]

---

[2] See https://www.oecd.org/dac/financing-sustainable-development/development-finance-standards/official-development-assistance.htm (accessed on 20 December 2023).

Against this backdrop, raising official development assistance flows should be an integral part of support to developing countries in advancing climate-compatible development paths. A commitment by just those countries making up the Group of Seven to meet the 0.7 per cent official development assistance target would generate an additional $150 billion annually, albeit still at the bottom of the range needed.

c. More active central banks

Central banks are not only at the apex of the national financial architecture but also play a key role in shaping the international agenda. Much can be done to better align their activities with climate and development goals, and indeed to set the rules and regulations for the entire financial system. Some central banks in both developed and developing countries have been implementing climate-related policies to guide and direct finance for several years now (*Trade and Development Report 2019*) and are considered to have made small contributions in greening monetary policy (Dikau and Volz, 2021; Siderius, 2022).

Yet, much more could be done. At the very least, central banks would have to move away from their goal of "market neutrality" for interventions, which in practice means maintaining the status quo, including favouring high-carbon firms over newer or alternative ones. More ambitious interventions would centre on dealing with medium- and longer-term risks rather than short-term crisis abatement, ideally supported by the international group of central banks, the Network for Greening the Financial System (NGFS). This could include monetary policies and regulatory frameworks that would help realign finance with decarbonization targets, including incorporating liability and financial risks into the lending practices of commercial banks to include climate-exposure risks. Such measures would more effectively regulate their lending choices (Schoenmaker, 2021; Boneva et al., 2022).

Some banks already have variable interest rates or reserve requirements for loans that are compatible with the Paris Agreement (see e.g. *Trade and Development Report 2019* for a survey; Simms, 2021; UNCTAD, 2023c). This could be more formalized if central banks and financial regulators integrated specific climate-related (or indeed development-related) goals into their mandates. This might encompass references to limiting global warming to 1.5 degrees, full biodiversity recovery by 2050 and designing transition plans for achieving these targets. Such a change in approach would improve policy coherence. It would enable monetary authorities to better support the fiscal action of Governments for tackling the climate and biodiversity crises and their anticipated negative economic and social impact.

Explicit nominal targets for climate and biodiversity would also enable monetary authorities to adopt a longer time horizon, crucial for navigating the challenging implementation of a just transition over the next decades. Sustained policy support and public investment for consistent implementation over several decades will not be possible based on emergency law and piecemeal action, as was feasible for a comparatively short-lived crisis such as the COVID-19 pandemic. With the absence of such nominal anchors, monetary authorities may keep vacillating between timid support and an outright rejection of considering the environmental dimension of their actions or inaction.

"The 11 largest European commercial banks have fossil fuel assets on their balance sheet amounting to 95 per cent of their equity. If fossil fuel assets were decisively stranded, they would likely go bankrupt."

The World Wildlife Fund for Nature has called for central banks and financial regulators to take on board the principle of tailoring their policies based on scientific considerations and to discriminate against firms whose activities are "always environmentally harmful" (World Wildlife Fund, 2022), such as fossil fuels.[3] Financial institutions investing in, providing underwriting services to or lending to fossil fuel sectors or associated companies could face higher regulatory capital and more stringent liquidity requirements. Furthermore, capital add-ons could be imposed for concentration risk if they fail to urgently reduce their exposure, as well as higher systemic risk buffers. Indeed, the 11 largest European commercial banks have fossil fuel assets on

---

[3] As an example, a large network of NGOs proposes to consider as "always environmentally harmful" all businesses listed on GCEL and GOGEL as well as businesses active in 13 subsectors identified using the 8-digit Global Industry Classification Standards. See *Call to Action to Ensure Transition to a Net-Zero and Nature-Positive Economy*, WWF (2022).

their balance sheet amounting to 95 per cent of their equity. If fossil fuel assets were decisively stranded, they would likely go bankrupt, raising the question yet again of whether to bail out firms that are too big to fail (Giraud et al., 2021).

A small number of central banks and financial regulators have started making modest steps forward in relation to these policy options. For instance, the European Central Bank discloses the list of its bond holdings by sector and company. The Bank of Finland has committed to making its investment portfolio carbon neutral by 2050 and has set intermediary goals for divesting from coal, oil and gas. The Bank of England, the European Central Bank and the Federal Reserve have started to run climate stress tests, and the Central Bank of South Africa has conducted a survey among banks about the consequences of climate risk. There are many other positive examples. Discussions are ongoing, notably in the context of the Network for Greening the Financial System. Implementation is too slow, however, with a tendency for smaller steps that preserve the status quo rather than bold action (Alliance climatique suisse, 2022).

Such plans are also relevant for multilateral development banks, which remain heavily involved in fossil fuel financing (e.g. Urgewald 2023a, 2023b, 2023c). This is despite calls for aligning their activities with Paris Agreement goals (Group of 20, 2022). Related to this is the way that multilateral development banks interact with national development banks, and how climate finance is linked with development finance – an area where there is still little research. In a recent study of 10 multilateral development banks, only two banks had this as an objective (Marois and Maradon, 2023). Policy changes to help this could include banks codeveloping a clear, simple, and standardized template or set of metrics to track existing financial cooperation. Also, governing boards of banks could require their institutions to meaningfully and transparently report on financing Sustainable Development Goals, as well as the climate reporting that many are now doing (ibid).

Insisting on climate disclosure could be imposed either by central banks or by government regulation. Whichever route is taken, this is needed because voluntary disclosure is not sufficient. This is already happening in some places. The French Energy Transition Law of 2015 mandates listed companies to disclose how climate risks are managed, providing a legislative environment that has accelerated the transition of French banks – including BNP Paribas – away from fossil fuels. Other examples include the stock exchanges of Johannesburg and Sao Paulo, two of the earliest innovators in requiring sustainability disclosures. Standard and Poor's Ratings Services have identified climate change as a key megatrend affecting sovereign bonds. In Brazil, banking regulations require socioenvironmental risk management (UNEP, 2015). Similarly, the Government of the United Kingdom has made it mandatory for the largest businesses in Great Britain to disclose their climate-related risks and opportunities, following the recommendations of its Taskforce on Climate-related Financial Disclosures.[4]

2. New and evolving market-related instruments

Can some of the new market-related instruments help developing countries chart a different path? With due consideration to the cautionary note about the limitations of these instruments, there can be little doubt that crowding-in private finance to a clearly defined transition strategy is important.

Since the twenty-sixth session of the Conference of the Parties in Glasgow, one new model to emerge is the "Just Energy Transition Partnership." Several countries have started or are negotiating these with donor countries and multilateral development banks, including Indonesia, Senegal, South Africa and Viet Nam. The value of these initiatives rests in how they seek to marry the financial and structural challenges that will face many developing countries in the coming decades, and how they highlight the need for a more integrated strategy.

However, more will be required if these partnerships are to deliver the expected developmental benefits. One issue is that the funds provided fall far short of what is needed: South Africa received just $8.5 billion from its five partners (France, Germany, the United Kingdom, the United States and the European Union) yet asked

---

[4] See https://www.gov.uk/government/news/uk-to-enshrine-mandatory-climate-disclosures-for-largest-companies-in-law.

for $84 billion to help move away from the use of coal. To go even further and achieve net zero, South Africa estimated that $250 billion was needed. Other concerns relate to the terms of the finance, a reliance on loans rather than grants and unclear conditionalities (box VI.2).

Other market-related initiatives, such as the Clean Development Mechanism developed under the Kyoto Protocol, have been disappointing. The larger economies in Asia (China and India) attract by far the largest share of projects and proceeds; sub-Saharan Africa captured less than 2 per cent of the market (Newell et al., 2023). Similarly, the Sustainable Development Mechanism created under the Paris Agreement further shows that market-driven mechanisms suffer the same old problems, in that the poorest and most needy regions and groups are not covered or not at sufficient scale (ibid). Since at least one quarter of the world's carbon emissions are now covered by some form of carbon pricing, international carbon pricing is frequently invoked as the way forward (*The Economist,* 2023).

However, the evidence is not encouraging for a myriad of reasons, distorted market outcomes being just one of them (Krogstrup and Oman, 2019). This distracts from the need for more proactive policy levers to tip the balance of risk and return against fossil fuel assets and towards just transitions.

Another example of innovative instruments involves the growing use of debt-for-nature swaps and debt relief, linked to climate action. There is growing interest in the search for financial mechanisms to induce producers to leave fossil fuel reserves safely in the ground (Muttitt and Kartha, 2020) and to conserve nature more generally. Many debt-distressed countries have fossil fuel reserves that could be used to repay debt. The "swap" concept reverses the equation, suggesting that these reserves could potentially help countries that resist extraction and keep their reserves in the ground. However, debt-for-nature swaps have been criticized for entailing lengthy negotiations, being expensive to establish for little fiscal space and creating challenges with ringfenced financing for environmental activities while other development goals remain underfinanced (*Trade and Development Reports 2019* and *2021*). As well as addressing such challenges, for swap initiatives to be effective, they need to be combined with broader debt relief interventions and expanded financing (UNCTAD, 2019).

Box VI.2 Learnings from South Africa and the Just Energy Transition Partnership

In South Africa, the Just Energy Transition Investment Plan (JET IP) raises concerns that reach beyond the small scale of the funds received and focus on the overall composition of the whole funding package. From the outset, South Africa expressed that it needed to implement a holistic approach to cope with the challenges of energy transition and transformation, given the millions of workers and households dependent on its precarious system of electrification based around mining dirty coal. The country has been experiencing frequent and long-lasting power cuts, with complete lack of electrification for many people. At the same time, it fears the social, economic and employment impacts of change. The Plan highlights a need to invest in retraining and skills development, social support and a path to economic diversification that includes innovation and localization, as well as investment in new forms of climate-aligned infrastructure (JET IP, 2022). However, this ambition is not backed by the actual financing provided by international partners.

According to recent analysis by the Institute of Economic Justice (IEJ) in South Africa, the problem lies not just in the small scale of finance available, but in how the finance is provided. Most of the $8.5 billion is offered in the form of loans (81 per cent) and guarantees (15 per cent). Grants constitute only 4 per cent. There are risks that repayment obligations will compound the already fragile financial position of the country, even if most of the loans are concessional (around $5.3 billion, compared to $1.5 billion in commercial loans, $1.3 billion in guarantees and just $0.3 billion as grants). Other concerns stem from the fact the JET IP model follows so-called "de-risking" approaches typical of blended finance and thematic bonds. While almost 90 per cent of the finances granted are for electricity infrastructure, very little is apportioned for the "justice" element associated with transitional risks, economic diversification and innovation and skills development, which receive just 0.3 per cent to 0.1 per cent.

Such deals might encourage the privatization of public goods, due to their emphasis on the use of public–private partnerships. Investment through private commercial loans is earmarked for potentially profitable wind and solar energy, but all other elements (decommissioning coal plants, transmission and grid strengthening, distribution and batteries) are considered to require concessional loans from development finance institutions or government support. This may lead to future privatization that will reduce affordable energy access and government revenue sources.

Some of the financial and legal risks associated with the package stem from its reliance on debt instruments and private capital markets that may bring greater exposure to external dynamics and shocks. This is especially pertinent given the contingent reliance on the State for the de-risking part of the partnership. Bringing in external investors who follow foreign regulatory jurisdiction is another risk, as is evident in disputes elsewhere in the world. In the context of South Africa, it is feared this could include tensions with its human rights framework.

Underpinning these concerns is a general lack of transparency about the nature of conditionalities, interest rates, terms, grace periods, State obligations and exposure to the currencies involved in the financing package. Furthermore, important developmental benefits are absent. The plan in its current form only provides minimal support to help develop green industries locally or to meet the social security needs of affected communities and workers. If similar models are rolled out in other countries, this raises the risk of perpetuating an already unstable, unequal and anarchic international debt architecture.

Source: Institute of Economic Justice and Climate Finance for Equitable Transitions (2023).

While central banks and financial authorities need to take the lead by insisting on common instruments, supported by using regulations and not relying on voluntary disclosure, there is an important supplementary role for private forms of (self) governance. The Investor Network on Climate Risk, formed by a group of institutional investors, examines opportunities and strategies for investment in clean energy and climate technologies. Its Clean Energy Investment Working Group involves collaboration between the Coalition for Environmentally Responsible Economies (CERES) investor network on climate risk and the Clean Energy Group. It aims to "develop an ongoing framework within which participants can explore the risks and rewards in making investments and allocating capital to the clean energy sector and other climate-related opportunities" (Newell et al., 2023).

"In the fossil fuel sector, increasing disclosures would help clarify debates about exactly who is financing what."

Such initiatives from both public regulators and private investors are essential because the current lack of disclosure leaves investors in the dark about overstated assets and understated liabilities. This means markets are unable to allocate capital appropriately, undermining efforts to decarbonize the global economy.

In the fossil fuel sector specifically, increasing disclosures would help clarify debates about exactly who is financing what. Differences in estimates for developed country lending and investment vis-à-vis developing countries can be linked to whether underwriting or concessional lending is included (Ma and Gallagher, 2021). Similar research in the energy sector finds that an extremely high share of potential emissions from the world's largest energy firms are controlled by a handful of investors and shareholders, including through major actors such as BlackRock, Vanguard and Fidelity Investments (Dordi et al., 2022; UNCTAD, 2023; Reclaim Finance, 2023). As long as high-carbon remains more profitable than clean energy sources, there is no incentive for these firms to make a clean energy shift. Requiring them to calculate and disclose their true climate exposures would help ensure shareholders were fully informed about future financial risks. It would also reward those firms that decided to shift.[5]

3. Divestment and redirection of existing funds

Divestment and redirection of existing expenditure have the significant advantage that the funds already exist and do not need to be raised. Furthermore, they automatically "turn off the taps" that are making matters worse. Doing so, and doing it in a way that ensures developmental and equitable impacts of the change, will require a good deal of policy and regulatory support at the international level.

a. Fossil fuel subsidy reform

One of the most visible and challenging examples of where the misalignment of the financial system is damaging both economy and environment concerns fossil fuel subsidies. The scale of public finances flowing into these subsidies is enormous, exacerbating climate inequalities and crowding out other, and potentially much better uses of scarce public funds. The issue is, however, much more nuanced than first appears.

The most recent estimates by IMF argue that global fossil fuel subsidies in their various forms cost a record $7 trillion in 2022, that is, 7.1 per cent of world GDP. This figure is composed of explicit and implicit subsidies amounting to $1.3 trillion and $5.7 trillion, respectively (figure VI.5 and table VI.1). While the former measures the amount that Governments effectively disbursed to reduce both the production cost of fossil fuels and the price paid by consumers, the latter represents the difference between the market price of fossil fuel and their effective cost to society, including negative externalities on health and the environment, as well as foregone consumption tax revenue (Black et al., 2023). The latter, therefore, can be understood as a shadow cost rather than a direct one, but the former represents actual expenditure that could potentially be redirected to other purposes.

Other estimates of the size and scale of subsidies vary depending on the methodologies used. The 2022 figure is admittedly sharply higher than previous years, owing to the energy crisis triggered by the war in Ukraine. The fact is these subsidies remain high even after a decade and a half of multilateral commitments to cut them.

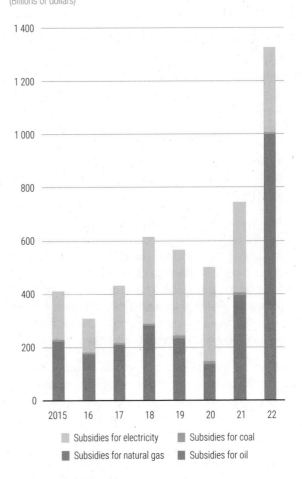

Figure VI.5 Despite years of multilateral pledges, fossil fuel subsidies fly high

Fossil fuel subsidies by fuel type

(Billions of dollars)

Source: UNCTAD calculations based on IMF data as described in Black et al. (2023).

VI

---

[5] In reference to Article 2.1 (c) of the Paris Agreement, the limitations of current disclosure are considered to be a major impediment.

Table VI.1 Even a small reduction in subsidies would help, as producer subsidies total $51 billion

Fossil fuel subsidies, by type, 2022

(Billions of dollars unless otherwise indicated)

	Implicit fossil fuel subsidies	Explicit fossil fuel subsidies	Total fossil fuel subsidies	Producer fossil fuel subsidies	Producer fossil fuel subsidies (as a percentage of explicit fossil fuel subsidies)
Low-income countries	18	8	26	0	0.0
Lower-middle-income countries	711	224	935	6	2.7
Upper-middle-income countries	3 093	643	3 736	27	4.2
High-income countries	1 887	452	2 339	18	4.1
Global	5 710	1 326	7 036	51	3.9

Source: UNCTAD calculations based on IMF data as described in Black et al. (2023).
Note: Explicit fossil fuel subsidies measure the undercharging of the supply costs of fossil fuels (i.e. the amounts disbursed by Governments for fossil fuel production subsidies and fossil fuel consumption subsidies); implicit fossil fuel subsidies measure the undercharging for environmental costs as well as the forgone consumption tax revenues caused by fossil fuel subsidies.

b. Why and how fossil fuel subsidies must be phased out

Fossil fuel subsidies pose challenges not only due to their magnitude, but their tendency to crowd out other uses of government revenues. Contributing to the issue is how and where fossil fuel prices distort true economic and environmental costs. IMF data including implicit and explicit subsidies indicates a high proportion of these subsidies relates to the coal sector, at $2 trillion, that is, about 30 per cent of the total. Coal is one of the oldest sources of fossil fuels and known to be particularly dirty, provoking widely recognized environmental and health risks. It is also a likely centre for future financial and economic shocks, as coal sector assets lose their value and when the millions of people working in the sector lose their livelihoods (*Trade and Development Report 2019*). Reform of the coal sector is a policy priority in many countries including Indonesia and South Africa, as discussed below.

An immediate challenge with phasing out "inefficient" subsidies is that this category has no coherent or formal international definition. Economists would say that the different types of subsidies are so intertwined it is not meaningful to distinguish some as "efficient" or "inefficient". All are distortionary (and hence "inefficient") even in the narrowest definition of the term. All subsidies artificially lower the price of fossil fuels relative to potential substitutes. This leads to production and consumption that is higher than would otherwise be the case, especially in energy-intensive sectors such as power and transport. The interlinkages between demand and supply provoke a self-reinforcing cycle; subsidies designed to support fossil fuel exploration and production will inevitably encourage not only greater production but also consumption, because they lead to lower prices.

However, outside the abstractions of economic modelling, the impact of phasing out fossil fuel subsidies varies depending on the perspective. In advanced economies, subsidized consumption of fossil fuels may be considered excessive in the presence of alternative sources; in the global South, where alternative sources of electrification and energy are lacking, subsidized consumption may be insufficient to meet the essential needs of households and firms.

If the aim of Governments is to support poor households and reduce inequality, fossil fuel subsidies are not the way to do it. Subsidies often make inequalities worse because they are a blunt instrument that is usually not targeted by income (UNDP, 2021; World Bank, 2012). Even so, the relatively small benefit to the poorest decile can be nonetheless extremely important; it may mean the difference between having electricity or none at all. Such arguments to help poor households (and small businesses) were particularly pressing during the energy price hikes of 2021 and 2022.

Given this background, any efforts to cut fossil fuel subsidies need to acknowledge the complexities and asymmetries of producers and consumers. Stopping the "untold billions" of subsidies (Victor, 2009) has proved hard to do. One reason is that fossil fuel subsidies have been paid out for decades, and this systemic support over time created an entire ecosystem of big firms, enterprises and interest groups with political power. Lobby groups in the industry spend hundreds of millions of dollars to protect their position (Moser and Ashley, 2014; and others, within a substantial body of literature on this).

Shedding light onto these distributional matters could potentially help support the case for providing support to low-income households in other, less high-carbon intensive ways. At the same time, resistance can come from consumers as well as producers. Events in Morocco in 2015, Mexico in 2017 (International Institute for Sustainable Development, 2022) and the *"gilets jaunes"* (yellow vests) movement in France in 2018 illuminated some of the social pain and tensions evident when Governments try to close off the subsidy tap, if no compensatory instruments have been provided. At the same time, lessons can be learned from more positive examples – including approaches used in Ghana, Indonesia, Zambia and other countries. In these cases, it was important that subsidy savings were used to build social welfare, health care and education systems (Laan et al., 2023).

Looking ahead, the world is likely to see a checkerboard of different paces of transition and change across regions and countries, maybe even within countries. In a recent study of nationally determined contributions (NDCs), researchers found that few had what was described as a "transition plan" (Jones, 2023).

The fact that all countries have signed the pledge of Sustainable Development Goal 12 to reduce subsidies, yet so many do not have a NDCs transition plan, does not auger well for future efforts to cut subsidies or to wind down fossil fuel production. An added constraint is that many developing countries' NDCs are conditional on receiving adequate climate finance – which as noted above, has still not been forthcoming.

c. The most feasible targets

Given these challenges, initial steps may need to be small, but their implementation is urgent. For immediate purposes, the rapid phase out of explicit producer subsidies would seem the most obvious contender, and suppressing consumer subsidies would follow, in an appropriately sequenced manner. This needs to be done fairly and not threaten the essential needs of the poorer half of the population. But even in the case of the former, there are likely to be significant political and economic challenges, particularly in fuel-exporting developing countries.

Consequently, it is imperative to prioritize the reduction of subsidies in advanced economies. Developing countries currently lack the financial capacity to transition to new sources of foreign exchange generation and to provide the same level of protection to their populations. Additional capacities are required for these crucial tasks. As mentioned above, production subsidies only account for $53 billion, a fraction of total fossil fuel subsidies. However, this sum is highly significant compared to other sources of development and climate finance. Addressing production directly now would also have the double ecological benefit of reducing volumes of fossil fuels, while recognizing that there needs to be a means of ensuring the poorest households are still able to access renewable and affordable energy.

As entire economic systems tend to be highly dependent on fossil fuel, there are concerns in many countries that reducing subsidies – even just the subset of producer subsidies – would hurt economic activity and slow growth and development. In some countries, subsidies for production are used to ensure access to remote and rural areas, where other energy sources are not currently available. Hence, another strategy would be to simultaneously boost the use of renewable energy sources as an alternative. These are still only in the early stages of development in most countries and much needs to be done before they can be relied upon to even partly replace fossil fuels as a reliable source of energy. Moreover, there is the additional challenge, as shown in other sections of this chapter, that many developing countries have State-owned fossil fuel sectors that they rely upon for revenue. A switch to renewables will bring not only a drop in revenue for Government, but higher imports and the costs of intellectual property rights for the technologies needed to make the shift. A great deal more needs to be done to make sure the shift to renewables brings with it the desired benefits in terms of fiscal revenues, bottom of the pyramid benefits, job creation and industrialization.

Recent evidence on decoupling (Haberl et al., 2020; Wiedenhofer et al., 2020; Parrique et al., 2019) stresses that it is difficult, if not impossible, for Governments wanting to transition away from fossil fuels and cut subsidies to do so without reducing their existing energy use and economic activities (box VI.3). The impact of reducing subsidies will be extreme, yet to do nothing brings risks, including being further locked into stranded assets and the subsequent financial, social and economic shocks this will bring (*Trade and Development Report 2019*) on top of the physical shocks. However, this is not yet an option for developing countries, many of which will likely still need to increase emissions. For low-income and other developing countries, it is extremely unlikely that they can consider implementing subsidy reforms until developed countries take the lead. For developed countries, this involves not only scaling back their own subsidies but extending financial and technological assistance to help developing countries in their subsidy reduction efforts.

Box VI.3 The case of Indonesia: Financing reform of the palm oil and fossil fuel sectors

The Government of Indonesia grapples with significant challenges in domestic financing due to its dominant role in the country's financial sector, particularly in supplying financial debt instruments, given the limited size of financial entities, such as pension funds. Government debt creation is constrained by internal rules established after the Asian financial crisis to prevent capital flight. In 2019, Indonesia initiated tax expenditure and revenue reforms to elevate tax revenues from a low 10 per cent of GDP, a substantial challenge compared to advanced countries. There are also immediate challenges with respect to international finance, one of which is its high cost. This is a critical constraint even before the question of directing the finances raised towards emission reducing purposes – which can be another constraint if there is insufficient interest from investors.

In the palm oil sector, Indonesia has reconsidered the role of trade policies. Indonesia is the world's largest exporter of palm oil. Hence, it significantly contributes to international carbon emissions.[a] The Government has embarked on a programme to increase efficiencies in palm oil production and limit growth, and this is funded through export taxes. While expanding the moratorium on new plantations initiated in 2011 will likely have a significant ecological impact, the policy will increase pressure on fiscal resources. A large portion of the taxes generated from palm oil exports will be needed to support the transition of impoverished farmers; thus far, the bulk of export taxes raised on palm oil has been devoted to the biofuel programme.

In the energy sector, the Government has set a target of 31 per cent renewable energy by 2050, up from a target of 23 per cent by 2025. In 2021, actual performance in renewable energy reached 11.7 per cent. There are no plans for new coal power plants, except for those already at the financial closing or construction stage. In addition, the national electrical utility company will need a transition subsidy of approximately $4.8 billion to reach its 2030 targets and cover costs related to stranding assets, decommissioning coal plants, early retirement compensation for existing contracts with private energy providers, State coal revenue losses, tax income losses and policy incentives for redeployment of labour, capital and natural resources. So far, external sources of funding for this are small: they include REDD+[b] funding from Norway and a transition project from the Asian Development Bank. In February 2023, Indonesia and the Treasury of the United States announced the creation of a secretariat for a Just Transition Programme with the United States and European partners.

Source: UNCTAD.

---

[a] See https://theicct.org/palm-oil-is-the-elephant-in-the-greenhouse/.

[b] REDD stands for reducing emissions from deforestation and forest degradation; REDD+ includes "fostering conservation, sustainable management of forests, and enhancement of forest carbon stocks".

D. CHANGING THE RECORD: BUILDING A CONSISTENT FINANCIAL ECOSYSTEM THAT ALIGNS CLIMATE AND DEVELOPMENT FINANCE

The previous sections have described some tensions and inconsistencies where the ambitions of the Sustainable Development Goals and low-carbon agendas are constrained or contradicted by the practice of not adequately financing the investments to achieve them. The notion common in financial approaches that risk can be transferred, and that this is somehow similar to making a transformational investment, has led to an overreliance on the State as the holder of risk and underinvestment when it comes to providing key elements of the climate-consistent development agenda. Additionally, it fuels enthusiasm for risk insurance products designed to transfer sovereign and corporate risks stemming from extreme weather and other climatic shocks.[6]

As suggested by Kedward et al. (2023), the alternative to a market-led, risk-reduction strategy is a "market-shaping" approach that could be achieved through public policy. International cooperation and regulatory measures also need to be coherent with the ambition of increasing and redirecting finance to development and climate. This includes revisiting the role of multilateral lenders, as often discussed, to better centre their mission on transformational development strategies that are also low-carbon and equitable and provide global public goods. As this chapter has suggested, the current lending model needs to be reformed to better support developmental lending without repeating the public cost–private profit mistakes of some previous models.

"Protecting and expanding policy space is critical to enabling developing countries to pursue just transitions. This involves making use of infant industry protection, local content requirements, trade policy, looser forms of intellectual property rights and industrial policy to capitalize on opportunities in a new low-carbon economy."

More positively, momentum is already gathering, especially among many European States, to exit the Energy Charter Treaty, because it inhibits more ambitious action by restricting the policy space of Governments to wind down fossil fuel activities. There are calls to protect the policy space of developing countries to support their own low-carbon industries through revisions and exemptions to restrictive trade agreements. Protecting and expanding policy space is critical to enabling developing countries to pursue just transitions. This involves making use of infant industry protection, local content requirements, trade policy, looser forms of intellectual property rights and industrial policy to capitalize on opportunities in a new low-carbon economy. However, achieving this requires deeper revisions to trade and investment treaties.

Efforts to build support for and activate the levers described above to create a financial system compatible with tackling climate change need to be guided and underpinned by existing principles, such as "common but differentiated responsibility and respective capabilities", "special and differential treatment", "polluter pays" and so on. These are well established in international law and provide a basis for articulating respective obligations between richer and poorer countries. Equity in all its dimensions needs to take centre stage and should guide the selection of financial levers used to raise and redirect finance. As described in the experience of South Africa and the Just Energy Transition Partnerships, the challenge for how fossil fuel-dependent countries can change their energy systems and contingent economic structure, while also supporting the people and businesses that have evolved around it, is a crucial justice issue. Moreover, if the transition is not just, it will not be sustainable.

---

[6] These include, for example, the Caribbean Catastrophe Risk Insurance Facility, which mixes parametric insurance and regional risk-pooling across Governments, and the InsuResilience Global Partnership for Climate and Disaster Risk Finance and Insurance Solutions.

More concretely, existing principles of special and differential treatment on international economic rules and common but differentiated responsibilities on climate action, in their procedural, distributional and intergenerational dimensions, provide a starting point for establishing who pays and how, and who should be the primary beneficiaries of international support. This in turn will be a function of who is able to secure participation and representation in the key bodies making the decisions about global climate finance and global financial governance more broadly. This inevitably means returning to sensitive questions about voting rights and regional representation in major funding bodies as well as the access to those key bodies of civil society groups working with communities on the frontline of climate change and development.

Some of these guiding principles might be conceived of under a more encompassing umbrella such as a Global Green New Deal (as described in detail in *Trade and Development Report 2019*). The original New Deal in the United States in the 1930s sought to tackle economic insecurity (akin to the challenge of the current just transition), the predatory nature of finance (echoing the current need to contain the financialization of climate action) and address infrastructure gaps and regional inequalities (comparable to the persistent challenges in today's hyperglobalized society). The New Deal was to achieve all this in the context of a deep and persistent global recession, similar to the threat of a possible "lost decade" that the world is facing today.

Green new deals would have their own particular features that reflect local needs and priorities. But a number of shared elements would provide their collective identity, including a massive investment push in a series of interconnected public goods, and a series of coordinated policy measures that enable industrial transformation and investment-led growth models. These approaches at a national level would need to be supported by corresponding initiatives at the global level:

- Global rules should be calibrated toward the overarching goals of social and economic stability, shared prosperity and environmental sustainability and be protected against capture by the most powerful players.

- States should share common but differentiated responsibilities in a multilateral system built to advance global public goods and protect the global commons.

- The right of States to policy space to pursue national development strategies should be enshrined in global rules.

- Global regulations should be designed both to strengthen a dynamic international division of labour and to prevent destructive unilateral economic actions that prevent other nations from realizing common goals.

- Global public institutions should be accountable to their full membership, open to a diversity of viewpoints, cognizant of new voices, and have balanced dispute resolution systems.

This conversation takes place against a background of calls by UNCTAD and others for a "new Bretton Woods" (Gallagher and Kozul-Wright, 2021). It also unfolds at a time when other constituencies are questioning whether there needs to be a new dedicated global climate bank (*The Economist*, 2023).

However, without a fundamental shift in how funding priorities are set and the ways in which finance is governed, such a move would be unlikely to address many of the issues raised here. Notably, these include representation of poorer countries and social groups, overoptimism about the role of and lack of regulation around private finance and continued financing of many of the drivers of the climate crisis that people around the world face – including, but not only, fossil fuels.

There is an additional issue of whether Governments, as shareholders of development banks, will allow them to do the kind of lending required. One constraint continues to be the straitjacket of requiring triple A ratings. This opens the door for long-standing calls for a new kind of credit rating agency with expertise in development finance institutions, as well as the need for a bolder approach on the part of the banks themselves, given the assurances from agencies that higher leverage could be used without risking the rating (*Trade and Development Report 2019*).

The fact is, there is no simple answer. Simply redirecting a small percentage of global financial assets will not suffice. What is urgently needed is a determined and comprehensive overhaul of the entire global financial system. This task is undeniably complex, given the intricate interplay of diverse actors and institutions, each with distinct mandates, thresholds, and financing methods. However, only through a strategic and precise approach to these complexities can a financial landscape be established that is truly conducive to global development. This is not just a call for change; it is an insistence on a profound reconfiguration that aligns the global financial system with the imperatives of sustainable and inclusive progress.

E. CONCLUSION

The reason the world is facing a compounding climate and development crisis is not for lack of finance. It is due to the maldistribution and misalignment of finance in ways that undermine and contradict social and developmental needs and not only fail to respect environmental limits, but also challenge them.

Many of the actors currently dominating the global financial landscape are ill-suited to the challenge of delivering the transformative change now called for by the International Panel on Climate Change and many others (IPCC, 2018). A fundamental realignment of purpose, mandate and operating procedures is needed. Questions need to be asked regarding who (which countries, communities and social groups) finance should serve, as well as its purpose (which specific goals), and finally which governance mechanisms need to be employed towards these ends. These enquiries are crucial to ensure that financial contributions align with, rather than undermine, the goals outlined in the Paris Agreement and the broader Sustainable Development Goals (Newell et al., 2023). It is essential to undo the narrative that the primary role of public finance is to harness private finance for delivering public goods and services.

"The COVID-19 pandemic has shown that, if political and social will is present, it is possible to change the record."

The COVID-19 pandemic has shown that when the will is there, Governments and their institutions can use their power to mobilize vast amounts of capital (McDonald et al., 2020; Gutierrez and Kliatskova, 2021; Griffith-Jones et al., 2022) for the welfare of their citizens, to restrict harmful activities, encourage the repurposing of industries and intervene to protect the most vulnerable groups in society. This is not to say that all choices made were perfect. Rather, it shows how, if political and social will is present, it is possible to change the record.

One of the most effective ways to do this today would be to address the world's continued dependence on fossil fuels head-on; to stop financing new exploration of fossil fuels, to wind down the most problematic and dirty activities and to shift to renewable sources as widely as possible. Starting to turn off the fossil fuel tap, which causes the vast majority of global CO_2 emissions and is a main driver of global warming, would be a good first step. Development benefits can and should go hand-in-hand and need to be at the forefront of any coordinated strategies to ensure the transition is just and backed by political support.

VI

REFERENCES

African Development Bank, Asian Development Bank, Asian Infrastructure Investment Bank, European Bank for Reconstruction and Development, European Investment Bank, Inter-American Development Bank Group, Islamic Development Bank, New Development Bank and World Bank Group (2021). *2020 Joint Report on Multilateral Development Banks' Climate Finance*. Available at http://www.ebrd.com/2020-joint-report-on-mdbs-climate-finance (accessed 15 December 2023).

Alliance climatique suisse (2022). *Les Étapes de la Transition pour la BNS et la FINMA.* Geneva.

Attridge S and Engen L (2019). Blended finance in the poorest countries: The need for a better approach. Research Report. Overseas Development Institute. London.

Barrowclough D and Finkill G (2021). Banks, bonds and petrochemicals: Greening the path from the Copenhagen Agreement, through Covid and beyond. UNCTAD Research Paper No. 69.

Barrowclough D, Gallagher KP and Kozul-Wright R (2021). *Southern-Led Development Finance Solutions from the Global South*. Routledge. London and New York.

Bergman N (2018). Impacts of the fossil fuel divestment movement: Effects on finance, policy and public discourse. *Sustainability*. 10(7):25–29.

Bhattacharya A, Calland R, Averchenkova A, Gonzalez L, Martinez-Diaz L and Van Rooij J (2020). *Delivering on the $100 Billion Climate Finance Commitment and Transforming Climate Finance*. The Independent Expert Group on Climate Finance.

Black S, Antung A, Parry I and Vernon N (2023). IMF Fossil Fuel Subsidies Data: 2023 Update. Working Paper No. 2023/169. International Monetary Fund.

Bloomberg.com (2023). Oil's net zero scenarios are science fiction. 2 February.

Boneva L, Ferrucci G. and Mongelli FP (2022). Climate change and central banks: What role for monetary policy? *Climate Policy*. 22(6):770–787.

Caldecott B (2017). Introduction to special issue: Stranded assets and the environment. *Journal of Sustainable Finance & Investment*. 7(1):1–13.

Chancel L, Bothe P and Voituriez T (2023). *Climate Inequality Report 2023: Fair Taxes for a Sustainable Future in the Global South.* World Inequality Lab.

Christophers B (2022). Fossilised capital: Price and profit in the energy transition. *New Political Economy*. 27(1):146–159.

COP26 (2021) Climate Finance Delivery Plan: Meeting the US$100 Billion Goal. Available at: https://webarchive. nationalarchives.gov.uk/ukgwa/20230401054904/https://ukcop26.org/wp-content/uploads/2021/10/ Climate-Finance-Delivery-Plan-1.pdf (accessed 8 September 2023).

Dikau S and Volz U (2021). Central bank mandates, sustainability objectives and the promotion of green finance. *Ecological Economics*. 184:2–20.

Dordi T, Gehricke SA, Naef A and Weber O (2022). Ten financial actors can accelerate a transition away from fossil fuels. *Environmental Innovation and Societal Transitions*. 44:60–78.

Gabor D (2019). *Securitization for Sustainability: Does it Help Achieve the Sustainable Development Goals?* Heinrich Böll Stiftung. Washington, D.C.

Gabor D and Braun B (2023). Green Macrofinancial Regimes. Available at https://osf.io/preprints/ socarxiv/4pkv8/ (accessed on 5 October 2023).

Gallagher KP, Kozul-Wright R (2021). *The Case for a New Bretton Woods.* Polity Press. Cambridge.

Gallagher KP, Bhandary RR, Ray R and Luma Ramos (2023). Reforming Bretton Woods institutions to achieve climate change and development goals. *One Earth*. 6 October 2023.

Giraud G, Nicol C, Benaiteau S, Bonaventure M, Chaaoub V, Jego M, Tsanga A, Mitteau G, Philpott L, Poidatz A, Schreiber P (2021). *Fossil Assets: The New Subprimes? How Funding the Climate Crisis Can Lead to a Financial Crisis.* Reclaim Finance. June 2021.

Green New Deal (2008). *A Green New Deal*. New Economics Foundation. London.

Griffith-Jones S and Ocampo JA, eds. (2018). *The Future of National Development Banks*. Oxford University Press. Oxford.

Griffith-Jones S and Barrowclough D (2022). Counter-cyclical responses: How development banks helped the Covid-19 recovery and lessons for the future. Research Paper No. 290. Agence Francaise de Développement. Paris.

Group of 20 (2022). *Boosting MDBs' Investing Capacity. An Independent Review of Multilateral Development Banks' Capital Adequacy Frameworks.* Published with the support of the 2020 Italian and 2022 Indonesian G20 Presidencies.

Group of 20 (2018). *G20 Eminent Persons Report on Global Financial Governance*. Group of Twenty.

Gutierrez E and Kliatskova T (2021). *National Development Financial Institutions: Trends, Crisis Response Activities, and Lessons Learned*. EFI Insight-Finance. World Bank. Washington, D.C.

Haberl H, Wiedenhofer D, Virág D, Kalt G, Plank B, Brockway P, Fishman T, Hausknost D, Krausmann FP, Leon-Gruchalski B, Mayer A, Pichler M, Schaffartzik A, Sousa T, Streeck J and Creutzig F (2020). A systematic review of the evidence on decoupling of GDP, resource use and GHG emissions. Part II: Synthesizing the insights. *Environmental Research Letters*. 15(6):065003.

Hausfather Z and Friedlingstein P (2022). Global CO_2 emissions from fossil fuels hit record high in 2022. *Carbon Brief*. 11 November.

Humphrey C (2018). The role of credit rating agencies in shaping multilateral finance: Recent developments and policy options. Policy Paper for the Inter-Governmental Group of 24. Group of 24. Washington, D.C.

IEA (2022). *World Energy Investment 2022 Datafile*. International Energy Agency.

IEA (2023a). *World Energy Investment 2023*. International Energy Agency.

IEA (2023b). *World Energy Investment 2023. Methodology Annex*. International Energy Agency.

Institute of Economic Justice and Climate Finance for Equitable Transitions (2023). Submission to the Presidential Climate Commission on South Africa's Just Energy Transition – Investment Plan. Submitted by the Institute for Economic Justice and the Climate Finance for Equitable Transitions.

International Institute for Sustainable Development (2022). Background Note on Fossil Fuel Subsidy Reform. Geneva.

Jain M, Sharma GD and Srivastava M (2019). Can sustainable investment yield better financial returns: A comparative study of ESG indices and MSCI indices. *Risks*. 7(1):15.

JET IP (2022). South Africa's Just Energy Transition Investment Plan (JET IP), for the initial period 2023–2027. The Presidency of South Africa.

Jiborn M, Kander A, Kulionis V, Nielsen H and Moran DD (2018). Decoupling or delusion? Measuring emissions displacement in foreign trade. *Global Environmental Change*. 49:27–34.

Jones N (2023). Nearly half of recent climate pledges plan to keep extracting fossil fuels. Guest post on *Carbon Brief*. Available at: https://www.carbonbrief.org/guest-post-nearly-half-of-recent-climate-pledges-plan-to-keep-extracting-fossil-fuels/

Kanemoto K, Lenzen M, Peters GP, Moran DD, and Geschke A (2012). Frameworks for comparing emissions associated with production, consumption, and international trade. *Environmental Science & Technology*. 46(1):172–179.

VI

Kedward K, Gabor D and Ryan-Collins J (2022). Aligning finance with the green transition: From a risk-based to an allocative green credit policy regime. UCL Institute for Innovation and Public Purpose. Working Paper Series 2022/11. University College London.

Krogstrup S and Oman W (2019). Macroeconomic and financial policies for climate change mitigation: A review of the literature. IMF Working Papers No. 185. International Monetary Fund. Washington, D.C.

Laan T, Geddes A, Bois von Kursk O, Jones N, Kuehne K, Gerbase L, O'Manique C, Sharma D and Stockman L (2023). *Fanning the Flames: G20 Provides Record Financial Support for Fossil Fuels.* Energy Policy Tracker.

Liddle B (2018). Consumption-based accounting and the trade-carbon emissions nexus. *Energy Economics.* 69:71–78.

Lubis C, Doherty D and Young W (2022). Investment requirements of a low-carbon world: Energy supply investment ratios. *BloombergNEF.* 6 October.

Ma X and Gallagher K (2021). Who funds overseas coal plants? The need for transparency and accountability. Policy Brief No. 008. Global Economic Governance Initiative (GEGI). Global Development Policy Centre. University of Boston.

Marois T, Stewart J and Marodon R (2023). From multi-to national-and back again: Realising the SDG potential of public development banks. Research Paper No. 267. Agence Française de Développement. Paris.

Matsumoto C, Monteiro R, Rial I and Sakrak OA (2021). Mastering the risky business of public–private partnerships in infrastructure. Departmental Paper No. 2021/010. International Monetary Fund.

McDonald DA, Marois T and Barrowclough D, eds. (2020). *Public Banks and Covid-19: Combatting the Pandemic with Public Finance.* Municipal Services Project, UNCTAD and Eurodad. Kingston, Geneva, Brussels.

Moser C and Ashley M (2014). *The Fossil-Fuel Industry Spent Big to Set the Anti-Environment Agenda of the Next Congress.* Center for American Progress.

Munir W and Gallagher K (2018). Scaling up lending at the multi-lateral development banks: Benefits and costs of expanding and optimizing MDB balance sheets. Working Paper No. 013. Global Economic Governance Initiative (GEGI). Global Development Policy Centre. University of Boston.

Muttitt G and Kartha S (2020). Equity, Climate Justice and Fossil Fuel Extraction: Principles for a Managed Phase Out. *Climate Policy.* 20:1024–1042.

Newell P, Daley F, Mikheeva O and Peša I (2023). Mind the gap: The global governance of just transitions. *Global Policy.* 14(3):425–437.

Nick S and Thalmann P (2022). Towards true climate neutrality for global aviation: A negative emissions fund for airlines. *Journal of Risk and Financial Management.* 15(11):505.

OECD (2016). 2020 projections of climate finance towards the USD 100 billion goal. Technical Note. Organisation for Economic Co-operation and Development. OECD Publishing.

OECD (2022). *Multilateral Development Finance 2022.* Organisation for Economic Co-operation and Development.

OECD (2023). *Global Outlook on Financing for Sustainable Development 2023.* Organisation for Economic Co-operation and Development.

Oxfam (2023). *Climate Finance Shadow Report. Assessing the delivery of the $100 billion commitment.* Oxfam. United Kingdom.

Parrique T, Barth J, Briens F, Spangenberg J and Kraus-Polk A (2019). *Decoupling Debunked. Evidence and Arguments against Green Growth as a Sole Strategy for Sustainability. A Study Edited by the European Environment Bureau.* European Environment Bureau.

Pietsch A and Salakhova D (2022). Pricing of green bonds: Drivers and dynamics of the greenium. Working Paper Series No. 2022/2728. European Central Bank.

Reclaim Finance (2023). *Throwing Fuel on the Fire: GFANZ financing of fossil fuel expansion.* Available at https://reclaimfinance.org/site/en/2023/01/17/throwing-fuel-on-the-fire-gfanz-financing-of-fossil-fuel-expansion/ (accessed 8 September 2023).

Rickman J, Falkenberg M, Kothari S, Larosa F, Grubb M and Ameli N (2023). The systemic challenge of phasing out fossil fuel Finance. DOI: https://doi.org/10.21203/rs.3.rs-3121305/v1 (accessed 8 September 2023).

Schoenmaker D (2021). Greening monetary policy. *Climate Policy*. 21(4):581–592.

Scott K and Barrett J (2015). An integration of net imported emissions into climate change targets. *Environmental Science & Policy*. 52:150–157.

Siderius K (2022). An unexpected climate activist: central banks and the politics of the climate neutral economy. *Journal of European Public Policy*. 30(8):1588–1608(21).

Simms A (2021). *The Case for an Ecological Interest Rate*. New Weather Institute. London.

Stiglitz JE (2019). People, Power, and Profits: Progressive Capitalism for an Age of Discontent. Penguin Publishers. United Kingdom.

Studart R and Gallagher KP (2016). Infrastructure for sustainable development: The role of national development banks. GEGI Policy Brief No. 007. Global Economic Governance Initiative.

Sweeney S (2020). Weaponizing the numbers: The hidden agenda behind fossil-fuel subsidy reform. *New Labor Forum*. 29(1):87–92.

The Economist (2023). A new Bretton Woods. 25 February.

Tienhaara, KR, Thrasher B, Simmons A and Gallagher K (2022a). The energy charter treaty's protection of 1.5°C-incompatible oil and gas assets. GEGI Policy Brief No. 021. Global Development Policy Centre. University of Boston.

Tienhaara KR, Thrasher B, Simmons A and Gallagher K (2022b). Investor-state disputes threaten the global green energy transition. *Science*. 376(6594):701–703.

Urgewald (2021). Global Coal Exit List. Available at: https://www.coalexit.org/ (accessed 8 September 2023).

Urgewald (2023). *Investing in Climate Chaos*. Available at: https://investinginclimatechaos.org/ (Accessed 8 September 2023).

Urgewald (2023a). *World Bank Evolution Roadmap fails to curb financial flows to fossil fuels*. Available at https://www.urgewald.org/en/shop/world-bank-evolution-roadmap-fails-curb-financial-flows-fossil-fuels (Accessed 8 September 2023).

Urgewald (2023b). *AIIB Energy Strategy: Still sticking to gas and oil, no fossil energy exit in sight*. Available at https://www.urgewald.org/en/shop/aiib-energy-strategy (Accessed 8 September 2023).

Urgewald (2023c). *Investing in Climate Chaos*. Available at: https://investinginclimatechaos.org/ (Accessed 8 September 2023).

UNCTAD (2015). *Trade and Development Report 2015: Making the International Financial Architecture Work for Development.* (United Nations Publication. Sales No E.15.II.D.4. New York and Geneva).

UNCTAD (2019). *Trade and Development Report 2019: Financing a Global Green New Deal.* (United Nations Publication. Sales No E.19.II.D.15. New York and Geneva).

UNCTAD (2021). *Trade and Development Report 2021: From Recovery to Resilience – The Development Dimension*. Chapter V. (United Nations publication. Sales No. E.22.II.D.1. Geneva).

UNCTAD (2022) *Trade and Development Report 2022*: *Development Prospects in a Fractured World – Global Disorder and Regional Responses.* (United Nations publication. Sales No. E.22.II.D.44. Geneva).

UNCTAD (2022) Financing for development: Mobilizing sustainable development finance beyond COVID-19. Intergovernmental Group of Experts on Financing for Development, Fifth Session. 21–23 March. Geneva.

UNCTAD (2023a). *World Investment Report - Investing in Sustainable Energy for All*. (United Nations publication. Sales No. E.23.II.D.17. New York).

UNCTAD (2023b). *Green Finance and Decarbonization of Petrochemicals: Slim Pickings in a Crucial but Hard to Abate Industry.* (United Nations publication, Geneva).

UNCTAD (2023c). *The Least Developed Countries Report: Crisis-Resilient Development Finance.* (United Nations publication. Sales No. E.23.II.D.27. Geneva).

UNDP (2021). *Alternative Uses of Pre-Tax Fossil Fuel Subsidies Per Year*. United Nations Development Programme. New York.

UNEP (2015). *The Financial System We Need: Aligning the Financial System with Sustainable Development*. United Nations Environment Programme. Nairobi.

UNEP, SEI, Climate Analytics, E3G and IISD (2023). *The Production Gap: Phasing Down or Phasing up? Top Fossil Fuel Producers Plan Even More Extraction Despite Climate Promises.* Stockholm Environment Institute, Climate Analytics, E3G, International Institute for Sustainable Development and United Nations Environment Programme.

UNFCCC (2021) Report of the Conference of the Parties serving as the meeting of the Parties to the Paris Agreement on its third session, held in Glasgow from 31 October–13 November, 2021.

UNFCCC (2022). Report on progress towards achieving the goal of mobilizing jointly USD 100 billion per year to address the needs of developing countries in the context of meaningful mitigation actions and transparency of implementation. Technical Report. UNFCCC Standing Committee on Finance. United Nations. Bonn, Germany.

United Nations (2023). Our Common Agenda – Reforms to the International Financial Architecture. Policy Brief No. 6.

Victor D (2009). *Untold Billions. Fossil-Fuel Subsidies, Their Impacts and the Path to Reform.* Global Subsidies Initiative (GSI) of the International Institute for Sustainable Development (IISD). Geneva.

Vivas D, Barrowclough D, Contreras C (2021). The ocean economy: Trends, impacts and opportunities for a post COVID-19 blue recovery in developing countries. Research Paper 137. The South Centre. Geneva.

Volz U (2017). *On the Role of Central Banks in Enhancing Green Finance*. United Nations Environment Programme. New York.

Warmerdam W (2022). GFANZ financiers of the fossil fuel expansionists – Finance research methodology. Reclaim Finance. Available at: https://reclaimfinance.org/site/wp-content/uploads/2022/12/Profundo_GFANZ-report-Research-methodology-.pdf (accessed on 8 September 2023).

Wiedenhofer D, Virág D, Kalt G, Plank B, Streeck J, Pichler M, Mayer A, Krausmann F, Brockway P, Schaffartzik A, Fishman T, Hausknost D, Leon-Gruchalski B, Sousa T, Creutzig F and Haberl H (2020). A systematic review of the evidence on decoupling of GDP, resource use and GHG emissions. Part I: Bibliometric and conceptual mapping. *Environmental Research Letters*. 15(6):063002.

World Bank (2012). *Indonesia Economic Quarterly: Redirecting Spending*. Washington, D.C.

World Bank (2023). *Evolving the World Bank Group's Mission, Operations and Resources*. Washington, D.C.

WWF (2022). *Call to Action to Ensure Transition to a Net Zero and Nature Positive Economy*. World Wildlife Fund for Nature.

Xu J, Marodon R and Ru X (2021). Mapping 500+ development banks: Qualification criteria, stylized facts, and development trends. Research Report No. 2. The Institute of New Structural Economics. Peking University. Beijing.